93-2069

NEGOTIATING THE FUTURE

NEGOTIATING THE FUTURE

A Labor Perspective on American Business

*Barry Bluestone and
Irving Bluestone*

BasicBooks
A Division of HarperCollins*Publishers*

Library of Congress Cataloging-in-Publication Data
Bluestone, Barry.
Negotiating the future: a labor perspective on American business / Barry Bluestone and
Irving Bluestone
p. cm.
Includes bibliographical references and index.
ISBN 0-465-04917-6
1. Industrial relations—United States 2. Management—United States—Employee
participation. I. Bluestone, Irving. II. Title.
HD6957.U6B55 1992
331'.0973—dc20   91-59007
CIP

Designed by Ellen Levine

93 94 95 CC/HC 9 8 7 6 5 4 3

To our beloved Zelda and M. E.

Contents

PART II
FROM THE GLORY DAYS TO TROUBLED TIMES

PART III
FROM THE ADVERSARIAL WORKPLACE TO
EMPLOYEE INVOLVEMENT

PART IV
TOWARD AN ENTERPRISE COMPACT

Preface

During World War II, the older of us (Irving) was a production grinder at the General Motors's Hyatt Roller Bearing Division in Harrison, New Jersey. My department produced aircraft engine bearings for fighter planes and bombers. Manufacturing to extremely close tolerance for both size and finish was essential—one defective engine bearing could mean a downed plane and the death of its crew. High-carbon steel was used to produce these bearings, and my job was to grind the outside diameter of the outer race (the outside ring of the bearing) to plus or minus 0.0002 inch. The floor inspector made an occasional spot check for size on the mechanical gauge that was on my workbench alongside the machine.

I was interested in learning about the high-carbon steel used in bearings because I thought having more knowledge about the metal would help me perform the job better. So I borrowed a book from the public library and brought it to the plant to read during my lunch break. The book lay on my workbench next to the gauge. My foreman, passing by, picked up the book, thumbed through it casually, then turned to me and asked: "What the hell are you doing with this?" I told him why I was reading it. His prompt reply was: "Look here, you don't need a book to do your job. Just do the job as you've been told and grind the damned races to spec. That's all I want you to do." He put the book on the bench and walked away.

A year or so later, as a member of the local union shop committee,

I was involved in negotiations on contract provisions governing layoffs, recall rights, and other subjects related to seniority. The union had submitted various proposals to management, which had responded with its counterproposals. Discussions seesawed back and forth for more than a year with no real progress toward an agreement. One day the labor relations director, management's chief negotiator, opened the meeting with a new approach: "We are willing to withdraw all of our seniority proposals, and I'm asking that you withdraw all yours. Let's start with a clean slate. You fellows prepare a brand-new proposal from scratch, with every *i* dotted and every *t* crossed, complete with occupational groups and flow charts. We'll review it and get back to you. Maybe that will give us both a fresh start."

We weren't making any progress anyway, so we decided that the suggestion made a lot of sense. In a couple of days we came up with a full-blown seniority agreement proposal. We figured we had covered every possible eventuality of seniority-rights protection and submitted it to the labor relations director. He said they would review it and get back to us in a week.

The following week we came to the bargaining table. At the labor relations director's chair lay the document we had given him. He opened the discussion by explaining that he had studied our proposal together with the plant manager and had reviewed it with the plant superintendent and other operations personnel. He noted that management would have great difficulty living with some of the provisions but, rather than continuing to haggle and hassle any further, they were prepared to accept the proposal exactly as we had written it. With that he stood up and leaned across the table toward the chairman of our shop committee. The chairman, avoiding his outstretched hand, grabbed our proposal from the table, tore it in half, and exclaimed: "No, sir. If that proposal is good for you, it can't be any good for us!"

These irritating experiences elicit a knowing smile from me today, but, multiplied a thousandfold, they aptly describe the failings of what was, and unfortunately in too many settings still is, the traditional work organization—a workplace that exhibits the self-defeating mindset that the individual worker is no more than an adjunct to the company and that the natural relationship between management and labor must be hierarchical and adversarial, an advantage for one inherently meaning a disadvantage to the other.

Negotiating the Future rejects this brand of zero-sum thinking in favor of what many of our readers may see as a revolutionary approach to rebuilding labor-management relations in the United States. We shall argue that because of old-fashioned thinking and orthodox ways of doing things, America is failing to meet the global economic challenge. We are certainly not the first to say this, nor will we be the last. But we shall argue that the cornerstone in the rebuilding of America lies in reshaping the fundamental relationship between employees and management and creating a new work culture. Appropriate fiscal and monetary policies and adequate investment in advanced technology are necessary preconditions for an American economic renaissance, along with investments in public infrastructure, education, and training.

We contend that no matter how fine-tuned these macro policies, the nation's economic engine will not run smoothly until relations in the workplace are radically and democratically reorganized. At the risk of seeming anachronistic or utopian, we shall explain how labor unions—with a new function and purpose—can play a critical role in this reorganization. And we shall explore why and how managers must be willing to adopt a completely new modus operandi with regard not only to the workplace but to the way they run their entire enterprise.

Making the changes we suggest will not be easy. When profits are squeezed and stockholders revolt, management is under enormous pressure to cut costs. Labor becomes the prime target. Venerable firms like IBM hint at the first layoffs in their history. General Motors closes fourteen more plants. Caterpillar threatens to hire replacement workers. Faced with growing job insecurity, unionized workers react with outrage. Nonunion workers respond more quietly, but their impact on the company is often as devastating. Low morale leads to less commitment to productivity, quality, and innovation. All of this must be changed if America is to compete successfully in the global economy.

Fortunately for the country, there is evidence that in important sectors of the economy both labor and management have taken the first tentative steps toward such a reinvention of labor-management relations. The purpose of this book is to urge both sides to take much longer strides. Instead of simply treating workers better, management must be willing to share decision-making authority with them. Instead of workers' input being limited to the factory floor or the outer office, labor must be brought into the inner circle where the strategic decisions about the enterprise are made. Instead of trying to jettison their unions, management must be willing to welcome them as a constructive force in what we call an Enterprise Compact. Instead of viewing the company as its mortal enemy, labor must be willing to change with the times—focusing its energy on achieving a better life on the job while concurrently improving the competitiveness of the enterprise. Indeed, in recognition of the requirements of the global marketplace, we believe that labor and management have more in common than in conflict. Finding a new structure for labor-management relations that rests on common interests and mutual concerns is, we argue, a sine qua non for economic prosperity if not outright survival.

In part, our own experiences and understanding of how the world has changed have led us to these conclusions. One of us grew up during the Great Depression of the 1930s, the other during the turbulent 1960s. We are both trying to understand better the exigencies, but also the promise, of the 1990s. The older of us began work in a General Motors factory in the early 1940s and retired as a vice president of the United Auto Workers union almost forty years later. His son, the younger of us, spent summers on a Ford assembly line, working his way through a doctorate in economics at the University of Michigan. The older of us was motivated by the struggles of organized labor to make a better world for workers. The younger of us was influenced by the Port Huron statement, the founding document of Students for a Democratic Society—in particular, the statement's endorsement of a form of democracy in which all individuals have central roles to play in making the decisions that most affect their own lives.

The two of us, father and son, have pooled our various talents and experience to write what we hope will be seen as a forthright account of what has gone awry in the American economy and what might be done to make it right again. We each have our biases, but we have attempted to be objective—not an easy task with this subject. Often we did not see eye to eye on issues, more because of our different vantage points than because of fundamental differences over what appeared on the horizon. In the process of writing this book, we have learned a great deal from each other, and surely about each other.

In this effort, we have accumulated a large number of debts. Scores of friends, new and old, helped us to understand better the issues we were trying to confront. Close colleagues provided us with both gentle encouragement and, when needed, not so gentle criticism; both were badly needed. As usual, Ben Harrison was there as best friend and knowledgeable associate. Our publisher, Martin Kessler, helped us to focus our ideas. And most important of all, our wives, who also double as mother and daughter-in-law, did much more than patiently abide the thousands of hours we put into this project. Time and time again, when frustrated by our own inability to comprehend the other's point of view, one or the other of these wonderful partners in our lives—and sometimes both together—would step in to clear the air and persuade us to look at the other's perspective. As virtually everyone in our family knows, without Zelda and M. E. this book might never have seen the light of day.

PART I

INTRODUCTION

CHAPTER 1

A New Vision for American Enterprise

For most of its citizens, America's integration into the global economy in the 1980s was a difficult process. And the next decade promises to be one of continuing adjustment, sometimes painful. Unless America does a better job in competing in the 1990s than it did in the 1980s, more and more people will find their standard of living getting worse.
—*Karen Pennar,* Business Week, *Special Report,* Can You Compete? *(1990)*

Life in the American workplace is changing. In fact, our very economic survival requires it to change. Firms—and unions in industries where they continue to play a vital role in labor relations—are caught up in a whirlwind of experiments with "employee involvement," "quality circles," "problem-solving teams," "autonomous work groups," and "participative management." Along the way, "worker empowerment" has become part of the lexicon of some of America's toughest CEOs.[1] Company brass are ordering line supervisors to show greater respect for employees who not so long ago were treated as expendable cogs in a vast production machine. Teamwork, cooperation, and mutual trust are in; adversarialism is out. In this age of being "prepositionally correct," managers are supposed to talk *with*, not *at*, their work force. These are refreshing trends—but they are at best baby steps at a time when American industry requires a revolutionary leap in labor-management relations to boost its productivity, improve the quality of its products, and step up its rate of innovation.

THE END OF THE GLORY DAYS

The economic pressure for a labor-management revolution is of very recent vintage. During America's economic "glory days"—roughly from 1947 through 1973—neither the repressed conflict in the authoritarian workplace nor the more carefully choreographed conflict in the union setting prevented stockholders from enjoying buoyant profits or workers from enjoying a modicum of employment security and a steadily rising material standard of living. In an economy isolated from international competition, "authoritarianism" and "adversarialism" were not inconsistent with a booming economy. If workers stood around while engineers and foremen tried to solve a machining problem because line employees were not expected to solve it on their own, nor in most cases even allowed to try, or if labor and management spent months bickering over a contract clause, there was enough slack in the system to permit it. Hardly anyone was losing sales or jobs to the Japanese or the Germans, let alone the South Koreans or the Taiwanese.

By the mid-1970s, however, it was becoming patently clear that the authoritarian/adversarial labor relations system had a serious shortcoming: it was not particularly effective at encouraging successful outcomes in domestic or international competition. Unfortunately, as foreign competitors built up a head of steam, the dominant response from management was not to build a strong coalition with its work force but precisely the opposite: to assault labor with demands from on high for wage and benefit concessions combined with diminishing employment security. Where organized labor was still strong, workers often responded by digging in their heels.

As one salient indicator of the failure of traditional labor-management relations, 30 percent of U.S. manufacturing plants operating in 1969 were no longer in production by the end of 1976.[2] Many had been relocated away from the communities where they had put down roots. Thousands more with once-proud names and venerable reputations disappeared altogether. Millions of workers lost their jobs.

William Abernathy, Kim Clark, and Alan Kantrow of the Harvard Business School summed up America's economic plight in their 1983 book, *Industrial Renaissance:* "The harsh truth is that the industrial landscape in America is already littered with the remains of once-successful companies that could not adapt their strategic vision to altered conditions of competition."[3]

By the time these highly respected management experts had published their economic call to arms, the fallout was evident. The United States had already experienced more than a decade of economic stagnation and entered a period described by Bennett Harrison and Barry Bluestone (the younger of us) as "the great U-turn."[4] After reaching record levels in 1965, the average profit rate across industries in the nation headed south for most of the next decade and a half. The Dow-Jones Industrial Average closed lower in 1979 than it had in 1965. Inflation-adjusted weekly earnings, which grew by a healthy 60 percent between 1947 and 1973, stopped increasing and headed down as well. Today, the typical paycheck in real dollar terms is 11 percent *smaller* than in 1973. Median family income, which had virtually doubled in a single generation after the war, stagnated throughout the 1970s and most of the 1980s—even as the number of two-income families rose sharply. The "effortless economic superiority" that America had come to know in the aftermath of World War II evaporated in one industry after another.[5]

For a time it was the blue-collar worker who bore the brunt of America's economic slide. But by the early 1980s, even white-collar workers were not safe from the new international competition. "The global economy spares no one," *Business Week* concluded. The myth, it warned, is that most Americans are going to prosper in the 1990s. The reality: "Without changes, much of the decline in living standards is yet to come."[6]

THE PROBLEM AT HAND: PRODUCTIVITY, QUALITY, AND INNOVATION

Sector-by-sector analysis of industrial performance reveals time and time again the same three critical factors that are contributing to U.S.

losses in world markets and therefore to declines in profits *and* wages, stockholders' dividends *and* employee security. First, productivity growth in the 1970s and 1980s fell well below previous postwar levels and continues to lag behind the growth rates achieved by our trading partners. This is particularly true in the labor-intensive service industries that have dominated job growth for more than a quarter-century. With wages and profits outstripping efficiency growth, U.S. production costs have increased relative to the competition with the inevitable consequence that many American goods have been priced out of the market.

Second, even when U.S. prices undercut the competition, the quality of our products often does not. By the early 1980s, Americans were buying Hondas instead of Chevys, not because they were cheaper—in fact, they were not—but because their performance was better, their fuel efficiency superior, and their frequency of repair lower. Sony TVs are purchased because their image is noticeably sharper and their color reproduction more lifelike and vivid.

Third, in a world where technology grows exponentially and consumer tastes are remarkably fickle, American firms have fallen woefully behind in new product development and innovation. VCRs and Nintendo games perennially dominate Christmas sales, yet not a single one is designed or built in the United States. Today, we can add the laptop computer, the fax machine, and the Hi-8 format video camcorder to the list of products for which the U.S. market share is essentially zero.

It is fair to ask why, after so much success in the early postwar years, the United States has fallen behind in productivity growth, quality, and innovation. Everyone has a pet answer. More than a decade ago, President Carter blamed an economic malaise that had gripped the nation; President Reagan blamed big government, high taxes, and piles of government regulations; economists have tried to blame low family savings rates, too little business investment, OPEC oil prices, the rush of women into the labor market, declines in R&D spending, inflation, the shift to services from manufacturing and mining, and the postwar baby boom. No one knows for sure. Despite a Herculean effort at statistically deciphering what caused industrial efficiency to slip from a healthy 3.0 percent annual growth rate during the 1950s to no better than 1.3 percent during the 1980s, economic statisticians have been able to explain only a small fraction of the sharp decline. The oft-mentioned culprits of unsatisfactory savings rates and anemic capital investment, the shift in production from manufacturing to services, rising energy prices, and government "over-regulation" are apparently responsible for much less than half of the loss. After dozens of attempts, the consensus conclusion is that much of the decline is due to "un-measured factors."[7]

In this day of measuring everything, what's unmeasured? One of the two leading contenders, by the economists' reckoning, is an unspecified change in the nature (not the amount) of new technology. It seems we are investing in new technologies, but apparently not using the right ones. The other unmeasured factor, and by far the more intriguing, is a failure of corporate managers to manage resources effectively. It is not that managers have developed some form of corporate amnesia when it comes to effective decision making, but that new times require new means and apparently too many corporations have not developed them. If this proves right—and the evidence seems more and more convincing—then an economic renaissance requires much more atten-tion to labor-management relations, human resource management, and the like and less to such factors as tax cuts to promote capital investment or more industry deregulation. That productivity growth has been lowest in the labor-intensive service sector—indeed, negative in some nonmanufacturing industries, including finance and insurance, real estate, and construction—suggests that how labor is utilized in the firm may very well be a dominant reason for the collapse in U.S. productivity in recent years.[8] The level of capital investment and the amount of new technology introduced into the production process may be less important than how labor and management work together to get the most out of the capital and technology available. Getting labor-management relations right, we shall argue, is the key ingredient in building an American economic renaissance.

One revealing bit of data demonstrating the importance of organiz-ing work effectively within the business enterprise can be found in a major study of corporate efficiency conducted during the late 1970s by Theodore H. Barry Associates, a management consulting firm. In constructing an "anatomy of a work day," the study found that, on average, only 4.4 hours of a typical employee's work day are used productively. On the order of 1.2 hours are lost because of personal and other unavoidable delays, while 2.4 hours are "just wasted." Nearly 35 percent of the wasted time is due to poor scheduling of workers; 25 percent is due to unclear communication of assignments;

and 15 percent is due to improper staffing. The remaining "waste" is due to uncoordinated materials handling, absenteeism, and tardiness. Moreover, the loss in productivity is greater among white-collar than among blue-collar workers. Such inefficiency is not anywhere near as common in Europe and Japan.[9] This research does not suggest that labor is lazy in America; it demonstrates that workers are poorly managed, that their intelligence, skill, and motivation go underutilized, and that too often they are treated as expendable.

CORPORATE ATTEMPTS AT BOOSTING WORKER PRODUCTIVITY

As international competition squeezed profits, some firms concluded correctly that they needed to get more than 4.4 hours of work out of an 8-hour day. To their discredit, however, and for many firms their demise, corporate leaders often went about it in precisely the wrong way. They rolled up their sleeves, took a deep breath, and proceeded to imitate a management style pioneered by the Prussian military. Because of its now infamous CEO, the most publicized case is Eastern Airlines. One business journalist who followed the airline during its turbulent flight to bankruptcy, Aaron Bernstein, writes that Frank Lorenzo "represented the get-tough approach to management that Ronald Reagan had revived when the President fired striking air traffic controllers in 1981."[10] Instead of maintaining the high level of labor-management cooperation that had been forged in the company before his arrival, Lorenzo swerved 180 degrees in a misguided attempt to save his once high-flying airline. Intimidating employees into a work speedup and forcing unprecedented wage and benefit cuts, he so alienated them that they were ultimately willing to sacrifice their jobs to get rid of him.

In April 1990, in the wake of one of the most bitter strikes in recent American history, and only four years after Lorenzo had taken over Eastern and the management of its 38,000 employees, a New York bankruptcy court declared him unfit to run the company. Eastern's logo disappeared from the sky and all its employees lost their jobs. Most of them looked on with open hostility as Lorenzo walked away from the

company with $28 million in cash plus a three-year "golden para-
chute" worth $75,000 a month.[11] In another celebrated case, Fred
Currey, the CEO of Greyhound Lines, deliberately broke a bus drivers'
strike against his company, in the process driving his firm straight into
Chapter 11.[12]

Most CEOs are not as intemperate as Lorenzo or Currey, but they
often bring about the same results. In attempting to meet the competition, they rely on wage cuts and the furloughing of thousands of their
workers, often sacrificing the very employee loyalty and high morale
they desperately need to boost productivity, quality, and innovation.

Eastern and Greyhound represent one end of the labor-
management continuum, but as we noted at the beginning of this
chapter, a growing number of companies are much closer to the opposite pole. In their 1984 nationwide compendium, *The 100 Best Companies
to Work for in America*, Robert Levering and his colleagues Milton Moskowitz and Michael Katz identified the best companies as those that
had transcended the manipulative framework of traditional management and achieved a sense of "we are all in it together." According to
their criteria, a good employer exhibits the following behavior:

1. The company makes people feel that they are part of a team or,
   in some cases, a family.
2. Management encourages open communication, informing people of new developments and encouraging them to offer suggestions and complaints.
3. Management stresses quality, enabling people to feel pride in the
   products or services they are providing, and
4. Internally, the enterprise reduces the distinctions of rank between
   top management and those in entry-level jobs.[13]

Donnelly Corporation, a Michigan-based manufacturer of mirrors,
windows, and glass products especially for the auto industry, ranked as
one of Levering's 100 Best Employers. As he and his colleagues note,
Donnelly "operates on the notion that people can be responsible
human beings, even in the workplace. They don't have to be *told* what
to do; they can decide for themselves."[14] The goal at Donnelly is
worker self-management. The firm has removed time clocks from its
factory floor and put everyone on salary. Employees work in teams of
eight or nine, each team being responsible for its own production goals

within overall company objectives. There is a rule at the company that no one can be displaced by technological improvement. All grievances are reviewed and employee policies set by a plantwide committee with two-thirds of the membership comprised of production workers. All Donnelly employees share in profits through a bonus system.

Hewlett-Packard, another of the 100 Best, has adopted many of these same practices. There are no time clocks; workers share in profits; jobs are "permanent," with virtually no layoffs; and management abides by a code of employee involvement (EI) principles that includes assuring its employees, in the company's own words, "respect and dignity, self-esteem, recognition, participation, security and permanence."[15] The 3M Corporation, famous for Scotch tape and a producer of 45,000 other products, has over 350 "quality circles" throughout its nearly 100 plants worldwide.

The type of approach adopted by Donnelly, Hewlett-Packard, and 3M may seem to involve nothing more than simple common sense, but in practice it is radically different from the traditional autocratic method of managing private business enterprise, and, for that matter, agencies of the public sector. As late as 1984 so few firms had adopted this way of doing business that, Levering notes, out of hundreds of thousands of firms, "it was hard to find 100 companies that were good enough to make the book."[16]

THE EMBRYONIC STATE OF EMPLOYEE INVOLVEMENT AND ECONOMIC DEMOCRACY

Enlightenment takes time to catch on. Thomas Peters and Robert Waterman stressed a decade ago in their best-seller, *In Search of Excellence,* that "if you want productivity and the financial reward that goes with it, you must treat your workers as your most important asset."[17] Yet getting management to embrace and genuinely implement this perspective is no easy task. Both management and labor suffer from what John Maynard Keynes saw as the difficulty not with new ideas but in escaping old ones.[18] Only a handful of firms have taken industrial relations much beyond the archaic model of boss as order-giver, employee as order-taker.

In the industrial era that began in the late nineteenth century, accepted managerial practice called for workplace institutions all framed with the single objective of maintaining strict control over employees—essentially, putting no trust in them at all. While there were experiments with paternalistic welfare systems, particularly during the 1920s, and another try at "human relations" systems later on, in the 1930s and 1940s, the pattern for much of the twentieth century was set by Frederick Winslow Taylor and his most renowned disciple, Henry Ford. Taylor, the father of "scientific management," advised his clients that they could maximize productivity by centralizing all work-floor knowledge in management, removing all "brain work" from the shop, and assigning individually defined, minuscule tasks to each worker in the enterprise. Henry Ford made headlines with his $5-a-day wage, while instituting the mind-numbing moving assembly line and tight control over his employees both inside and outside the plant. For the money, men lined up for blocks to become Ford workers, though they despised the assembly line and were wary of the close monitoring.

Ford's notions about his workers were plain and simple. As he put it, Taylor's method was great for monotonous minds:

> Of necessity, the work of an individual must be repetitive—not otherwise can he gain effortless speed which makes low prices and earns high wages. Some of our tasks are exceedingly monotonous . . . but then, also, many minds are monotonous—many men want to earn a living without thinking, and for these men a task which demands no brains is a boon.[19]

With the level of education in the work force rising rapidly after World War II, the proportion of Henry Ford's "monotonous minds" surely declined in the population. Yet contemporary surveys suggest that many employers have not weighed the implications of this trend. Despite the sage advice of Peters and Waterman on the asset value of a company's employees, *Fortune* magazine reported in late 1989 that the "trust gap" between top management and labor is growing, not shrinking.[20] One management consulting firm, the Hay Group, drawing on ten years of survey data covering hundreds of companies and thousands of employees, concluded in a 1988 study that the attitudes of middle managers and professionals toward the workplace are becoming more like those of hourly workers, historically the most disaffected in American society.[21]

In an even larger study, the Opinion Research Corporation of Chicago surveyed 100,000 middle managers, supervisors, professionals, salespeople, and technical, clerical, and hourly workers who worked for Fortune 500 companies. The disheartening results are summarized in table 1.1.

Every group of workers was more alienated from top management near the end of the ego-gratifying 1980s than right after the 1981–82 recession. By 1988, only a bare majority (54 percent) of middle managers felt their companies were treating them with respect and consideration. Only 42 percent of professionals and 30 percent of hourly employees felt this way. *Fortune* concludes pessimistically that "relations between employer and employed are not good, and at an especially dicey moment. Just when top management wants everyone to begin swaying to a faster, more productive beat, employees are loath to dance."[22]

Part of the problem is that even among firms proclaiming their commitment to reform, hierarchy on the factory floor or in the office complex has scarcely diminished. Reform stops well short of the execu-

TABLE 1.1

The Growing "Trust Gap"

		Positive Response	
		1983	1988
"Is the company treating	Managers:	63%	54%
you with respect and	Professionals:	49	42
consideration?"	Hourly:	39	30
"How would you rate	Managers:	68	52
the ability of top	Professionals:	53	40
management?"	Hourly:	41	30
"When top management	Managers:	85	78
puts out information,	Professionals:	80	73
how do you feel about it?"	Hourly:	65	55

Source: Opinion Research Corporation, as reported in Alan Farnham, "The Trust Gap," *Fortune,* December 4, 1989, p. 57.

tive suite. In more enlightened firms, employees are being given more decision-making leeway on the job, but they remain barred from any role in the strategic decisions made "upstairs." They are being given responsibility to redesign their own jobs, but are rarely, if ever, consulted about the design of their company's products, the technologies used in their production, or the advertising programs used to lure their customers. The chasm between hourly and salaried employees, and between supervisors and the supervised, has hardly been bridged. As a result, the typical company in the United States is using only a fraction of its collective brainpower.

In unionized industries, management's otherwise unfettered right to rule the work force continues to be circumscribed by union contract, and the workplace itself is run more democratically. Yet even here, in most instances the present demarcation between the rights and responsibilities of employers and those of employees is drawn sharply in hundreds of pages of fine print and enforced rigorously within a structured adversarial environment. If not exactly class warfare, the present framework of labor-management relations in shops, offices, and factories throughout the nation remains largely antithetical to what America needs most: much higher productivity, much better quality, more innovation, and far more employment security and job satisfaction.

Wave after wave of layoffs is compounding the problem. Just when the most prudent managers are concluding that people are truly their most valuable resource, one series of layoffs after another convinces employees of exactly the opposite. The "lean and mean" strategy employed by the bulk of firms trying to cope with intensified competition has no doubt contributed mightily to the results reported in table 1.1. By the beginning of the 1990s, even many of the enlightened firms that made Levering's 100 Best List were under intense pressure to consider layoffs for the first time in their histories.[23]

The source of the pressure became abundantly clear in a December 1991 meeting between John Akers, IBM's CEO, and skeptical Wall Street stock analysts concerned about the announced wholesale restructuring of the bluest of the blue-chip corporations. Akers's plans were met with approval only after he repeated an earlier assertion that IBM's practice of not laying off workers would "clearly be on the table" if the company could not improve results through voluntary severance.[24] That very afternoon, Big Blue's stock on the New York Stock Exchange went up $1.25—a small rebound after months of declining to $85 per share from a high of $138 earlier in the year. Throwing loyal employees out of work may please Wall Street, but it obviously does little to reverse the growing trust gap felt by workers. Pink slips are a poor prescription for building teamwork and worker loyalty among those lucky enough to keep their jobs after the latest cutback.

THE TRACK RECORD ON EMPLOYEE INVOLVEMENT

For all the recent publicity about the new corporate culture, employee involvement, teamwork, and employee participation, one question lingers even when no layoffs are contemplated: Does the strategy work? If one sifts through opinion surveys of managers and workers, combs through econometric studies by savvy statisticians, consults scores of case studies, and listens to innumerable anecdotes, one is drawn to the disconcerting conclusion: sometimes yes, usually no. In some cases productivity improves; in a few it declines; in most not much happens at all. The same is true for improvements in quality. This is not a consoling finding from management's perspective, and certainly not for those who pin their hopes on employee involvement as a restorative of American economic prowess. But it is not surprising.

Closer examination of the data suggests that employee participation is a success for all "stakeholders" in the enterprise only in those cases where it is pursued vigorously, thoroughly, openly, with full commitment and mutual trust. Simply going through the motions is useless. For firms like Donnelly, Hallmark, and 3M, which have made employee participation the core element of their corporate cultures, it has paid off handsomely. When these companies say "no layoffs," they mean it—at least when they are not faced with a catastrophic economy. When they ask workers to design their own jobs, they keep their hands off. But many, if not most, firms go through the motions but do not entertain the substance. Too many, as Peters and Waterman conclude, fall prey to the "lip service disaster and the gimmicks disaster."[25]

At Donnelly, the maker of glass products for the auto industry, employee participation has worked because it is at the core, not the fringe, of the company's philosophy. Between 1975 and 1984, productivity measured as real dollar sales per employee went up 110 percent—a compounded rate of efficiency growth of better than 7 percent per year, five times greater than the national average.[26] Today Donnelly continues to adhere to its policy of worker empowerment, and it has paid off. Despite the grave recession that struck the auto industry in the early 1990s, Donnelly continued to expand and remained profitable throughout this period. Its employment has more than doubled since 1985, partially as a result of successfully building up, through quality products, its sales volume to all ten major Japanese automobile plants operating in the United States. The company openly credits its success to "employee empowerment."[27]

It is hardly coincidental that when William Seidman, the tough former chairman of the Federal Deposit Insurance Corporation (FDIC), and his colleague Steven Skanche went searching for U.S. companies that maintained their competitive edge, they found one thing in common among the success stories: virtually all had implemented substantial labor-management innovations aimed at empowering workers. Como Plastics Corporation, for example, has used employee teamwork and problem-solving teams to boost their productivity and profits. Worker involvement in cost-reduction teams and in the setting of productivity targets at the America Seating Company has done the same. Emphasizing participative management in solving production problems boosted profits at Dana Corporation, Honeywell, Motorola, and, until recently, Procter & Gamble.[28]

Beyond the general rule of direct investment of workers in decision making are two additional factors that substantially increase the odds of success. One is a system of financial reward for employees through profit or gain sharing. When workers as a group share the rewards of improved productivity, quality, or company profitability, the motivation to make participation work for the company pays off more handsomely. Seidman and Skanche found this to be true in a range of firms, including Diamond Fiber Products and Certified Grocers, where employee rewards are tied to performance.[29]

The other factor correlated with the success of employee involvement programs may come as a shock. It is the presence of a labor union. Participation turns out to work best when it is organized jointly between union and management and when workers have a voice independent from management that cannot be unilaterally stifled by "the boss." Mixing adversarial and cooperative relations—negotiated within a context where employees are represented by legally constituted and recognized unions—proves in one study after another to be the most successful form of employee involvement for all stakeholders. When a union gets involved with a company pursuing worker empowerment, employee morale appears to be highest and productivity and quality improve the most.

REBUILDING LABOR UNIONS FOR ECONOMIC SUCCESS

The fact that participation works best in union environments from the *company's* point of view as well as the *employees'* is not as surprising as it may seem. Historically, many of the initial experiments in creating a new corporate culture began in the union sector with the full participation of organized labor. In the auto, steel, and communications industries, unions actually led the way, often against the wishes of the corporate leadership who sat across from them at the bargaining table.

The synergy of union-management joint action is a relatively new phenomenon in the American workplace. What we call the "traditional workplace contract" provides little in the way of joint participation outside of wage and benefit determination, job security provisions, and working conditions. For decades, adversarial collective bargaining, punctuated periodically by strikes, won for many union members a rising standard of living based on a wage formula that combined an "annual improvement factor" plus a "cost-of-living allowance" to keep up with inflation. In successive rounds of collective bargaining, "fringes" were added to the traditional union contract: employer-paid health insurance, pensions, life insurance, vacation pay, holiday pay, and a host of other benefits. Union-negotiated contracts enhanced job security through seniority provisions and a formal grievance process.

Having won this array of protections, and in the context of an expanding economy, unions were generally willing to cede strategic decision making to top-level management. Virtually all traditional union contracts contain the equivalent of General Motors's "Paragraph 8"—a management-rights clause that leaves to management the exclusive right to make all decisions in the firm not explicitly dealt with in the written agreement.

There have been, however, notable attempts at transcending the limits of the traditional workplace contract. As early as 1967, delegates to the United Auto Workers collective-bargaining convention approved a resolution that dealt with the basic objective of humanizing the workplace and affording employees a greater measure of respect, dignity, and participation on the job. As chief administrative assistant to Walter Reuther, the union's president, Irving Bluestone (the elder of us) wrote that resolution. In part, it read:

> The work place is not a penal colony; it must be stripped of its air of coercion and compulsion; imaginative new ways must be found to enable workers to participate democratically in decisions affecting the nature of their work. There is no reason why human and democratic innovation must continue to lag behind technological innovation in the plants and offices.[30]

When the UAW first brought what it called the "quality of worklife" issue to the bargaining table at General Motors, the company scoffed at the idea. But by 1973, GM agreed to begin implementation of the union-proposed, jointly sponsored "Quality of Worklife Improvement" program, which became known as QWL. While it was couched in terms of dignity and participation that were foreign to the company, General Motors slowly came to recognize that QWL could help the company as much as its workers. QWL encouraged employees to play a meaningful role in boosting the quality of their own work lives, and in doing so led to improved efficiency and product quality as well. By the 1980s, with imports carving giant market shares out of the hides of domestic producers, both corporate management and union leaders increasingly saw in "joint action" one of the few remaining avenues for fulfilling the common interests of management and labor alike.

Even Roger Smith, the former chairman of General Motors whose work experience was devoted to the finance side of the business, eventually voiced his support for the changed work culture advocated by the union. At the spring 1985 groundbreaking for the new multimillion-dollar UAW-GM Human Resource Center in Auburn Hills, Michigan, Smith told the celebrants that management across the country had to fundamentally change its attitude toward its employees and their unions:

> No longer are the adversarial union-management roles of the past appropriate for today's environment. Instead, a teamwork approach

is needed. . . . [It] will encompass such new approaches to problem-solving as Quality of Work Life and joint union-management strategies. Such an approach seems to us the only way American *business* can effectively compete in the future; the only way American *unions* can stay strong and viable; the only way American *employees* can enjoy job satisfaction and job security.[31]

Taking such a stand, which goes against hallowed tradition, is not easy for corporate or union leaders. Managers must answer to their stockholders and sometimes hostile corporate raiders, while union officials must carefully explain their positions to their members whenever they depart, even marginally, from what is taken to be the politically correct position.[32] Advocating "cooperation" is still controversial enough to keep many from speaking up. As former Secretary of Labor John Dunlop has noted, those labor leaders who support joint action or who see the need for improved enterprise productivity are often labeled by those who oppose these concepts as "class collaborationists" who have "sold out to the bosses" and signed "sweetheart deals."[33] Corporate CEOs who advocate democratization of the workplace are often accused of precisely the same crimes by their more traditional business colleagues.

What is beginning to win over a small but steadily increasing number of corporate leaders to the union perspective on joint management of the workplace is the success that teamwork is enjoying where it has been vigorously and genuinely implemented. In union settings at Xerox, Ford, General Motors, Preston Trucking, Corning Glass, A. O. Smith, Honeywell, AT&T, LTV Steel, and in the public sector in the Bureau of Motor Equipment in New York City's Sanitation Department, union-management joint action has led to well-publicized improvements in productivity, quality, and innovation.

By no means has the adversarial relationship between labor and management completely disappeared at any of these firms. But the intrinsic and inevitable conflict over wages, benefits, and employment security is more easily mediated in the presence of joint action over a growing number of issues, from the design of individual jobs to the factory environment, employee assistance, apprenticeship training, health and safety, and a host of other matters.

Joint action in the workplace represents a healthy start toward rebuilding labor-management relations in American industry—but, as we shall argue, it is only a first phase in what must be a more ambitious departure from past practice. Central to our argument is the desirability of expanding the role of organized labor, not eliminating it.

THE CASE FOR EXPANDING THE UNION ROLE IN AMERICAN BUSINESS

Suggesting that unions might be the critical missing element in a national campaign for global competitiveness may seem farfetched even to those sympathetic to organized labor. After all, in many industries unions are in retreat. With only one in six American workers now represented by a union and the proportion declining, one might question the relevance or role of organized labor in bringing about an economic renaissance throughout America. Even if one were convinced that unions play a positive role in boosting productivity, quality, and innovation in the workplace, it seems unlikely that one-sixth of the work force could make much difference. Hence even strong supporters of unionism may have their doubts about how much can be gained through union-management joint action.

More dismissive are the critics who maintain that whatever else they do, unions do nothing to improve a company's competitiveness. Robert M. Kaus, writing in *Harper's Magazine* in the aftermath of the ill-fated air traffic controllers' strike, is typical of union critics. Kaus writes that "the actions [of unions] often seem to lie at the root of many of our problems, economic and otherwise." Reiterating oft-repeated claims, Kaus notes that the industries that are most heavily unionized, like autos and steel, are the most apt to be losing the competition with the Japanese; that unionized urban transportation systems "lose riders and fall into squalor as fares rise to pay the ever higher salaries of the ever smaller numbers of transit workers"; that the dominant teachers' union has resolutely opposed all attempts to weed out mediocre teachers; and that "everywhere that unionized businesses have been losing in the marketplace, they (and their unions) have turned to government to bail them out, at the public's expense, through protectionism or government subsidy." Indeed, Kaus suggests, it is "the very system of collective bargaining [that] affects the nature of business enterprises in ways that make the salvation of American industry, and renewed prosperity for American workers, hard to imagine.''[34]

Many of these criticisms resonate with the public. In some circles, there remains a deep resentment of unions. A decade ago, politicians, used-car dealers, and union leaders shared one thing in common: all received low ratings in polls soliciting popular opinion about the admirable qualities of people in various occupations. As late as 1981 only half of Americans had a favorable view of labor leaders, and fully two out of five Americans viewed them with hostility.

In some cases, unions have brought this on themselves. In the incessant struggle to maintain job security for their members, there is often enormous pressure on unions to retain outdated work rules or jurisdictional lines that hamper productivity, that encourage employers—even some generous ones—to move operations to nonunion regions, and that alienate the consuming public. The most flagrant examples receive great attention. After the diesel locomotive replaced the steam-driven railroad engine, the locomotive engineers' union insisted on maintaining a fireman on board to stoke a nonexistent coal-burning furnace. There are stories about electricians refusing to change lightbulbs because that task was not explicitly written into the job description. Even political struggles within local or national unions sometimes spill over onto the bargaining table and now and then contribute to a strike that might have been avoided. Union leaders can be as stubborn as management when it comes to contract demands, and workers themselves have been known to compel their leaders to take a strike action that turns out to be in no one's interest. In just one example, at the start of the school year in the fall of 1991, the school-bus drivers in Boston exasperated parents and school board members by striking for the third time in six years in a bid to gain another pay raise—at a time when teachers were being laid off.[35]

Although this type of behavior demeans the union movement, the relatively few instances in which unions cross the boundary into unjustified treatment of a firm or of the public interest are isolated. They tend to be played up in newspaper and television accounts, while the more mundane day-to-day workings of good union-company relations are ignored. The big-screen image of roughneck local union officials depicted in Marlon Brando's classic film *On the Waterfront* is much more likely to color public opinion than are the reams of unheralded statistics showing that 99 percent of union-management disputes are settled without strikes, intimidation, or violence. So too is the revelation on CBS-TV's "60 Minutes" of Teamster executive salaries of $400,000 and more—a corrosive, if not corrupt, practice that was terminated with the stunning victory of the union's reform slate in late 1991, a slate committed to eliminating the union's ties to underworld activity.[36]

There is no question that the vast majority of unions are democratic and not corrupt. Even union critics admit this fact, and public support for organized labor is once again on the rise. In a 1991 Roper poll, 62 percent of respondents had "great" or "fair" confidence in labor leaders, while only 27 percent held a negative image of them.[37]

But unions are not merely less harmful than critics like Kaus suggest; overwhelming evidence now demonstrates that even the most traditional ones have actually performed well for companies and for their workers. Statistical studies by Richard Freeman and James L. Medoff in the early 1980s, since replicated by other scholars, indicate that in most industries unionized establishments are more productive than nonunion establishments, while in only a few are they less efficient. The quality of the products is also superior in unionized companies.[38]

There are good reasons for this seemingly counterintuitive finding. Unionized employers normally have a lower rate of turnover, thus spend fewer resources on training new workers. Unions also keep managers on their toes, forcing them to strive harder to improve productivity in the face of union demands for higher wages. Ironically, it is precisely this last reason that often leads managers to shun unions in the first place.

TOWARD A NEW BRAND OF UNIONISM IN THE UNITED STATES: THE THREE-TRACK SYSTEM

Major changes in the role and purpose of unions have been under way for more than two decades. Most unions today recognize that to maintain employment security for their members, they must pay close attention to the economic condition of the firms where their members work. This has driven some unions to emphasize productivity and quality even more so than management. It was the UAW that insisted on "quality networks" in the auto industry, well before management came around to accepting their worth.

The structure and role of unions within key industries have been changing since the mid-1970s. In auto, in steel, in communications, in textiles and apparel, in the electrical goods industry, and selectively in trucking and the public sector, the traditional workplace contract has been expanding into what we call a three-track system. *Track 1* represents the standard adversarial position between labor and management over the familiar set of issues negotiated since the 1930s, and in some industries even earlier: wages, benefits, and working conditions. Added to this function is now *Track 2*, which provides for direct individual employee participation in such activities as jointly sponsored teams involved in making various workplace decisions. Finally there is *Track 3*, direct union involvement in a range of decisions and the administration of activities customarily reserved as management prerogatives.

While Track 2 involves employees directly in decisions in their own "neighborhood" within the workplace, Track 3 is built around joint committees comprised of representatives of management and the union throughout the establishment. Track 1 remains adversarial in nature, but the two new tracks reflect generally nonconflictual joint action. In return for sharing more power at the workplace and upgrading job satisfaction, firms agreeing to the expanded contract do so with the expectation of improved productivity and quality. What has therefore been evolving is a mixed system of labor-management relations: joint action to expand the size of the economic pie; adversarial relations when it comes to dividing it.

FROM THE WORKPLACE CONTRACT TO THE ENTERPRISE COMPACT

In the Jewish festival of Passover celebrants rejoice in the efforts of Moses to free his people from bondage in Egypt and to bring them to the land of Israel. After the Passover meal, "Dayenu" is often sung. Roughly translated, *dayenu* means "it would have been enough." Those assembled at the Passover feast repeat *dayenu* as the leader recounts every step of the way from the safe passage through the Red Sea and the giving of the Ten Commandments to eventual arrival in the Promised Land.

When it comes to the present state of employee involvement and joint action, we believe that *dayenu* is not an appropriate response. To be successful for both management and labor, there are many more miles to travel and hurdles to overcome. EI and the three-track system, while reversing nearly a century of rigid Taylorist control, are but the first tentative steps toward something much broader, certainly more exhilarating, and ultimately much more powerful as a foundation for an American economic recovery.

The expanded Workplace Contract, when implemented genuinely and comprehensively, can change the culture of production, whether of goods or services, in the direction of improving employee satisfaction and thereby boosting the efficiency of each individual job. But, limited as it is to the problems of the factory floor or the office setting, it does not address the strategic decisions of the firm. The crucial factors that determine whether an enterprise flourishes or flounders, including pricing and accounting, design and engineering, advertising and marketing, investment and subcontracting, remain entrenched with top management. That is, the "directive" function—imbuing the enterprise with purpose, objectives, and goals—resides exclusively with management, outside the domain of the workers themselves or their union representatives. This simply is not enough. Given the track record of American industry, it is abundantly clear that management does not have all the answers.

At considerable risk of ruffling the feathers of long-enduring custom or of being accused of hopeless utopianism, we believe that the next giant step in labor-management relations—one that is already beginning to be taken in a handful of enterprises—will involve expanding employee participation to this upper level of decision making within the firm. Workers themselves and their union representatives need to be "brought into the loop" in all of these strategic areas of management. Ultimately, labor must begin to participate and take responsibility with management for decisions at *all* levels of the firm, from the shop floor to the boardroom. Economic success today requires that everyone from the janitor and the machinist to the secretary and the senior engineer have a role in the strategic decisions that affect the company's well-being. This even includes input in the pricing of the company's products, in the design of customer relations, and in the very investment decisions that determine the expansion or demise of the enterprise.

Progress toward this form of economic democracy will be slow and at times retrogressive. But we believe it will succeed because there is already embryonic evidence—which we review in chapter 8—that joint decision making at the strategic level of the firm is working to solve problems of productivity, quality, innovation, and employment security that have been largely immune to other strategies. By sharing decision-making power with its work force, management may feel that it is yielding control over decisions that it alone can pursue wisely. But, when done right, joint participation is a positive-sum game for managers and workers alike.

Saturn, the UAW–General Motors joint venture to conceive, design, and build a brand-new automobile with the full participation of the union, is perhaps the most advanced effort in this regard. From the very moment of its conception in 1982 through the construction of its $3 billion facility in Spring Hill, Tennessee, and finally in 1990 with the assembly of the first Saturn vehicle, the union was intimately involved in an extensive array of strategic decisions. In joint committees, management and workers combined forces to design collaboratively the physical plant, to choose every technology used within it, to produce a marketing and advertising strategy, and to develop the entire set of recruitment and education programs used to select and train the new GM division's work force.

The democratic process of decision making within the company begins with semi-autonomous teams on the plant floor and works up through concentric rings of empowerment all the way to division headquarters. At one end, team members in the factory are responsible for interviewing and recommending the hiring of their own colleagues. At higher levels within the organization, union representatives are co-equal with management in influencing decisions that in virtually every other work setting in America are the sole domain of management. Whether or not the Saturn automobile turns out to be a success in the marketplace cannot diminish its pioneering role as a full-scale experiment in labor-management relations.

What we envisage on a somewhat more distant horizon is a brand-new Enterprise Compact between labor and management that will go well beyond the three tracks of the expanded workplace contract and even beyond Saturn. A *contract* is essentially adversarial in nature, representing a compromise between the separate interests of each party to the agreement. In contrast, a *compact* is fundamentally a cooperative document, providing for a mutual vision and a joint system for achieving common goals that foster the general well-being of all stakeholders in a given endeavor. One of the best examples is the Mayflower Compact the American Pilgrims signed on November 11, 1620. This profound document declared:

> [we] doe by these presents solemnly & mutually in the presence of God, and one of another, covenant & combine our selves togeather into a civill body politick; for our better ordering, & preservation & furtherance of the ends aforesaid; and by vertue hearof to enact, constitute, and frame shuch just & equall lawes, ordinances, Acts, constitutions, & offices, from time to time, as shall be thought most meete & convenient for the generall good of the Colonie.[39]

In a modern setting, almost four centuries later, the Pilgrims' compact may provide just the right guidance for a new way of building cars and machine tools, or of providing banking services and hospital care.

In our model of the negotiated Enterprise Compact, the traditional roles of labor and management are sharply altered from current practice: labor takes on greater responsibility for productivity and quality—formerly managment's domain; management assumes a greater obligation to provide employment security—formerly a union concern. *Together,* management and the company's unionized work force work jointly to make decisions at every level of the firm right up through the hierarchy to the level now occupied by the company's CEO.

Whether one believes that traditional unions have benefited or hindered productivity and quality begs the question, for what we advocate is not an expansion of traditional trade-union structures or an atavistic return to the good old days of hardheaded adversarial collective bargaining. Instead, given the nature of the contemporary world economy, we believe it is necessary to build a new union movement based on the principle of a shared set of labor and management rights and responsibilities. This movement must continue in the organized sector of the economy and must spread to the unorganized.

The technical details of the Enterprise Compact must be negotiated between labor and management in much the same way that collective bargaining has been used to nail down the traditional Workplace Contract. But at the core of the Enterprise Compact, as we envision it, are seven major provisions:

1. The union and management agree to pursue mutually established productivity growth targets.
2. Wage and compensation goals are set consistent with productivity growth in order to maintain global competitiveness.
3. Price setting in the company is subject to joint action by union
   and management.
4. Quality is a "strikable" issue, to assure that products and service
   meet or exceed international standards.
5. Employment security is guaranteed for the company's work
   force.
6. Extra financial rewards are provided through profit and gain
   sharing throughout the enterprise.

Finally, at the very center of the Enterprise Compact and reinforcing
all other provisions:

7. The union and management agree to joint decision making
   throughout the firm, including labor representation on the company's Board of Directors. With this, the last remnants of the
   traditional Workplace Contract's "management-rights" clause
   are abolished.

We have no illusion that such radical change in labor-management
arrangements will occur overnight. Nor do we expect union representatives and corporate executives to suddenly develop an evangelical zeal
to make over their relations with the Enterprise Compact as a template.
But we do believe that a thrust toward democratizing American enterprise is practically inevitable as management and labor continue to be
frustrated by the pressure of global competition.

Why, one might rightfully ask, will organized labor risk abandoning
traditional methods for co-responsibility in the tricky task of managing
the enterprise? And why will management ever willingly surrender its
current prerogatives to an organization once, and still in most circles,
considered its adversary?

As for labor, union leaders increasingly recognize that all the gains
they have made through collective bargaining can go for naught if
management fails to pay adequate attention to productivity, quality,
and innovation. One or two seriously flawed management decisions
can wipe out more employment security than all the contract provi-

sions in the world can guarantee. A narrow focus on short-term profits at the expense of long-term market share may be fine for stockholders, who can instantly abandon the company simply by issuing sell orders to their stockbrokers. The consequences of this same narrow strategic focus are not so readily handled by workers forced to take wage and benefit cuts or to pay the ultimate penalty of losing their jobs.

For management, embracing the Enterprise Compact will no doubt come haltingly and with great skepticism. Under the compact, labor is required to take on greater responsibility, while management must surrender what it has historically considered its sacrosanct right. Given institutional inertia, neither will come easily, but the latter will almost surely generate more resistance. Only as its advantages prove successful in a few pioneering firms will additional companies be willing to take the leap toward the Enterprise Compact. This has always been the case with the initial efforts at employee involvement, and we have no reason to believe it will be different with this much more challenging form of economic democracy.

Nonetheless, we can foresee that some individual companies will take the first tentative steps toward the Enterprise Compact, perceiving in it their long-term interest. This is the case at Harvard Industries in Union, New Jersey, a UAW-organized shop that produces aerospace parts. After years of fierce labor-management conflict, the parties agreed in 1991 to joint decision making throughout the firm and capped the contract by jettisoning all semblance of a management-rights clause. A Plant Council comprised of union representatives and management has responsibility for manufacturing decisions. A joint Business Council including top UAW officials and top management executives is responsible for all strategic decisions.[40]

Management will inevitably learn from the best of the joint-action employee involvement experiments that fully involved workers really are the most productive. Increasingly, managers will also recognize that they do not have a monopoly on all the information or strategic knowledge needed to run a competitive business profitably. Their unions, particularly when committed to the principles of the Enterprise Compact, can make a unique contribution to a firm's economic success. They can organize workers for collective action in a way that management cannot, for a simple reason. Management must make decisions that benefit the stockholder, while the union must act to preserve the interests of its members. Since these two are not always synonymous, workers will always be reticent to give full allegiance to management's lead. In contrast, a union that has gained the trust of its members by serving their interests in terms of wages, working conditions, and employment security has the opportunity to organize the work force to achieve economic goals from which both the company and its work force benefit.

This organizational role of the union within the Enterprise Compact cannot be duplicated outside the union setting. In the absence of an independent union, workers always carry a residual apprehension of management, knowing all too well that a change in corporate leadership or in economic conditions can, with the unilateral stroke of a manager's pen, reverse hard-won gains, regardless of how much faith workers might have in the present ranks of management. For this reason, if none other, the formidable task of organizing workers for collective effort *in service to the entire enterprise* is better exercised by a union that is openly on the side of labor than by management, which must constantly divide its loyalty between its stockholders and its work force.

This argument has never been more cogently put forward than by Peter Drucker, one of America's most respected management consultants. Writing more than forty years ago, he made the implicit case for the Enterprise Compact:

> The answer, the only possible answer to the political duality of the industrial enterprise, is the labor union. Management with its political authority over the enterprise can neither be avoided nor be transformed, no matter what political, economic, or legal arrangements are tried. At the same time this governmental authority can never put the welfare of its subjects first; it cannot be legitimate. Hence the split has to be institutionalized, has, so to speak, to be built into the very structure of the government of the enterprise. The only way to make the government of the enterprise legitimate is through a counter power which represents the members against their government while at the same time itself forming a part of this government. The *union* is thus the institutional expression of the basic political tension of the enterprise.[41]

Eventually the drive toward an American labor-management relations system based on the tenets of the Enterprise Compact will build as more and more workers and corporate executives recognize that the

archaic ways of doing business—either authoritarian or adversarial—
serve no one's interest. As Abernathy, Clark, and Kantrow put it:

> As in any long-standing feud, some members on both sides will turn
> whatever comes to hand against their sworn enemies. But in this
> industrial version of the Hatfields and the McCoys, mutual intransi-
> gence is no longer acceptable as a principle of survival. In the face
> of stiff foreign competition, it is a blueprint for extinction.[42]

To avoid economic extinction, both labor and management will in
time work toward a new strategic relationship based on mutual trust
and co-responsibility with the Enterprise Compact as one particular
model to emulate.

Government can also play a practical role in fostering the new
compact. Changes in labor law can be used to nourish it, as can
education programs and local labor-management groups operating at
the local or state level. As unions strive to democratize the enterprise,
we believe their ability to organize the unorganized will be enhanced.
Successful experience with the Enterprise Compact should also dull
management's current appetite for a union-free environment.

Even the venerable National Association of Manufacturers (NAM),
historically never considered a great friend of labor, has begun to
change its spots. In what *Business Week* called an "extraordinarily strong
endorsement of participation or employee involvement," the Association predicted: "In the 1990s, we will witness a rapid revolution of
employee participation—a revolution that will transform the way work
is organized and managed."[43] We do not for a moment expect NAM
to endorse the Enterprise Compact, but we suspect its members will
study it carefully and not dismiss it out of hand. Indeed, movement in
this direction is already on the horizon. The Collective Bargaining
Forum, an organization of national union presidents and corporate
executives—including those from American Airlines, Ford Motor
Company, Inland Steel, ALCOA, CSX Transportation, and Ameritech—has taken as its objective the design of a "workable compact"
that includes commitment to the integrity of the union, the union's
commitment to the competitiveness of the enterprise, and worker participation "in decisions that affect them, including the development of
long-term business strategies."[44]

Management and labor will ultimately come around to the Enterprise Compact because it serves their mutual needs. In this spirit, Mike Bennett, the visionary president of the union at Saturn, has asked the right questions about the future of America:

> The real question for the 1990s is, "Can we, in organized labor and management, live without an enemy?" Without the communist threat to overwhelm us, who and what should we guard against? Without labor/management adversarialism, what would we each try to accomplish? What could we accomplish collaboratively? . . .
>
> There is a "peace dividend" in each of these examples. In the first, world peace in our time, and the diminished risk of mutual nuclear destruction and the opportunity to redirect valuable resources in directions that multiply the likelihood of increasing wealth for all Americans. However, whatever impact this "peace dividend" has in regard to the military budget and the redistribution of those re- sources, it is insignificant compared to the return to the American people when management and labor come to agreement on what it is they wish to accomplish collaboratively and then set about how to do it cooperatively, each as a full partner in the process. The return to society on this "peace dividend" far exceeds anything President Bush and Soviet leader Mikhail Gorbachev could expect. It vastly improves the outcomes of the utilization of resources, human and otherwise, in their moment of truth they each face.[45]

To negotiate the future, through the Scylla of heightened global competition and the Charybdis of obsolete industrial relations, will require that we negotiate—literally negotiate—a new future in labor- management joint action. We do not pretend to have a blueprint for this future, but we hope to provide some of the essential trail markers.

PART II

FROM THE GLORY DAYS TO TROUBLED TIMES

CHAPTER 2

The Glory Days and the Traditional Workplace Contract

Whatever else it has implied, the American Dream has meant the promise of continuing material advance and therefore of social opportunities for all citizens. . . . Belief in the American Dream—that progress indeed happens and the "best is yet to come"—is basic to the claim of American exceptionalism.

—"A View from Great Britain,"
Oxford Analytica, America in Perspective *(1986)*

To begin to understand the fundamental changes that labor and management must make to reestablish American competitiveness and enhance the nation's overall standard of living, it is useful to recall some recent history—in particular, the glory days of the first post–World War II generation and the special conditions that once made the United States the world's preeminent economic power.

Two years before the United States committed troops to the war effort in Europe and the Pacific, nearly 10 million Americans were unemployed—more than one-sixth of the entire labor force. The official jobless rate declined in 1940 and again in 1941, but on the eve of the American entry into World War II, nearly one in ten Americans remained without work.[1]

The war changed that abruptly. Between the beginning of 1942 and the end of 1945, the federal government spent more than $350 billion—nearly 45 percent of the gross national product—on the war effort. Auto plants were hastily converted to produce jeeps, tanks, and airplanes, operating on a twenty-four-hour-a-day schedule, seven days a week. Among others, Henry Kaiser's shipyards went into full production, building nearly 1,500 "Liberty Ships" and their successor, the "Victory Ships," in less than five years.[2] In industries seemingly far removed from war, bath towel manufacturers converted their operations to produce millions of yards of khaki, shoe manufacturers turned out millions of pairs of combat boots, and canners countless tons of Spam.[3]

America was back to work. By early 1943, just about everyone who wanted a job could find one. A large share of the labor force worked overtime to make up for the 15 million men and women who were serving in the armed forces.[4] By 1944, only 1.2 percent of the labor force was counted as officially "unemployed"—most only temporarily out of work while moving between employers who were desperate for their services.[5]

Yet, within months of the successful Allied invasion at Normandy, concern over the state of the postwar economy began to mount. "Doomsday" economists forecast that, come the armistice, sharp cuts in military contracting would lead to widespread unemployment. One widely quoted estimate had the United States returning to depression conditions with 19 million jobless.[6] Experts predicted that fewer than 10 percent of the 4 million workers in shipbuilding and aircraft would remain in these occupations after the war.[7] How to reintegrate into the labor force the millions who had served in the armed forces posed still another conundrum. The doomsayers prophesied that lower government spending would ripple through the economy, driving household consumption and business investment down while forcing GNP and employment back to depression levels. The most pessimistic among them painted visions of breadlines and desperation.

The immediate postwar period and the quarter-century to follow turned out, of course, quite differently. Instead of widespread poverty, there was unanticipated abundance. Workers' wages and benefits and corporate profits rose in tandem to levels unheard of before the war. Within a decade, millions of workers and their families were well on their way to earning incomes that brought them into the great American middle class. For the first time in the modern era, the majority of Americans lived in homes they owned—or at least co-owned with a bank. Fewer than 45 percent of all housing units had been owner-occupied in 1940, a proportion that had not increased since 1920; by 1960, home ownership was up to 62 percent, close to today's level.[8] The postwar boom also allowed working families to equip their new homes with a dazzling array of household appliances. In just the twenty years between 1950 and 1970, the proportion of households with telephones increased from 62 to 91 percent; the percentage with television, from 9 to 95 percent. Passenger car registrations more than doubled, from 40 million to 89 million—extraordinary for a country with only 63 million households.[9]

In retrospect, we know why the doomsayers' predictions fell so far from the mark. An historically unique set of domestic and world economic conditions, in combination with dramatic improvements in wages and benefits negotiated as part of the expanding traditional Workplace Contract, produced the preconditions for the most prosperous quarter-century in American history. Together, these forces created spectacular increases in consumer demand, business investment, and national output—and set the stage for a labor-management accord that provided workers with a growing claim on the rewards of a robust economy. The glory days would not endure forever, but for a quarter-century they represented an unparalleled economic opportunity for tens of millions of families who could still remember the dark days of the Great Depression. Most important, the threat of global competition was nowhere in sight.

ALL THE RIGHT INGREDIENTS FOR PROSPERITY

One good way to decipher this auspicious turn of events is to consider the basic "macro" equation for the economy: $GNP = C + I + G + X - M$. Total Gross National Product (GNP) is comprised of Household Consumption (C) plus Business Investment (I) plus Government Procurement (G) plus Exports (X) minus Imports (M). With the euphoria that accompanied the ticker-tape parades welcoming the troops home, every one of these GNP components broke simultaneously in favor of the economy.

The first element contributing to the postwar boom was enormous pent-up consumer demand. During the war, production of most consumer goods had been sharply curtailed and in some cases halted.[10] By March 1943, families needed cash *and* a ration coupon to purchase a long list of common household items.[11] After four years of war-imposed scarcity, Americans looked forward to junking their worn-out refrigerators and replacing household appliances held together with the proverbial chewing gum and baling wire. They wanted to replace the family automobile, or at least its treadworn tires. And many wanted new homes, particularly new tract houses in the suburbs.

Without the money to translate these burgeoning desires into purchases, there could not have been a boom in consumption. But with full employment and rising incomes during the war but little on which to spend their money, families stowed their savings in war bonds, bank accounts, and credit unions. All told, nearly $125 billion was socked away during the war, equivalent in today's purchasing power to nearly a trillion dollars. The blending of this gargantuan amount of liquid assets with nearly insatiable pent-up demand contributed to the most uninhibited spending spree in American history.[12] Consumption (C) flourished, putting millions to work, particularly in the manufacturing sector and in construction.[13]

To meet consumer demand, businesses had to convert their factories from the production of war goods to a market basket of peacetime commodities. By early 1946, General Motors, Ford, and Chrysler were back in the business of assembling passenger automobiles, along with Kaiser-Fraser, Willys-Overland, Nash, Hudson, Studebaker, and Packard. RCA was turning out television receivers in place of radar sets, and GE and Westinghouse were once again in the home appliance business. Over $300 billion dollars (in 1990 dollars) of new factories and office buildings were erected between 1946 and 1950. Another $420 billion of real dollar investment was poured into these plants in the form of new machinery and business equipment, from typewriters and dictaphones to entire assembly lines, from drafting tables to open-hearth furnaces.[14]

The new Investment (I) created millions of additional jobs—the number of workers in the construction trades alone (carpenters, electricians, structural steel erectors, painters, and roofers) more than doubled between 1945 and 1950[15]—and, even more important, provided the capital and technology to energize a spurt in productivity growth.[16] From 1949 through 1959, labor productivity—defined as the value of output per worker hour—advanced by an average of 3 percent a year, as much as 50 percent higher than the average for the first four decades of the century.[17] Such rapid efficiency growth permitted impressive gains in employee wages without sending rates of inflation soaring. Indeed, as long—and only as long—as these productivity advances were made could wages and profits rise without being eroded by equivalent increases in prices. As we shall see, this would change dramatically for the second postwar generation.

The government played a critical role too, as a direct generator of aggregate demand. Federal government purchases of military goods and services declined sharply at war's end, as predicted.[18] But in the postwar exuberance, nearly everyone failed to foresee the economic implications of the cold war with the Soviet Union and China and of U.S. involvement in the shooting war in Korea. By 1953, federal spending (G) had returned to $58 billion from a low of $14 billion in 1947.[19] The end of the Korean War reduced nominal Department of Defense spending, but by less than $10 billion.[20] The newly christened aerospace industry was once again hiring Class A machinists, riveters, and assemblers. Welders were back to work in the nation's shipyards as part of the new military-industrial complex.

Of course, the government's spur to economic growth was not limited to defense work. Under the G.I. Bill, the federal government provided $14 billion in education and job-training benefits, putting thousands of teachers to work boosting the skills and productivity of the work force.[21] Washington also agreed to underwrite 90 percent of the cost of what ultimately would be the 41,000-mile system of interstate highways.[22] Stunned by the successful launch of *Sputnik* in 1957, the government spent lavishly to catch up to and then surpass Soviet exploits in space. Spending on "human resources" back on earth expanded even more. From a consolidated budget of $10 billion in 1947 for education, training, health, income security, Social Security, and veterans benefits, the federal government doubled its spending by 1958 and doubled it again by 1966.[23]

State and city governments also played a critical role, shelling out nearly $200 billion to build and maintain streets, roads, and highways between 1947 and the end of the 1960s. They spent more than twice as much to build new schools and to hire teachers to educate a generation of baby-boomers who began reaching kindergarten in 1950.[24] Thus the reduction in post–World War II total government spending was nowhere near as cataclysmic as many had feared. Contributing directly to the Great American Jobs Machine, public-sector agencies added over 8 million new staff to their payrolls between the end of the war and 1973.

AMERICA'S NEW ROLE AS GLOBAL LEADER

Equally crucial to America's glory days was the dawning of U.S. global hegemony.[25] Under the Truman Doctrine and the Marshall Plan, the United States committed over $13 billion in foreign aid between 1947 and 1953 to help rebuild Europe and thus contain Soviet expansion[26]—an enormous amount, by any standard.[27]

In the process, Marshall Plan loans and grants generated a bonanza for American industry: as much as 80 percent of the original assistance came back to U.S. firms in the form of American exports (X). Ultimately, for every hundred dollars' worth of production for domestic consumption, the United States had the advantage of producing and selling an additional ten dollars' worth of goods abroad.[28] Americans were being put to work in record numbers not simply to satisfy the voracious appetite of U.S. consumers but to help feed, clothe, and reindustrialize the nations of Western Europe and the Far East. At the time, no one could fathom the extent to which American aid would help to create the nation's own future competition.

As if all this were not sufficient to ignite a postwar economic boom of enormous proportion, the virtual disappearance of import competition (M) helped immeasurably. The saturation bombing of such industrial centers as Dresden and the total destruction of Japanese economic might at Hiroshima and Nagasaki meant that for years foreign competitors would have to concentrate on rebuilding their own industries before they could even contemplate exporting. Indeed, imports as a share of U.S. GNP did not recover their predepression level until nearly a quarter of a century after World War II ended.[29] As a result, American consumers had little choice but to buy products built with American technology and stamped "Made in the U.S.A." One did not need a Buy American campaign to maintain domestic employment: consumers might be dismayed on occasion by the quality of the U.S. goods they purchased, but their only alternative was to do without. In a period of conspicuous consumption and planned obsolescence, they bought.

THE OLIGOPOLY ADVANTAGE AND REGULATED MARKETS

The glory days were also a time when there was little domestic competition. Oligopoly—the control of individual product markets by a few manufacturers—dominated economic activity. Four-firm "concentration ratios," indicating the proportion of total sales in an industry attributed to the largest four producers, topped 70 percent in seventeen key industries.[30] Among these were motor vehicles, telephone and telegraph apparatus, aircraft engines and engine parts, photographic equipment and supplies, flat glass, turbines and turbine generators, household laundry equipment, and chewing gum.

Within each of these broad sectors, "administered pricing" prevailed despite the existence of antitrust legislation. Explicit price collusion was, of course, illegal. But nothing prevented Post or General Mills, for example, from raising their breakfast cereal prices to match an increase announced by Kellogg's, as long as the CEOs refrained from sharing price information over an otherwise perfectly legal game of golf. As a result, stockholders benefited, but labor employed in these sectors benefited as well. Unions could press for higher wages and benefits, and if productivity advances did not cover the extra cost, firms could simply boost prices without fear of losing customers to competitors. Oligopoly indemnified corporate profits and enhanced employment security.

One further factor contributed to the glory days: government regulation. Railroads and banks were first regulated during the Progressive Era; securities exchanges, motor carriers, commercial airlines, and communications were the objects of the second wave of government intervention during the New Deal days of the 1930s. Much of the legislation, particularly under the Roosevelt administration, was designed to restrict ruinous competition among industry members. Developed during the depression, its real impact was felt after the war.

In practice, the elimination of price competition in regulated industries provided guaranteed profits to stockholders and enabled unionized employees to win substantial wage and benefit improvements, with the assurance that if pay raises adversely affected profits, the government regulators would permit regulated firms to boost prices to cover their higher operating costs. Economists call the excess profits and wage premiums due to such market imperfections "economic rent."

These "rents" were prevalent in the airline industry, telecommunications (the latter as a result of the government-mandated AT&T monopoly), interstate bus transportation, and trucking. Limits on competition in the allocation of radio and television frequencies through the Federal Communications Commission had a similar impact. Finally, workers on federal construction projects benefited from government regulation, in this case from the Davis-Bacon Act. Under this law, workers employed on federal construction projects must be paid "prevailing wages" in the local labor market.[31] Since the Department of Labor historically has used the so-called 30 percent rule by which *prevailing* came to mean the pay for the highest 30 percent of construction workers in an area, Davis-Bacon required federal contractors to pay relatively good wages whether their employees were unionized or not.[32] Given the enormous boom in highway, road, sewer, school, and municipal building construction during the 1950s and 1960s, these regulations benefited millions of workers on public projects and in the process stimulated consumption and growth.

PROSPERITY AND PROFITS IN AN ADVERSARIAL AGE

The equation for unprecedented economic success was now complete: consumption, investment, government spending, and exports were all on a fast-moving escalator, while imports were trapped on the first floor. Meanwhile, oligopoly and regulation assured protected domestic markets. This extraordinary combination of factors pushed the overall unemployment rate below 3 percent in 1952 and 1953. Only rarely would the rate go as high as 6.5 percent during the entire quarter-century following the war. Over the same period, GNP growth averaged 3.7 percent. Given the "rule of 72," this meant that real GNP doubled in less than twenty years' time.[33]

In such an economic environment, it was hardly surprising that business and labor did exceedingly well. More than 130,000 new businesses were incorporated in 1946 alone; nearly an equal number were started in each year of the following decade.[34] Corporate profits more than doubled between 1946 and 1951, and continued their upward swing, reaching a peak in 1965.[35] Reflecting this trend, the Dow-Jones Industrial Average nearly quadrupled by the end of the 1950s.[36]

During this uniquely prosperous period in American history, organized labor was in the unusually comfortable position of being able to remind corporate leaders continually of the profitability of their operations and of how easily they could afford to offer better wages and benefits to their employees. With little threat from unemployment and high rates of organization in key industries, unions could more easily and successfully use the strike weapon to gain what they considered equitable settlements. Indeed, within a month after World War II ended, nearly 500,000 workers in factories across the country walked off their jobs in mostly effective attempts at winning wage adjustments to catch up with the inflation resulting from strict wage controls during the war, unmatched by equivalent controls on prices. In the following year, the most strikebound in American history, the number on strike spiraled to over 2 million as auto workers, meatpackers, electrical workers, and steel workers traded in their tools for picket signs.[37] In the years to come, the incidence of work stoppages would decline, but each year from 1947 to 1957 the Bureau of Labor Statistics counted an average of 370 major strikes, involving better than 1.5 million workers annually.[38]

In practice, the overwhelming majority of new labor agreements negotiated in the years after the war were concluded without resort to strikes or employer lockouts. Still, the fundamental nature of the relationship between management and labor was notably adversarial. If labor did not always see corporate leadership as its sworn enemy, and if management did not always see unions as an absolute threat to the free enterprise system, both sides oftentimes appeared to act on such perceptions during contract negotiations. Indeed, the result of even "successful" rounds of collective bargaining produced something closer to an uneasy truce than a stable partnership. Union leaders felt they had to remain tirelessly vigilant against management efforts to undermine the agreements made at the bargaining table, while management often had fears that the unions in their shops would search incessantly for ways to take advantage of loopholes in the contract in order to eke out further gains for their members at the expense of profits.

Organized labor and management fought their battles in many arenas. Besides the bargaining table, both sides fought in the courts and in Congress. Management sought injunctive relief from union picket lines and boycotts. Unions tried to obtain court rulings against management practices that allegedly violated national labor laws. Both sides lobbied the federal government as well as state and local governments for laws that would benefit their side.

During the glory days, however, the often acerbic adversarial process produced benefits for both workers and stockholders. Employment security turned out to be fully compatible with rapidly rising wages and benefits because markets were protected from domestic competition through oligopoly and regulation and from global competition by the economic devastation that World War II had visited on much of the rest of the world. And profits were protected by the sheer growth in the size of markets. Most important, rapid productivity growth ratified the wage and benefit package without unduly eroding dividends or capital gains. Job growth reduced labor's anxiety about technological progress that ordinarily would have spelled labor displacement. With more than enough work to go around, employers could promote experienced employees and thereby provide fresh job opportunities for those who lined up at the employment office. Moreover, as long as economic growth was maintained, there was little reason to question management's ability to run the enterprise. With wages rising and employment relatively secure, it appeared to most workers that management was making the right strategic decisions. In short, a sensational growth economy supplied the foundation for an unusual capital-labor accord founded on orchestrated conflict.

In retrospect, the causation between economic growth and the strength of organized labor ran both ways. In the heyday following World War II, organized labor never represented much more than about a third of the total work force.[39] Yet unions played a pivotal role in maintaining postwar prosperity, not only for their own members but for the nation as a whole. The contract demands made by organized labor and the settlements it ultimately concluded with management provided workers with better wages and benefits and reasonably steady employment—both of which contributed to higher consumption levels and therefore higher GNP and employment. In a real sense, the rise of unions in the postwar era and the expansion in the scope of the negotiated labor agreement were every bit as important to producing the glory days as the pent-up demand and pent-up savings from the war or the investment, government, and export-led booms that followed.

Indeed, without the increasing wages and benefits won by unions, it is unlikely that the immediate postwar consumption and investment boom could have sustained the glory days for much more than a decade. "Wage-led" growth sustained the boom for a quarter of a century.

THE TRADITIONAL WORKPLACE CONTRACT

Labor's gains in the heyday following World War II were codified in what we call the traditional Workplace Contract, as introduced in the last chapter. The contract varied from industry to industry and from one firm to another, but the essentials were the same in mining and on construction sites, in transportation and communications, inside blue-collar plants and white-collar offices, and ultimately in schools and in a large part of the public sector. During the glory days, the contract provided workers with steadily increasing wages and benefits, job security, a voice in establishing and enforcing working conditions, and greater dignity on the job. It constrained management to deal with a legally constituted union over a range of work-site issues, but it stopped short of providing workers or their representatives with any meaningful input into the strategic decisions of the firm beyond the workplace per se. Thus the Workplace Contract provided labor with a measure of control over wages, but not corporate investment; over who was laid off, but not over who was hired; over working conditions in a factory or mine, but not over the nature, the prices, or the quality of the product or service produced.

Looking back over nearly half a century of labor agreements in key industries throughout the economy, we can discern the basic elements of what constitutes the traditional Workplace Contract. While the typical labor agreement in force today spans hundreds upon hundreds of pages of negotiated provisions, its major elements can be distilled into seven basic points:

1. The annual improvement factor and cost-of-living adjustment (AIF/COLA) wage formula.
2. Extensive collectively bargained job-related benefits.

3. Seniority-based layoffs, recalls, and transfers, including consideration of seniority in promotions.
4. Negotiated conditions of work, work rules, and job classifications.
5. Grievance and arbitration machinery to resolve disputes over interpretation of the contract.
6. On-site union representation and a union security provision.
7. Retention of management prerogatives over many workplace issues and virtually all strategic enterprise decisions.

As a whole, these constitute the basis for labor-management relations in most organized firms in the country. Many nonunion firms have unilaterally adopted a good number of them, despite the absence of union pressure. A brief discussion of each of the Workplace Contract's chief provisions can help illuminate the nature of labor-management relations during the glory days.

THE AIF/COLA WAGE FORMULA

On any list of what employees want most from a job, decent wages always rank near the top. For their own reasons firms, both union and nonunion, desire a reasonable formula for determining pay rates and periodic wage increases. Unions, in negotiating for higher pay, also like to have credible grounds for their wage demands. In the aftermath of World War II, one method for setting wages gained prominence. It was born out of the 1948 contract negotiations between the United Auto Workers and General Motors. Variations on this formula still dominate wage setting under many union contracts.

The actual formula was brought to the bargaining table by management.[40] Charlie "Engine" Wilson, the president of General Motors, was unalterably opposed to any union incursion into managing the enterprise. But Wilson, along with GM's legendary chairman, Alfred Sloan, was well aware of his employees' demands for an equitable share of the company's and the nation's emerging prosperity. During the 1945–46 strike negotiations, the UAW's vice president and chief negotiator at GM, Walter Reuther, had argued for a 30 percent wage increase to cover lost purchasing power due to price inflation during the war. Reuther explained that the company could meet this demand and maintain healthy profits without raising auto prices. The corporation flatly rejected the concept of wage protection against inflation in

1946, but two years later found the union's argument persuasive. At Wilson's own personal instruction, GM's bargaining team introduced the concepts of the "annual improvement factor" (AIF) and the "cost-of-living adjustment" (COLA).

The idea behind the AIF was that each year workers should receive a wage increase equal to the long-term average growth in *national* productivity. Wilson concurred with the view that as the nation became more productive, his own workers were due a share of the gains as a matter of course. Moreover, reasoning as an engineer, he figured that if he was required to negotiate with a union, he wanted a technically sound, presumably indisputable basis for setting annual wage adjustments. Tying pay increases to measured productivity growth, Wilson thought, would do both. At the bargaining table, the UAW agreed to AIF as a method for determining annual wage increments.[41]

Here an important historical note is in order. In subsequent negotiations in the auto industry and elsewhere, the underlying concept of annual wage improvement was maintained, but the direct relationship to measured national productivity growth was dropped. While labor leaders and management continued to agree that yearly pay increments should be related broadly to advances in productivity (and profitability), the original Wilson AIF formula was abandoned; wage increases were no longer anchored firmly to measured increases in national industrial efficiency. In the course of negotiations, the AIF tended to settle in at 3 percent across the board, with variations from time to time depending on economic circumstances.[42] Before the explosive growth in import competition, abandonment of strict "productivity bargaining" posed little problem for companies or unions. But in the 1970s and 1980s, as we shall see, it would herald serious problems for both.

In addition to AIF, Wilson was responsible for designing the first COLA formula for the auto industry. It was originally structured so that future inflation would not reduce the workers' standard of living. Specifically, workers would be given a quarterly adjustment to their wages based on increases in the official government consumer price index (CPI).[43] In a matter of just a few years following the 1948 UAW-GM contract, variations on this particular COLA formula would be adopted in the steel industry, in the electrical goods and machine tool industries, in the postal service, and in a host of other sectors throughout the economy. By 1977 more than 60 percent of all major union contracts in the private sector had a cost-of-living provision, and many unions in the public sector tried to follow suit.[44]

The combination of AIF and COLA permitted employees the income security to buy into the American dream.[45] At the same time, profits were protected. In fact, despite the generous wage gains in the first few years following World War II, profits throughout much of American industry continued to grow faster than workers' earnings. With the AIF/COLA provision in effect, profits were 51 percent higher in 1948 than in 1947 in the auto industry, and in the first quarter of 1949 nearly 35 percent higher still.[46] Over the full spectrum of American industry, corporate profits rose from $17 billion in 1946 to $39.9 billion in 1951, topping $50 billion by the end of the 1950s.[47] With AIF and COLA, American business came to the realization that higher wages tied to rising productivity were not necessarily incompatible with higher profits. Indeed, just the opposite was true. If enough firms bought into the formula, AIF/COLA actually contributed to each company's bottom line by boosting overall aggregate consumer demand.

JOB-RELATED BENEFITS

The second element in the traditional Workplace Contract was the expansion of what was once called fringe benefits—today so extensive that the term *fringe* has been dropped. In one industry after another, benefits such as paid holidays, jury-duty pay, vacation pay, the night-shift premium, life insurance, medical insurance, sickness and accident plans, pensions, and supplemental company-paid unemployment benefits all gained prominence in the bargaining process.[48] In the nonunion sector, these benefits were provided by many employers as a supplement to wages or, in some cases, as a partial substitute for them. Nonunion firms often matched the Workplace Contract provisions negotiated in the organized sector as part and parcel of a strategy to remain union-free or simply to attract well-qualified employees.

The prominence accorded job benefits as part of the total compensation package in the typical U.S. firm derives from the fact that none of these benefits is mandated by government as employment-related entitlements. This is far different than in many European countries, where the law requires firms to provide vacation and holiday pay, and the government itself furnishes medical coverage. American workers receive these benefits only if their employer agrees to offer them as part of a union contract or if nonunion employers offer them voluntarily, presumably to entice workers to join their firm.

Since World War II, unions have devoted as much effort to expanding benefit coverage as they have to winning wage increases. As a result, losing a job in the United States remains much more painful than in Europe and elsewhere: here one loses not only a wage but many of the key benefits, particularly health-care coverage, that workers in nearly every other industrialized country take for granted.

SENIORITY PROVISIONS

Because a job is much more than simply a paycheck, job protection is another critical element in the traditional Workplace Contract. Seniority systems spread throughout the organized sector with hardly an exception. Who was laid off when work was slack and recalled to work when output recovered, who received promotions to higher-rated jobs when openings arose, and who had the right of transfer to a different work assignment or department remained for centuries at the sole discretion of management. From labor's perspective, this arrangement could be highly arbitrary and easily abused. Supervisors could reward their friends and punish their adversaries with little regard to whether a particular employee was capable of doing the work. The reward system in many a workplace resembled the worst aspects of Tammany Hall. Not uncommonly, nepotism and favoritism governed who would be retained and who would be summarily released. Even when the system was not corrupt, it was often seen as inequitable. Older employees who had given their best to the company for decades were released with impunity to make way for younger workers eager to take their place.

Seniority provides a simple and consistent method for making decisions about layoffs, recalls, and transfers. The beauty of seniority rules is that they are generally nonarbitrary and virtually tamper-resistant. Each worker has an easily identified "seniority date"—usually the day he or she hires in at the company. In cases of layoff, management is required to follow the rule of "last hired/first fired" within the context of negotiated occupational groups and an agreed-upon "flow chart."

Unions insisted on this system and management acceded to it, for no better formula could be found that avoided the potentially capricious nature of supervisor choice. The only thing that needed to be worked out—and labor and management fought bitterly over it—was how to arrange the seniority system. Management often insisted on the narrowest work unit for the purposes of applying seniority, while unions demanded plantwide or even companywide "bumping rights" to protect workers with the highest seniority.[49] Lines of demarcation between the crafts and lesser-skilled positions were maintained, but within the broad category of "production work" the union sought and often won plantwide seniority protection.

WORK RULES AND JOB CLASSIFICATIONS

The next element of the postwar Workplace Contract was the establishment and retention of defined conditions of work, specific work rules, and job classifications. Without negotiated work rules, managers have the right under law, with limited restrictions, to use workers as they wish. Judicial opinion commonly accepts an implicit contract between employee and employer granting the employer rights over the employee for the duration of the workday. This is essentially the "property right" of management.

One of the earliest encroachments on this property right was the organized attempt, particularly in the manufacturing sector, to stop "speedup." Whether in apparel or textiles or auto and steel, workers were constantly forced to battle against an excessive demand for output. Union negotiators therefore insisted on contract provisions that would wrest from management its absolute control over the work effort put forward by its employees.

Under labor-management agreements, management's discretion over the use of workers is also constrained by a contractually established web of rules covering a broad array of workplace conditions, including hours of work and work assignments. While construction and craft unions have led the fight to maintain reasonable—although arguably, in some cases, overly restrictive—procedures and classifications, the practice of establishing narrowly defined jobs and encasing them in detailed rules was first and foremost a management invention. Under the tutelage of Frederick Winslow Taylor, employers began to apply "scientific management" in the early part of this century. As we shall see in chapter 5, Taylorism took Adam Smith's "division of labor" to its ultimate extreme. Every job was broken down into its component elements and assigned to individual workers. Rigid rules were formulated by management to guide workers in their every motion. The goal was to use a combination of the least-skilled labor to construct the most complicated and sophisticated products.

Under the Workplace Contract, labor turned the rigidity of work standards, work rules, and lines of job demarcation to its own advantage—improving health and safety on the job and enhancing job security. Management initially set the production standard, but workers protested an unfair work pace. The union, by negotiating a fair standard tied to a reasonable work pace, fought speedup and conserved jobs.

Maintaining narrowly defined job classifications for skilled workers also provided a form of job security. Functions of tradesmen such as the electrician, the millwright, and the carpenter were defined, and the union made certain that these jurisdictional lines were not crossed. As part of the rules, unions also demanded that supervisors supervise, not do work assigned to employees. The foreman who hauls a box of parts to a worker or picks up trash lying in the aisle may well be the target of a grievance for performing work to be done by employees in the bargaining unit.

The system did little to enhance creativity on the job or assure the highest level of efficiency. But in an era of mass production, sharp lines of job demarcation could bolster job security without seriously compromising what was considered by managers to be efficient production methods.

GRIEVANCE MACHINERY

Even the most carefully drafted contract between two parties cannot hope to resolve all potential disputes. Each particular case is replete with specific circumstances the parties to the contract could not have foreseen. In real life the "devil is in the details," and the details are often not in the contract. The fifth element in the traditional Workplace Contract established a formal mechanism for resolving differences over interpretation of the contract when the agreement is either ambiguous on a particular subject or the two sides are at odds over specific language. By analogy, the grievance machinery does for the union contract what the legal and court system does for the U.S. Constitution: it interprets contract provisions and resolves disputes.

Practically all collective-bargaining agreements contain elaborate machinery for this purpose. With a formal grievance procedure, the worker can "have his day in court" by filing a complaint when he or she feels the contract is not being upheld. To many a worker, the grievance system is among the most important benefits of union membership—as important as the wages and benefits won at the collective-bargaining table. The latter can be matched by the nonunion employer, but the enforceable grievance process is found only in the organized sector of the economy. It provides the individual worker with the necessary clout to challenge management over disciplinary cases and over the negotiated provisions that govern the workplace. It also provides for binding impartial arbitration if the grievance is not resolved within the established grievance procedure. Where management has not betrayed the trust of labor, or given the appearance of betrayal, and where unions have not abused the system, the grievance process has worked well. A smoothly functioning, equitable dispute-resolution mechanism preserves employee rights under the contract and can help avoid costly work stoppages.

To represent its members adequately in the shop, unions have fought for and won on-site representation. This allows the union to have individuals elected by employees at the work site to service their members whenever complaints are raised against management. Such a visible presence provides workers with the assurance that they are not alone when they file a grievance and permits the union representative to attempt to settle disputes before they go through the grievance process, mediation, or arbitration.

Management generally agrees to the grievance process and on-site union representation because the alternative—the equivalent of guerrilla warfare on the plant floor—may be even more costly. While established to meet the needs of employees, properly functioning grievance machinery has served the needs of management as well.

UNION SECURITY PROVISIONS

Under federal law, management is obligated to recognize a union and to bargain in good faith with it when a majority of the employees in a bargaining unit designates the union as their collective-bargaining agent. Federal law also requires that the union provide its services to all the employees in the unit. This includes employees who are not members of the union and pay no dues. Unions see this as the equivalent of representation with no taxation.

It is the usual practice, therefore, for a union to demand that a "union security" clause be written into the labor contract. Except where prohibited by state legislative action under paragraph 14b of the Taft-Hartley Act, the demand is almost invariably for a "union shop" provision.[50] This requires every employee in the bargaining unit to become a member of the union and to pay the established dues as a condition of employment. The argument, of course, is that since all the represented employees must by law receive the same benefits of the union-negotiated contract, all should help defray the cost of providing the union's services.

Unions customarily also propose a contract clause establishing a voluntary "checkoff" of dues. As a convenience, employees who voluntarily sign a checkoff card have their dues deducted from their paychecks as they might for contributions to the United Way or for the payroll savings plan. Management then transmits the dues to the union. Those who prefer not to sign a checkoff card can pay their dues directly to the union.

The union shop clause, even in the thirty states that permit it under 14b, is by no means universally included in the Workplace Contract. Like wages, benefits, seniority, work rules, and the grievance procedure, it must be successfully negotiated with management.

MANAGEMENT RIGHTS

Bringing the previous six provisions into the workplace represented genuine victories for labor. But management resolutely refused to retreat from what it considered its innate right to make the big decisions in the company. To preserve this "right," it is not surprising that management's invariable response to the legal obligation to bargain with a union is to insist on a tightly worded "management-rights" clause in its labor contracts. Such a provision assures that management will retain the decision-making authority over all issues not explicitly delineated in the contract (or precluded by federal, state, or local law). From a large number of union contracts we have devised a sample provision that serves to highlight the emphasis management places on protecting its own decision-making powers:

Typical Management-Rights Clause

Management prerogatives and the exercise thereof shall be unqualified, shall remain exclusively in the Management and *shall include without limitation all matters not covered by this Agreement* as well as the following, to the extent that the following are not limited or modified by the terms and conditions of this Agreement:

(a) The prerogative to hire, promote, assign to shifts, maintain discipline and efficiency, discharge and discipline all employees for a justifiable reason.

(b) The prerogative to determine the type of work to be performed, the location of work within the plants, the schedules of production, the schedules of working hours and the methods, processes and means of manufacture.[51] [Emphasis added.]

Constitutional law buffs may immediately recognize the parallel between the management-prerogatives clause and the last article of the original U.S. Bill of Rights, which reserves all powers not explicitly delegated to the federal authorities "to the States, respectively, or to the people."

Under the "residual thesis" of management rights, managers can delegate rights to employees and unions through collective bargaining, but they reserve the right to all "residual matters" not specifically detailed in the contract.[52] In the modern labor agreement, the "residual matters" include a host of items concerning the day-to-day operations in the workplace and, assuredly, decision making at higher levels of the enterprise. They include control over the design and engineering of the product or service; the methods, means, and processes of manufacture or provision of a service; all pricing decisions; the determination of quality standards; control over subcontracting and production location decisions; determination of all financing and investment activity; and unilateral control over decisions bearing on where to locate and when to expand production, or, for that matter, when and under what circumstances to close down all or part of an operation.

The point is that the traditional contract intrinsically makes a sharp distinction between issues within the workplace and those at the level of the enterprise. The former are subject to collective bargaining and thus are the joint decision of labor and management in the normal course of events. The latter are solely the prerogative of management, regardless of how critical these decisions may be for the employment security or the general well-being of the work force—or, for that matter, the health and well-being of the organization itself.

The battle over management rights has a rich postwar history. Within five months of the formal end of World War II, management and organized labor were already jockeying for control over decision making. A *Washington Post* editorial in January 1946 noted that "the question how far employees should have a voice in dictating to management is at present one of the hottest issues before the country."[53] Acknowledging that executive decisions over pricing policy or the very nature of the product could impinge on job security, leading unions attempted to cajole management into "opening the books." They suggested to management new products including the "Small Car Named Desire," a 1949 UAW idea for a low-priced, compact, fuel-efficient automobile.

In general, management disregarded such suggestions and staunchly refused to make strategic information available to workers or their unions. In a widely distributed company pamphlet, "Here Is the Issue," General Motors, for example, argued that "a look at the books is a clever phrase intended as an opening wedge whereby the unions hope to pry their way into the whole field of management. It leads surely to the day when union bosses, under threat of strike, will seek to tell us *what* we can make, *when* we can make it."[54] GM was certainly not going to permit this, nor would any other company.

Ultimately, under pressure from their members, most unions focused their efforts on making the pay package more lucrative, providing more generous benefits, and tying job security to seniority. They eased off on their demands for more strategic input in the firm. No union could entice its members to endure a strike over the price or quality of the product. Better wages, pensions, and medical coverage were much closer to what workers wanted. With employment expanding and job security reasonably assured, most workers were willing to leave strategic decision making to company executives. After all, some argued, that is what they are paid to do.

For all practical purposes, the major battle over management rights in strategic decisions was over by the end of the 1940s. Unions had cemented the right to co-manage vital workplace issues, but corporate executives retained the sole right to manage the enterprise. This separation of control has continued, more or less intact, to the present day. The historic five-year contract between the UAW and GM in 1950 typified this new labor-management accord: AIF/COLA was firmly entrenched as the method for setting wages; employer-paid pensions were negotiated; vacation and holiday pay were improved; the seniority system remained the basis for shifting employees or reducing payroll; the grievance machinery including arbitration continued intact; work rules were jointly determined; and a union security clause was now sacrosanct.[55] In return, the management-rights clause continued unchanged as a constraint on labor's power within the company.

Calling the 1950 contract between the company and the union "the treaty of Detroit," *Fortune* magazine led the cheerleading for the business community when the negotiations were successfully concluded:

> GM may have paid a billion for peace [but] it got a bargain. . . . General Motors has regained control over one of the crucial management functions . . . long-range scheduling of production, model changes, and tool and plant investment. It has been so long since any big U.S. manufacturer could plan with confidence in its labor relations that industry has almost forgotten what it felt like. The full consequence of such a liberation of engineering and production talent can as yet only be guessed, but one estimate from Detroit is that in planning freedom alone the contract is worth 15 cents per man per hour to the corporation.[56]

Similarly, the union extolled the progress that had been achieved with the 1950 contract on behalf of its members and their families. Walter Reuther, who now as president of the union led the negotiations, stated to the press:

> We believe that this new agreement is not only a tremendous step forward in improving the economic conditions of General Motors workers and in stabilizing labor relations in General Motors, but that it points the way for the same improvements and stabilization throughout American industry. . . . It recognizes that workers have a right to a constantly improving standard of living and that they have a right to share in the benefits of greater production made possible through technological progress without additional human effort.[57]

"Sympathetic" pressure and pattern bargaining assured that the gains made at GM were not limited to auto workers.[58] The key features of the postwar workplace contract spread throughout much of the nation's basic industry, providing a powerful boost to workers' earnings and thereby a mass market for the bounteous output of private enterprise.[59] The dialectic between the postwar economic boom and the Workplace Contract was complete.

SPREADING THE UNION GOSPEL

Auto workers were not alone during the glory days in securing large wage gains and job security through the provisions of the Workplace Contract. Union membership expanded as workers in one sector after another sought the benefits and protections that organized employees enjoyed. During World War II, more than 4 million new workers joined national unions. In the following decade, union membership grew by another 3 million plus.[60] Wage and benefit patterns set in one industry spread rapidly to others. Unions regularly borrowed contract language from each other to bring to the bargaining tables in their own industries. As Otto Eckstein and Thomas Wilson found in their pioneering research in the mid-1960s,

> while no one industry is always the leader in establishing [a] pattern, autos and steel probably play more of a leadership role than the others. But whoever initiates the pattern, it has a very considerable influence on all subsequent settlements in the group. . . . The cement and aluminum settlements follow the steel settlement, and rubber and plate glass tend to follow the auto settlement.[61]

By one count, workers during this period were covered under more than 150,000 separate union contracts.[62] For production workers in the motor vehicle industry, the UAW had won average real weekly earnings gains of 67 percent between 1947 and 1970.[63] In the basic steel industry the gain was no less, at 68 percent; in electrical machinery, 60 percent; and in the machinery industry, 64 percent. The chemical industry led all others, with better than a 70 percent increase in average wages. The same held true in the nonunion sector, where companies like IBM, Motorola, Delta Airlines, Grumman Aircraft, and Burlington Mills copied personnel policies and matched compensation patterns established through collective bargaining in unionized firms.[64]

Those outside the manufacturing sector generally began with substantially lower wages at the end of the war, but often received proportional wage gains that approached those in basic industry. This was true despite the fact that few workers in these industries were members of trade unions. Nonsupervisory workers in wholesale trade saw their weekly wages rise by 63 percent between 1947 and 1970, while those working in banks, insurance companies, and real estate offices realized a gain of 60 percent. Workers in the retail trade sector, including clerks and inventory stockers, lagged behind, but even they were able to secure gains that averaged 56 percent during this twenty-three-year period.[65]

With such gains in the private sector, those who worked for government demanded the right to join unions as well. Unionization in the public sector dates back to the nineteenth century with the emergence of labor organizations among federal employees in the postal service and the government printing office. However, the rapid growth in public-sector unions at the federal, state, and local levels received major impetus only after President Kennedy's pathbreaking Executive Order 10988, issued in January 1962.

The presidential decree granted the right of federal workers to form, join, and assist an employee organization, although it set limits on the scope of bargaining. (Congress, for instance, holds the power to determine unilaterally the major economic provisions governing the employer/employee relationship.) President Nixon, in his Executive Order 11491, added features to the earlier order that strengthened grievance procedures, provided for exclusive recognition for a single union in such bargaining unit, and established a Federal Labor Relations Council to help resolve major policy disagreements.

As an indirect result of President Kennedy's Executive Order and succeeding presidential and congressional action, public-sector unionization increased at the state and local levels as more and more state, county, and city governments recognized the rights of their employees to organize and engage in collective bargaining. Associations of firefighters and police officers reorganized themselves as bona fide unions for the purpose of collective bargaining and worker representation. Teachers' unions enjoyed a particularly dramatic expansion. In response to the rise of the American Federation of Teachers, the National Education Association (NEA), originally created as a professional organization eschewing collective bargaining, became one of the nation's largest unions with more than 2.1 million members. It now aggressively pursues collective-bargaining agreements in the twenty-seven states where public employee unions are sanctioned. In sixteen others, NEA has negotiated "de facto" contracts despite the absence of a public-sector bargaining law.[66] By 1990, more than 43 percent of all government workers were represented by unions, in contrast to less than 14 percent in private industry.[67] Even industrial unions like the UAW and the Communications Workers now represent state employees, including white-collar workers in colleges and universities.[68] Thus public-sector unionization moved into a more prominent role within the national labor movement both in the strength of its membership and in its effectiveness in contract negotiations.

Ultimately much of what was won at the bargaining table in both the public and private realms diffused to the unorganized sector. If this were not true, the wage gap between union and nonunion labor would have expanded considerably beyond the 15 to 20 percent differential of the late 1960s and early 1970s.[69] In contrast, data on wage disparity and family income inequality from 1947 to 1973 suggest that this was a period when inequality substantially *declined*. A common statistical measure of wage inequality, the variance in the log of annual wages and salaries, fell from almost 2.1 in 1963 to 1.6 by 1975.[70] Family income inequality began to decline soon after World War II and continued to do so through the late 1960s as new elements of the workplace contract were being negotiated in the union sector and then adopted in the unorganized sector.[71] To be sure, certain industries such as auto and steel outpaced the average, but overall the United States became a more egalitarian society as a result of the traditional Workplace Contract.

AN EPHEMERAL TRIUMPH

In a real sense, the U.S. economy of the first postwar generation was a triumph not only of Keynesianism and market regulation but equally of the classical theory associated with Say's Law: supply creates its own demand. The wages paid to workers in the course of producing goods and providing services, and paid to stockholders in the form of dividends, gave workers and stockholders the very means to purchase that which was produced in the first place. Thus a "virtuous cycle" was established in which higher wages and profits created the demand for ever-higher levels of output and employment, ultimately contributing to further rounds of real wage gains and quarterly dividend checks. Today we refer to this virtuous cycle as "wage-led growth," since roughly three-quarters of the "supply" of purchasing power comes in the form of wages and salaries. For its part, the Keynesian contribution came in the form of continued high levels of government spending supplementing the high-wage, high-consumption, high-growth private economy that had been jump-started at war's end.

For decades the Workplace Contract worked, and for the most part worked well. Over time many managers learned to live with it, indeed even to prosper by it. The postwar Workplace Contract hardly fulfilled labor's demand for true "industrial" democracy, nor did it radically change the drudgery of most factory or office work, but no one could deny its powerful impact on changing the very meaning of social class in America.

To be sure, the rising tide of the new labor-management relations did not lift all ships. Even as the economy expanded and the equal-pay-for-equal-work principle was enforced in union contracts, national prosperity was by no means shared equitably between men and women or between whites and blacks. In 1948, the official unemployment rate for nonwhite men was 5.8 percent, compared with 3.4 percent for white men. More than twenty years later, and despite major gains in civil rights legislation, the gap was no smaller: 7.3 percent versus 4.0 percent. The median annual wage of black men who worked year-round full-time in 1970 was only two-thirds as great as that of their white male counterparts.[72] The ratio of black to white *family* incomes was but three-fifths, a proportion eerily reminiscent of Article II, Section 2, of the original U.S. Constitution, which stipulated (until ratification of the 14th Amendment in 1868) that each Negro would be counted as three-fifths of a white for purposes of apportioning congressional seats.[73]

Nonetheless, few—especially those who had known the despair of the Great Depression—would deny that America, confident of its global prowess, had transformed itself into a rich and self-satisfied nation in less than twenty-five years' time. *If* prosperity and profits had endured, the Workplace Contract would likely have spread throughout the economy. Unfortunately the national economy faltered, and the postwar Workplace Contract that had taken a generation to construct no longer fulfilled its goals of greater security and a continually rising standard of living supported by healthy enterprises. With onrushing global competition and the outsourcing of work to low-wage areas and nations, with a slowdown in productivity growth, and with the demise of the other economic conditions that had promoted the glory days, profits plummeted, real wages declined, layoffs and plant closings made short shrift of employment security, and union membership tumbled. The traditional Workplace Contract, with its emphasis on a clear-cut division in decision-making authority, could no longer work its magic for management or for labor.

CHAPTER 3

Goodbye to the Glory Days

This perception of ebbing economic power has to take account of the fact that the overwhelming superiority of the American economy in the years following World War II grew out of extraordinary circumstances that could not be sustained. The American lead was bound to erode as other countries recovered from the devastation of the war and rebuilt their industrial base.
—The MIT Commission on Industrial Productivity *(1989)*

America has failed to adjust to the new reality of a global economy, and we are beginning to pay the price.
—The Cuomo Commission Report on Trade and Competitiveness *(1988)*

The first conspicuous sign of economic trouble could be seen at every gasoline pump in the summer of 1974. Galvanized by American support of Israel during the Yom Kippur War—initiated by Egypt the previous October and joined by other Arab nations—the ministers of the Organization of Petroleum Exporting Countries (OPEC) successfully mounted an embargo of petroleum shipments to the United States, causing oil prices to soar. By the end of 1974, gasoline prices had jumped 50 percent.[1]

Everything else produced from petroleum, from heating oil to the vinyl used in phonograph records, immediately became more expensive. In a desperate attempt to maintain their profits in the face of sudden increased costs, U.S. firms raised their prices. Workers, in turn, tried to maintain the real value of their incomes by demanding wage increases and insisting on full implementation of the cost-of-living adjustments in their contracts. The inevitable result was a price-wage spiral. The original OPEC-led oil-price inflation was ratified and then multiplied by a real-life game of hot potato, as everyone tried to pass the oil "tax" on to everyone else. Inflation, which had climbed only 3.4 percent between December 1972 and December 1973, rose by 8.7 percent the following year and a record-shattering 12.3 percent the next.[2]

American citizens were waking up to the fact that their economic well-being was no longer sheltered from events in the rest of the world. Hikes in consumer prices so outstripped wage increases where COLA was not in effect that within two years of the initial oil embargo, real average weekly earnings in the private sector of the economy had plunged to the level prevailing almost a decade earlier.[3] Eight years of wage increases had been wiped out in two.

Yet the *real* import problem was just beginning to reveal itself. It was a consequence not of the shutting off of the oil spigot but of the opening of the import valve through which practically everything else flowed. Western Europe and Japan had taken the better part of a full generation to rebuild their war-torn economies. But as they did, they put in place the most modern of technologies, introduced the most sophisticated of high-tech products, and developed labor-management-relations systems that helped boost the productivity of their industries. When it came to steel, for example, the Europeans and the Japanese introduced the high-productivity basic oxygen furnace (BOF) almost as soon as it was developed in Austria in 1952. By contrast, the first BOF capacity was not introduced at a major U.S. steel firm until eleven years later.[4]

In one sector after another, the Europeans and the Japanese launched lower-priced products to compete with those made in America. In a matter of years, they had a competitive edge not only on price but often on quality and new product design. In autos, foreign producers were the first to offer radial tires, disk brakes, fuel-injection systems, and multivalve, high-output, fuel-efficient engines. At the beginning of their recovery, foreign competitors merely substituted their own products for the ones they had purchased as imports from the United

States (paid for, in many cases, with Marshall Plan dollars). By the 1970s, however, they had succeeded in producing enough to supply domestic needs as well as to export en masse to the rest of the world. Their favorite destination was the immense consumer market in the United States.

As foreign productive capacity came on line, America's share of world production fell. Some loss of share was expected, but in key industries the decline was precipitous. In 1950, for example, the U.S. had produced nearly half (47 percent) of the total world output of raw steel. Within a decade, the share was down to one-quarter (26 percent), and by 1970 to one-fifth (20 percent). Today, the United States is responsible for less than one-tenth of the world's output of this basic commodity. In car and truck production, the story is much the same. The U.S. produced 8 million—or three-fourths—of the 10.6 million motor vehicles produced worldwide in 1950. By 1980, admittedly during a recession, America's production was exactly the same as thirty years earlier, but the rest of the world had increased its output from 2.5 million units to over 30 million—a jump of 1100 percent. The U.S. share of world production had fallen from 76 percent to 21 percent. In 1950, West Germany produced 3 percent of the world's cars and trucks and Japan, for all intents and purposes, none. By 1985, Japan's share of the world market exceeded U.S. production, making it the number-one motor vehicle producer in the world, while Germany had captured a full 10 percent of the market.[5]

A by no means exhaustive roster of U.S.-made products that have lost half or more of their world market share since 1950 now includes: automobiles, cameras, stereo equipment, medical equipment, color television sets, hand tools, electron microscopes, electric motors, food processors, microwave ovens, athletic equipment, computer chips, industrial robots, radial tires, machine tools, and optical equipment.[6]

What was happening in world markets was mirrored in the U.S. domestic economy. When Americans went shopping in 1960 for a new automobile, more than 95 times out of 100 they came back with a General Motors, Ford, Chrysler, or American Motors product built within the borders of the United States. Buying American-made held equally true when the recently affluent U.S. consumer went out for a pair of shoes, a radio, or a TV—or, for that matter, when American industry went out to purchase steel or to invest in new machine tools. But by 1970, the shift toward imports was under way. Transistor radios from Japan soon dominated the market, while Sony became the premier brand of color television in the United States. Even before the 1980s, foreign companies had captured the lion's share of the consumer electronics market. While U.S. producers of footwear, apparel, and automobiles did a somewhat better job of holding on to their customers, by 1986—as table 3.1 amply demonstrates—each of these industries had surrendered between 30 and 50 percent of its market to imports.

The shocker in all of this for Americans was the incredible speed with which the import revolution materialized. In 1969, the year Boeing introduced the 747 jumbo jet and Americans on the moon sent computer-enhanced pictures back to earth, the import share of GNP was 5.7 percent—*exactly the same level* as on the eve of the Great Depression forty years earlier, when the best method to traverse the nation was by steam-powered railroad and the telegraph was only then being supplanted by the telephone. Yet in the single decade of the 1970s the import share nearly doubled, to 10.9 percent, and then by the end of the 1980s rose to 14 percent. As for manufactured goods alone, excluding services, agricultural products, and energy resources, imports of merchandise in the mid-1980s were equal to 45 percent of the value of GNP originating in the U.S. manufacturing sector—more than *triple*

TABLE 3.1

Imports as a Share of U.S. Domestic Market
Selected Industries, 1960–1986

Industry	1960	1970	1979	1986
Consumer Electronics	5.6%	31.6%	50.6%	68.0%
Footwear	2.3	14.6	31.3	58.0
Machine Tools	3.2	6.8	24.6	50.0
Apparel	1.8	5.2	10.0	50.0
Automobiles	4.1	11.2	21.0	31.0
Steel	4.2	14.3	14.0	24.0

Source: "The Reindustrialization of America," special issue, *Business Week,* June 30, 1980, p. 8; Michael L. Dertouzos, Richard K. Lester, and Robert M. Solow, Made in America (Cambridge: MIT Press, 1989), figure 1.1, p. 5; Bernard A. Gelb, "Import Penetration During the Eighties; Anatomy of the Data," Congressional Research Service, September 16, 1986, table 1, p. CRS-2.

the 1969 rate of 13.9 percent.[7] According to one estimate, fully 70 percent of all U.S. manufacturing output now faces direct foreign competition.[8] A rising share of services also originates as imports, particularly in the areas of shipping, insurance, banking, and securities transactions. In short, foreign competition had exploded on an America lulled into complacency by more than a quarter-century of unchallenged economic hegemony.

THE IMPACT OF THE NEW WORLD ORDER ON CAPITAL AND LABOR

Competition, according to the textbooks, is responsible for spurring enterprise to build better products, offer better services, and do both at higher levels of efficiency. Indeed, the absence of a healthy rivalry on the playing field or in the marketplace usually breeds halfhearted, dull performance, ultimately of little benefit to the spectator or the consumer. A baseball team is always more interesting when it is in the thick of a pennant race than when it has clinched its division championship and is simply counting down the days to the league playoffs. One has only to witness the demise of the Communist systems of Eastern Europe and the Soviet Union to see how the near absence of economic competition created long lines at supermarkets and department stores for, by Western standards, not very desirable meats and vegetables and extraordinarily shoddy manufactured goods.

In this sense, there is no question that increased international competition has benefited the American consumer. Hondas were indeed better cars than the so-called import-beaters such as the Chevrolet Vega, with its balky engine, and the Ford Pinto, which ran smoothly but had the unfortunate drawback of occasionally exploding when involved in a rear-end collision. Sony TVs had sharper definition and better sound than American-built Sylvanias or RCAs. Moreover, the variety of goods available to the consumer has certainly been enhanced. Without the Japanese, it is unlikely that the U.S. public would be enjoying an abundance of ever-improving and cheaper VCRs, phone answering machines, fax systems, and Nintendo games—despite the fact that, at least in the case of videotape recorders, the original engineering was all done in the United States.

What has been deeply disturbing to Americans about the import explosion is not, of course, the abundance of better and cheaper products but the impact it has had on corporate profits, employment and wages, and the Workplace Contract. With the import surge that began in the early 1970s, profits sagged and manufacturing employment—along with average wages—fell. The resurgence of the economy in the second half of the 1980s helped to rebuild profitability, to stabilize the level of manufacturing employment, and to curb the downward trend in wages. Still, nearly eight years of uninterrupted economic growth were nowhere near sufficient to restore the American economy to the position it had held before the rest of the world began to use the United States as its number-one customer. In the process, "deindustrialization"—while not characteristic of the entire economy—became the best description for what was happening to a broad array of manufacturing industries including motor vehicles and parts, tires, household appliances, textile mill products, apparel, footwear, electrical distribution equipment, radio and TV receivers, and even chemicals.[9]

Profit rates—not jobs—were the first to suffer from the new competition. In 1965, overall corporate profitability, as measured by the net after-tax rate of return on assets, was a healthy 10 percent. By 1970, it had fallen to 6 percent and, by 1974, to about 4.5 percent, less than half of its postwar peak.[10] In individual manufacturing industries, the decline in net pretax profit rates ranged from one-third in rubber products, glass, and heavy electric equipment and one-half in farm machinery and machine tools, to two-thirds in radio and television equipment and motor vehicles. Pretax profit rates fell to as low as 3.1 percent in shipbuilding and 3.4 percent in railroad equipment.[11] At these rates it was more profitable for American firms to stow their investment dollars in commercial bank certificates than to reinvest them in plants and equipment. Reflecting these anemic corporate rates of return, the Dow-Jones Industrial Average sank to a level in 1980 below that which had prevailed fifteen years earlier. Stockholders were clearly dismayed and, in shareholder meetings, openly hostile.

If stockholders were unhappy with dismal profits, shrinking dividends, and the virtual disappearance of capital gains, the eventual impact on the American work force was far worse. An analysis of Dun and Bradstreet data suggests that between 1969 and 1976 overall employment increased by a healthy 9 million jobs. But the same data indicate that this *net* increase was due almost exclusively to a massive creation of jobs in the service sector, offsetting losses in manufacturing. Outright plant closing, and the migration of enterprise from one area of the country to another or out of the country altogether, produced a "gross" loss of 22 million jobs during this seven-year period.[12] Candee Harris, a former research analyst at the Brookings Institution, found that the loss of jobs to plant closing continued throughout the 1970s and into the 1980s. In large-scale manufacturing plants alone, Harris counted 900,000 jobs erased *each year* between 1978 and 1982—one out of every four jobs in large manufacturing facilities.[13]

By 1987, employment in manufacturing was actually lower than in 1966.[14] In one company after another, white-collar as well as blue-collar workers were given pink slips. Nearly a quarter of the production work force in the auto industry in 1978 would disappear by 1989; similarly more than half of those who build farm machinery and construction equipment disappeared from these industries in the course of a single decade.[15] In furniture, glass products, steel, metal products, machinery, food and beverages, textiles, clothing, paper, chemical products, and leather, employment fell below the levels achieved in the 1960s and 1970s.[16] The distressing consequences of plant closing on workers, their families, and their communities were all too evident in terms of unemployment, income loss, and physical and mental trauma.[17]

THE DISAPPEARANCE OF MONOPOLY PROFITS AND MONOPOLY RENTS

In an entire range of industries, the explosion in global competition had eliminated the "monopoly advantage" shared by stockholders and workers. Conventionally measured industry concentration ratios no longer contained much meaning. GM, Ford, Chrysler, and American Motors remained the only domestic producers of automobiles, but a dozen or more foreign companies, including BMW, Volkswagen, Mercedes-Benz, Renault, Peugeot, Saab, Volvo, Nissan, Honda, Toyota, and Mazda, eliminated any semblance of "administered pricing" or monopoly practice. Now if GM raised its prices, Ford and Chrysler might follow, but not necessarily Nissan or VW. As a consequence, boosting profits the old-fashioned way—by raising prices—no longer proved a viable strategy. If GM and its domestic rivals raised their prices, price-conscious consumers abandoned domestic showrooms for those containing foreign makes. The same proved true in steel, consumer electronics, machine tools, and at least two dozen other major industries.

As monopoly profits vanished, firms were left in a serious bind. If their unions continued to push for wage increases that exceeded productivity advances, the time-honored method of costlessly passing the difference on to customers would no longer wash. In this case, firms had an uncomfortable choice. They could raise their prices anyway, sacrificing market share; they could settle for lower profits and the enmity of their stockholders; or they could aggressively challenge the wage demands of their employees and insist on economic concessions. In the end they did all three, but concentrated overwhelmingly on the last of these options.

The consequences were essentially preordained. The price gap between domestic and foreign goods widened, making imports even more attractive. Lower profits angered Wall Street, pushing stock prices down and lowering bond ratings, making it more expensive for firms to obtain investment funds on the open market. Where wages were flexible, they declined. In those industries where unions fought to maintain the full array of previously won wage and benefit gains, they often succeeded.[18] But the cost in terms of jobs was usually enormous, as management exercised its rights under the management-prerogatives clause to reduce employment levels, to shutter plants, and to relocate activities. What made it difficult for unions to agree to wage and benefit concessions was management's time-honored obstinate refusal to open the books to prove the need for changes in the contract. The fact that many corporations continued to reward their top executives with large bonuses despite plummeting sales and declining market share did not make it any easier for unions to sell "concession bargaining" to their members.

What global competition did to former oligopolistically organized industries like auto and steel was replicated in the industries that faced government deregulation at the end of the 1970s and beginning of the 1980s. A good case in point involves commercial airlines. The authority of the Civilian Aeronautics Board (CAB) over domestic airline routes ceased in 1981, while its control over domestic fares and corporate mergers and acquisitions was terminated in 1983. At the end of 1984, the CAB, like the Cheshire cat in *Alice in Wonderland,* disappeared altogether, leaving behind barely a trace of its smile. Only safety regulations remain, the province of the Federal Aviation Administration.[19]

As soon as the CAB lost its authority to set routes, discount airlines jumped into the market. People's Express, in the few years before it went bankrupt, succeeded in undercutting existing fares to the point where the traditional national carriers were forced to cut theirs or lose critical market share. Dozens of new airlines entered the market and began to compete aggressively, especially on heavily traveled routes. The industry's monopoly profit, once available as a result of regulation, disappeared. Instead of assured profits, deregulation seemed to assure airline losses.

The Motor Carrier Reform Act of 1980 did to trucking what airline deregulation did to the airlines. The act gave trucking companies greater flexibility in setting rates and made it easier for new companies to enter the industry. Freight costs dropped as hundreds of small and mid-sized trucking companies competed head to head for business. Once again the equivalent of government-regulated oligopoly disappeared and, with it, the monopoly profits and economic rents that administered pricing permits. Similar legislation eliminated the de facto monopoly elements in intercity bus travel and on the railroads. The expansion of cable television under revised Federal Communications Commission regulations effectively eliminated the ABC/CBS/ NBC oligopoly that had dominated commercial TV since its invention. The ultimate result was open season on workers' wages and employment security. Why this was so can be seen by examining the options management faced as profits plummeted.

MANAGERIAL STRATEGIES TO MEET THE IMPORT CHALLENGE

For managers, how to regain lost profits in the face of foreign competition and government deregulation became the single-minded focus of attention. A nearly endless stream of business consultants and self-styled "gurus" expressed their opinion on the matter. Books like Tom

Peters's and Robert H. Waterman's *In Search of Excellence* became over-night best-sellers as executives searched for advice on how to run their companies profitably.[20]

To grasp the pressures faced by the typical executive in the 1970s and 1980s, it is helpful to understand how profit is generated and measured. Simply put, profits are equal to total revenue—the total value of what a company produces—minus total costs. Some meat can be placed on this bare-bones formulation by examining its separate components. Total revenue, or the value of output, is equal to the average price charged per unit of output times the quantity sold. A firm that sells 100 hula hoops at $1.00 each reaps a total revenue of $100. It is somewhat more complex than this for goods like autos and steel, but the fundamentals are identical.

Total costs are more complicated because there is a greater array of them. The most important are related to labor, capital, raw materials, taxes, and the costs associated with complying with government regula-tions. How important each of these is to the individual firm depends on the technology used in production and on the nature of the firm's products or services. The Fanuc plant in Japan uses robots to build robots at night after the workers have headed for home; it has high capital costs. The local restaurant, on the other hand, usually has a cost structure in which labor is the most expensive component.

Labor cost, at least in the abstract, is equal to the average value of wages and job benefits paid to each worker times the number of workers employed. Capital costs are normally calculated as the average interest rate paid on a given investment times the amount of plant and equipment owned. Raw material costs, ranging from the steel and glass that go into the final assembly of an automobile and the energy costs used to power the plant, to the wholesale cost of the foodstuffs pur-chased by a fine gourmet restaurant, are equal to the average price of the "inputs" times the volume purchased. Finally, taxes paid to federal, state, local, and foreign governments and the cost of complying with government regulatory costs must be factored in as well in calculating after-tax profits.

By this formulation, corporate executives facing a "profits squeeze" have *ten* different strategies that might be used to get their firms out of the red. Only two of these are on the revenue side. Profits can be augmented by either raising prices or increasing market share. In the best of all possible worlds (at least from the point of view of the firm, if not the customer), the exceptionally successful firm can do both. As noted earlier, before the import surge, annual price increases were the rule in many industries, and market share was normally maintained because there was little foreign competition. As the quality of foreign products improved, market share often could not be maintained even by holding the line on prices. To maintain their market positions, American firms would have had to *cut* their prices, *improve* their quality, or both.

As we shall discuss more thoroughly in the next chapter, too many firms in too many industries did neither. They did not know what their customers wanted; they did not produce products that customers would buy; and they almost always underestimated the prowess of their competitors. General Motors, for example, had so little curiosity about the market for its cars, according to the automotive analyst Maryann Keller, that it was not until 1985 that it established a consumer market-research division.[21] Consequently the executives at the world's leading automobile company did not know what auto buyers were saying about their wants and needs, and therefore could not understand why so many prospective customers were driving Hondas and Toyotas rather than Chevrolets.

Once the two revenue-side strategies failed, executives had no choice but to turn to the cost side of the ledger in their attempt to become competitive. Looking across the entire corporate horizon, it is abundantly clear that in one company or another, corporate managers experimented with all eight remaining strategies in the repertoire. In the auto industry, for example, companies moved to curtail the amount of high-priced steel in their cars, hoping to reduce their raw material costs. Today the average American-built car has hundreds of fewer pounds of steel than in the 1960s, not just because the typical car is now smaller but because much of the missing metal has been replaced by plastic. Unfortunately the attempts to reduce raw material costs ran into unforeseen barriers. The OPEC oil price increases in 1973–74 and 1979–80 not only increased the cost of energy directly but inflated the price of virtually all the new synthetics used as substitutes for other raw materials: "The U.S. automakers' gambit [to substitute plastic for steel] was defeated by decisions made in Saudi Arabia, Iran, and Abu Dhabi," as the price of plastic, rubber, and allied products doubled between 1973 and 1980.[22]

Defeated on raw materials, many firms tried to reduce their capital costs, either by patching up old equipment and running it longer or by simply curtailing all new investment. But this strategy was also doomed to fail, on two grounds. Cutting back on capital investment might boost short-term profits, but it practically assures long-term extinction. By not replacing aging plants and equipment, and by failing to install new machine technology, firms quickly found themselves producing obsolete products with old-fashioned tools. To make matters worse, the price of capital also began to rise, completely outside the control of corporate managers. The prime rate—the interest rate the major banks charge their most credit-worthy customers—remained at a reasonable 4.5 percent during most of the early 1960s. However, as the Federal Reserve Board (the "Fed") boosted the interest rate it charged its member banks in order to deal with rising inflation due to the Vietnam War, the prime rate rose—to nearly 8 percent by 1970 and 11 percent by 1974. With further Fed credit tightening at the end of the 1970s to deal with double-digit inflation, the interest rate charged to even the nation's most favored corporate customers exceeded 18 percent.

In short order, ten possible strategies were reduced to four: reduce labor costs by cutting the number of workers used in production; reduce labor costs by using cheaper labor or cutting wages; work politically to reduce corporate taxes; or work politically to soften or eliminate what corporate managers viewed as costly and meddlesome government regulations. In the vernacular of the day, it was time to get "lean and mean" and to "get the government off the backs of the people." Management got down to work on both. Across a broad array of industries, a frontal assault on the traditional Workplace Contract was mounted. In some cases the strategy succeeded, but it ultimately provided the coup de grace to the glory days that had served labor and the economy so well for a quarter of a century.

UNDOING THE WORKPLACE CONTRACT

Labor cost "containment" became an especially tempting target, since labor accounts for at least 70 percent of total costs economywide.[23] "Cutting" labor took many forms. One was to take advantage of cheaper wage rates in the Newly Industrialized Countries (NICs) by either establishing manufacturing operations there or by subcontracting for parts or entire assemblies from indigenous firms located in those countries. For years, American apparel manufacturers have had their clothing sewn in the Caribbean and in Mexican towns south of the Rio Grande. General Motors's Packard Electric division makes wiring harnesses for GM cars in Chihuahua and Ciudad Juárez, Mexico, while its Delco Electronics division builds engine controls, electronic dash displays, and air conditioners in other Mexican factories. Chrysler and Ford do the same for a range of auto-related parts.[24] Automobile companies are not alone in traveling to Mexico. The number of *maquiladoras*—manufacturing plants along the Mexican border established with U.S. government approval—expanded from 65 employing 22,000 workers in 1970 to more than 1,700 employing between 400,-000 and 500,000 in 1991.[25] By the late 1980s, most of the 100 largest U.S. manufacturing firms had at least one *maquila* in their stable of global factories.[26]

Moving abroad to cut labor costs is not restricted to traditional manufacturing industries. High-tech has moved swiftly to take up residence in the NICs. It is estimated that for its personal computers IBM purchases 70 percent of its components from firms operating abroad—indeed, from a veritable United Nations: Sri Lanka, Ecuador, Taiwan, South Korea, and Malaysia. Hewlett-Packard manufactures its printed circuit boards in Taiwan. Apple Computer builds parts for its personal computers in Singapore. The practice is so common that Akio Morita, the chair and co-founder of the Sony Corporation, cautions his American friends that this strategy of shifting output to low-wage countries will inevitably lead to the "hollowing of American industry."[27] There are American managers who privately fear that Morita is right, but faced with import competition, they have found it imperative to take advantage of hourly wage rates that in 1988 were as low as $2.43 in Hong Kong, $2.46 in South Korea, $2.71 in Taiwan, and $1.57 in Mexico.[28]

In addition to moving abroad to avoid high labor costs, firms during the 1960s and 1970s increasingly resorted to what the labor movement dubbed the Southern Strategy—shutting down older, unionized plants primarily in the North and setting up new nonunion facilities in the South, where organized labor is weak or nonexistent. One such firm is Du Pont Chemical. At the end of World War II, 94 percent of Du Pont's blue-collar workers were represented by unions. Since then, Du Pont has built manufacturing capacity in fifty-one new sites, and now only 35 percent of its production employees belong to unions.[29] According to Kochan, Katz, and McKersie, who have followed this activity closely, the union-avoidance location decision has become a prominent component of management's attempt to reduce labor costs. General Mills, Pepsi-Cola, Mead Paper, Weyerhauser, Mobil Oil, Goodyear, Firestone, General Tire, Uniroyal, Pratt & Whitney, and Piper Aircraft are among a large list of firms that opened nonunion facilities rather than expand their existing unionized operations.[30]

Of course, the cost of building new plants in new locations, training unskilled workers, and coordinating engineering, design, and production over long distances often made it more profitable for firms to maintain domestic operations but strive to cut labor costs at home. This meant accelerating the introduction of automation to reduce the number of workers on their payrolls or, more often, demanding concessions at the bargaining table. The disastrous recession of 1981–82, which generated an unemployment rate of nearly 11 percent, stung organized labor with such heavy layoffs that it agreed to wage cuts and other concessions that would have been unheard of just a few years before. The same is true of the recession of the early 1990s. Even the most militant national labor leaders recognize that the days of global isolation are over, and with them the days of economic rent. For years business executives had cried wolf whenever unions demanded higher wages or more benefits. Now, as one business journalist put it, "the wolf was at the door."[31]

With literally hundreds of thousands of auto workers on indefinite layoff in 1982, the UAW, for one, agreed to open negotiations early to ease the cost burden on the auto companies. The membership ratified a new contract that included the cancellation of the AIF at General Motors and Ford, leaving hourly wages where they had been in 1981. It also agreed to deferral of the cost-of-living adjustment, essentially temporarily freezing wages altogether. While an abrupt and painful departure from past practice, these cuts were minor compared with those at Chrysler. Among the conditions for the federal loan guarantee that saved the company from certain bankruptcy and thousands of workers from the loss of their jobs, the UAW was compelled for a period to accept dramatic wage cuts that left Chrysler's straight-time wage rates 20 to 25 percent below domestic competitors.[32]

In the trucking industry and others, concession contracts also became the norm. In the face of deregulation and the entry of nonunion competition, the Master Freight Agreement of 1982 covering some 300,000 teamsters included no general wage increase and weakened the cost-of-living clause.[33] After 1981–82, concessions spread like wild-fire from one industry to another. By 1984–85, according to the UCLA economist Daniel J. B. Mitchell, virtually every industry with unionized firms had gained concessions in the form of wage freezes or outright rescissions. These included metals, motor vehicles, retail food stores, machinery, meatpacking, the airlines, printing and publishing, health care, lumber and paper, construction, public transit, trucking, aero-space, textiles, chemicals, hotels and restaurants, communications, ap-parel, mining, and business services. All together, Mitchell counted firms in thirty-nine different industries winning wage concessions from their unions.[34] At the same time, unilateral wage and benefit reductions were commonplace in the nonunion sector.

In other attempts to extract labor-cost savings, first the retail food industry and then the airlines developed the "two-tier" wage system, under which newly hired workers are paid at a sharply lower rate than more senior employees doing the same work. These wage differentials are not merely for short probationary periods. In some cases it takes ten years or more to achieve the top rate for a given job classification. In others the two-tier system is permanent unless deleted in subsequent negotiations. By 1985 some 11 percent of all nonconstruction union agreements had such a provision; by 1988 nearly a third of the union-ized work force was employed in companies utilizing this "innovation," including the U.S. Post Office, American Airlines, and a large number of major construction firms.[35] Again, similar developments occurred in firms where workers were not represented by unions.[36]

Other firms cut their labor costs by substituting part-time workers for their full-time employees. Hiring women on "mother's hours" became a popular way to recruit a labor force "willing" to work for lower pay and fewer fringe benefits—or no benefits at all. Workers could be hired from places like Manpower, Inc., and Kelly Services. Full-time jobs could be split up into part-time jobs. The latter has become so commonplace that the United Food and Commercial Workers' Union estimates that perhaps half of its members are now part-timers.[37]

By 1983 the spread of wage and other economic concessions, two-tier wage systems, and part-time work was already beginning to show up as a "deceleration" in the rise of nominal wages and labor compensation, and thus a significant reduction in real wages after controlling for inflation. An hourly compensation index developed by the U.S. Bureau of Labor Statistics and analyzed by the Brookings Institution's Robert J. Flanagan indicates that in the manufacturing sector of the economy, total (nominal) compensation rose by only 3.6 percent in 1983 in the unionized sector and by only 4.7 percent in nonunion firms. This can be compared with 7.7 to 11.0 percent annual increases in both sectors between 1976 and 1981. Outside manufacturing, a similar deceleration in wages and salaries took place. Overall, in the private sector, wage gains in 1983 were only 40 percent as great as they had been in 1980, and more than a third of the unionized private-sector work force in 1983 received no wage increases at all or suffered what has been appropriately dubbed wage "givebacks."[38] What had begun as a gush of imports in the 1970s, combined with an economic recession in the early 1980s, ultimately led to a torrent of economic concessions by labor.

Other elements of the postwar workplace contract were also under fire. Rigid work rules and strictly defined job classifications, sacred to unions since at least the 1940s, were loosened in many industries. Management demands for relaxation of restrictive work rules and highly differentiated job classifications accompanied the shift from mass production to "flexible specialization."[39] As long as mass production held sway, the traditional Taylorist or Fordist system of reducing each job to the lowest common denominator was consistent with the rules and classifications that unions demanded in the name of job security. But under flexible manufacturing and small-batch production, where workers were required to produce a constantly changing array of products, strict work rules and narrow job classifications were no longer deemed "efficient."[40] Unions were fortunate if they could compel firms to provide greater employment security in return for relaxation of the rules and classifications that management argued most interfered with efficient operations. Essentially, many companies demanded and, in the face of economic catastrophe, received what only a decade before would have been considered extraordinary prerogatives regarding the use of labor within the workplace.

Still, in a growing number of firms, managers were unsatisfied with the concessions they won. They now fought not just for changes in the traditional Workplace Contract but for its total abrogation. Many resorted to outright "union busting." According to Michael Goldfield, a Cornell University political scientist, employers stepped up their efforts, on the one hand, to encourage union decertification elections and, on the other, to delay National Labor Relations Board (NLRB) certification elections. In retaliation, the number of unfair labor charges against employers filed by unions before the NLRB almost doubled during the 1970s.[41] In Goldfield's words:

> While the traditional weapons of the blacklist and blackmail, of spies and thugs, have not disappeared, new weapons have risen to prominence. These include the use of antilabor consulting firms, the large-scale growth of anti-union employer organizations, the rise in numerous illegal tactics, the engagement in lengthy election delays, and the lessening of the ready acceptance of union rights and prerogatives, even in traditionally unionized sectors. These manifold tactics, and their concerted, widespread application, have proven to be a major reason for union decline in this country.[42]

To round out the story of managerial strategies in an age of global competition, it is necessary to note that the corporate sector came to the government as well as to its own work force for assistance. In the new administration of Ronald Reagan, corporate lobbyists found a willing partner to help them rebuild profits by slashing federal taxes and government regulations. Reductions in the corporation income tax and significant liberalization of depreciation rules on new investments contributed directly to the bottom line. The effective marginal tax rate on corporate profits averaged better than 30 percent during the entire decade of the 1970s. After the Reagan tax cuts of 1981 and 1982, the rate was no more than half as much.[43] Cuts in Occupational Safety and Health Administration (OSHA) regulations and the retrogression in environmental protection rules under Secretary of the Interior James Watt and Environmental Protection Agency Director Ann Gorsuch also contributed to a resurgence in corporate profits.[44] The refusal for eight years to increase the minimum wage from $3.35 per hour effectively deregulated wages. Summarily discharging all of the striking air traffic controllers in 1981 and placing new "pro-management" members on the National Labor Relations Board effectively deregulated the rules under which organized labor and management had been bound.[45]

PROFITS AND THE PAYCHECK

With such an all-out effort, we might well assume that the corporate strategies ultimately succeeded. From one perspective, they certainly did. Annual adjusted corporate profits *doubled* between 1982 and 1987, placing them 50 percent higher than at their previous peak in 1979.[46] The auto companies led the nation in this profits recovery. General Motors's after-tax profits tripled, from $963 million in 1982 to almost $3 billion in 1986.[47] Ford, based on the enormous success of its new Taurus and Sable models, turned its U.S. after-tax profits around from a $2 billion *loss* to a $2.5 billion profit between 1980 and 1986. Bringing up the rear, the poorest of the Big Three, Chrysler, saw its pretax profits rebound from a calamitous $4.6 billion *loss* in 1981 to a $1.4 billion after-tax gain.[48]

Outside the auto industry, with such exceptions as basic steel, the improvement in corporate rates of return was impressive as well. In fabricated metals, reported pretax profits went up 138 percent between 1982 and 1987; in electrical and electronic equipment, the gain was 88 percent; and in chemicals, a staggering 160 percent.[49] Nationwide the profit *rate* as measured by the net after-tax rate of return on corporate assets rebounded smartly after its dramatic fifteen-year decline: by 1986, it was back up to 7 percent, about the same as in 1969, just before the great import challenge began.[50]

The stock market, reflecting encouraging corporate reports, responded in kind. A person who, at the trough of the recession in 1982, invested $10,000 in a mutual fund containing the thirty Dow-Jones industrial stocks would have had an account worth over $30,000 five years later. Those with some spare cash and who were sufficiently clairvoyant or lucky to invest in mutual funds such as the Fidelity Magellan portfolio did significantly better. Individual fortunes were made overnight as investors celebrated Reagan's "new morning" in America. Multimillionaires, the likes of Donald Trump and Michael Milken, made the headlines as often as popular movie stars did.

The profits boom plus deep tax cuts plus cheerleading from the White House touched off an economic recovery that lasted throughout much of the Reagan presidency. Nonetheless there was a darkly ominous side to the business boom of the 1980s. The economic revival was built on a dangerously unstable foundation, and its gains were extremely unevenly shared. What fueled production during the 1980s was not some profound recovery in global competitiveness but a domestic spending binge based on enormous and nonsustainable levels of debt. If "malaise" characterized the 1970s, the 1980s was a decade of extravagance in which consumers, businesses, and government all spent well beyond their means.

Between 1980 and 1989, personal consumption expenditures increased by $1.7 trillion in nominal terms. This was certainly good for business, but the problem was that families financed nearly a quarter of their increased purchases not from their current income but by borrowing from the future. Consumers increased their nonmortgage installment credit by nearly $420 billion during the decade, including an additional $180 billion in automobile loans and $140 billion through credit cards.[51] Such a debt-financed consumer boom could not last; the sluggish growth in spending in the early 1990s bears this out. Businesses, too, financed their spending through unprecedented levels of borrowing, converting equity into debt to finance leveraged takeovers and buyouts. And, of course, the federal government financed its spending by running triple-digit deficits from 1982 on.

What did not grow as fast were exports and investment. Table 3.2 provides the percentage increases in each of the basic components of GNP between 1980 and 1989. Note that the weakest performance is found in investment, the second weakest in exports. The fastest growth

TABLE 3.2

Growth in the Components of
U.S. Gross National Product
(1980–1989)

Imports	110.8%
Consumption	99.1
Government Spending	93.4
Exports	78.4
Investment	76.5
GNP	90.4

Source: Council of Economic Advisors, "Economic Indicators" (Washington, D.C.: Government Printing Office, October 1990), p. 1.

component was imports. This pattern of economic indicators suggests that the "recovery" of the 1980s did not come about because the U.S. had solved its competitiveness problem.

The same conclusion is warranted by the trend in real average weekly earnings. By 1990, the typical paycheck was worth 11 percent *less* than in 1973, near the beginning of the import surge.[52] Not only was the average lower but the distribution of earnings was also more unequal. The ratio of annual earnings of college-educated workers to high school dropouts in 1973 was 2.3 to 1. By 1987, it had expanded to nearly 3 to 1 as high school dropouts and even high school graduates—those most likely to have been employed in blue-collar manufacturing and now left to their own devices in the low-wage end of the service economy—suffered real dollar wage and salary losses.[53] Lower earnings contributed to declines in family income, so that those with only a fragile grasp on middle-class status found themselves jettisoned into the ranks of the "lower" class or outright poverty.[54] The proportion of the population in poverty at the end of the decade was actually higher than it was at the beginning.[55] Inevitably there was a decline in the size of the middle class itself. Katherine Bradbury, a senior economist at the Federal Reserve Bank of Boston, found that the proportion of families with incomes between $20,000 and $50,000 declined from 53 percent to 47.9 percent in the period from 1973 to 1984. Of the 5.1 percentage-point change in the size of the middle class, 4.3 percent fell by sliding down the income spectrum while fewer than 1 percent moved out by moving up.[56] The combination of debt-financed growth and income polarization is, of course, hardly a recipe for long-term economic success.

As outright recession darkened the skies at the beginning of the 1990s, as unemployment rates surged above 7 percent, and as profits once again slid downward, the realization began to sink in that something was terribly amiss in the nation's economy. The traditional Workplace Contract no longer worked—for workers, businesses, or anyone else. It began to dawn on management, labor, and government that during the 1980s we had done everything to give the appearance of prosperity, but we had failed to deal with the central factors that determine a nation's economic success: productivity, the quality of products and services, and innovation. As a result, the United States was actually not that much more competitive at the beginning of the 1990s than it had been a decade before.

CHAPTER 4

What Went Wrong?

When people forget how to produce goods, and that appears to be the case in America, they will not be able to supply themselves even with their most basic needs.
—Akio Morita, The Japan That Can Say "No" *(1990)*

It isn't easy to squander the enormous advantage of being the so-called first mover in an industry, let alone that of operating in the world's biggest market, yet time after time American corporations have managed the feat.
—Thomas A. Stewart, "Lessons from U.S. Business Blunders,"
Fortune *Magazine (1990)*

The ascent of international competition in the 1970s was unquestionably the proximate cause for the demise of the glory days. Yet it would be naive to blame the loss of manufacturing jobs, the decline in average wages, or the plunge in corporate profits on the Japanese, the Germans, or more generally on the imports that flooded American shores from abroad. While there is ample evidence of "unfair" trade practices that disadvantaged certain sectors of U.S. industry, neither these practices nor foreign economic prowess automatically triggered stagnation in domestic living standards or undermined the postwar Workplace Contract. On the contrary, increases in foreign incomes *could* have provided tremendously expanded markets for a broad array of American goods, as it did for U.S.-designed commercial airframes and jet engines, mainframe computers, pharmaceuticals, organic chemicals, and military weapons, all of which enjoy healthy trade surpluses with the rest of the world.[1]

For a much longer list of industries, the trade picture is not anywhere as favorable. But the problem does *not* lie so much in foreign economic proficiency as in the inability of U.S. enterprise to meet the global challenge posed by the European and Asian renaissance. As Alan Kantrow, a former associate editor of the *Harvard Business Review* and an expert on survival strategies for industry, writes, the conventional wisdom on what went wrong is replete with innuendo and a bevy of scapegoats. He notes that the usual lineup of suspects accused of destroying America's competitiveness includes "outrageous interest rates, runaway inflation, excessive regulation, one-sided trade practices, troublesome unions, and meddlesome bureaucrats." Much of the literature reads as though industry could be successful if only "the Japanese played fair or the Federal Reserve behaved or Lane Kirkland [the president of the AFL-CIO] were reasonable or OSHA disappeared." The refrain, Kantrow notes, "is familiar, appealing, even seductive. But it is profoundly misleading."[2] Fundamentally, Pogo was right: we have met the enemy and he is us.

What the evidence shows, and on this there is little dispute, is that the United States fell behind its global economic rivals in what we have already discussed as the three critical areas that spell economic success or failure for a nation: productivity, quality, and innovation. Sometime in the late 1960s or early 1970s, one U.S. industry after another began to fail because it could no longer satisfy the market imperatives of high-quality, innovative goods and services at reasonable prices—with profound consequences for managers and workers, for society as a whole, and for the Workplace Contract that had been so carefully constructed in the postwar period.

PRICE AND PRODUCTIVITY

When considering what determines the *cost* of goods and services, a vital component of price, economists always begin with productivity. In a "closed" economy, with no exports or imports, increases in productivity determine the growth rate of real earnings—that is, the nominal wage workers receive in their pay envelopes relative to the prices they pay as consumers. In an "open" economy, subject to world competition, productivity growth also determines changes in one country's standard of living relative to another. Nations whose firms enjoy strong productivity growth will see the relative prices of their goods decline and thereby win increased demand for their products. Countries with chronically low productivity growth can remain competitive in world markets only by lowering their own wages or by accepting lower profits. For example, if nominal wages and profits rise by 3 percent in the presence of a productivity gain of the same amount, prices can remain unchanged. However, if nominal wages increase faster than productivity, say, 5 percent versus 2 percent, prices will rise by the difference if firms are to remain profitable. We can call this relationship the "wage/price/profit/productivity nexus."

There is a natural logic to all of this. If, nationwide, workers have 5 percent more in their pay envelopes but total national output increases by only 2 percent, prices will inevitably rise because consumers have 5 percent more dollars with which to bid on only 2 percent more goods. To be sure, in the event of such slow productivity growth, workers as a whole could increase their wages without a concomitant increase in price, but this would mean a sharp reduction in dividends distributed to stockholders. Since corporations exist to increase profits for their stockholders, slow productivity growth unavoidably precipitates a Promethean battle between labor and management over who will be held harmless: consumers from higher prices; workers from lower wages; or stockholders from lower profits. For precisely this reason, the postwar Workplace Contract began to face stiff opposition from management when poor productivity performance brought into sharp focus the underlying tradeoffs involved in meeting the conflicting demands of consumers, workers, and corporate stockholders.

AMERICA'S PRODUCTIVITY RECORD

Just how poorly *has* the United States fared in the global productivity contest? There are those who argue that in terms of productivity growth, nothing has gone wrong. To them, the end of the glory days simply coincided with America's return to a normal period of economic growth after an extraordinary one.[3]

But this position is not widely shared. Summing up all the available data on the efficiency of the U.S. economy, MIT's Paul Krugman concludes bluntly that "the two decades since 1970 have seen the worst U.S. productivity performance of the century."[4] As table 4.1 demonstrates, productivity grew faster during the Great Depression than it has since 1969.

Krugman is hardly alone in his assessment of U.S. productivity. Martin Baily and Alok Chakrabarti of the Brookings Institution, two economists who have produced what are considered among the most accurate estimates of the nation's economic efficiency, ruefully conclude that the decline in productivity, at least as evidenced through the early 1980s, occurred in all but six of the twenty key manufacturing industries in the country.[5]

For the record, the United States was not the only country to see its productivity growth rate decline in the more recent postwar period. But compared with its leading competitors—France, Germany, Japan, and Britain—the United States has trailed the pack since the early 1950s, and the gap has not narrowed appreciably in recent years, as table 4.2 reveals. Japan's productivity growth in the most recent period is moving along at less than half the breakneck pace achieved during the first postwar generation (1950–73). Still, its annual average advance in the 1980s was nearly three times the U.S. rate, and higher than America's record pace during the glory days of the 1950s and 1960s. While

TABLE 4.1

U.S. Productivity Growth Since 1899

1899–09	1.8%
1909–19	1.8
1919–29	2.4
1929–39	1.6
1939–49	2.6
1949–59	3.0
1959–69	2.5
1969–79	1.2
1979–89	1.3

Source: Paul Krugman, *The Age of Diminished Expectations* (Cambridge, Mass.: MIT Press, 1990), p. 12.

TABLE 4.2

Labor Productivity Growth in Five Countries, 1950–1986

	France	Germany	Japan	Britain	U.S.
1950–73	5.01%	5.83%	7.41%	3.15%	2.44%
1973–79	3.83	3.91	3.40	2.18	0.80
1979–86	3.24	1.88	3.06	2.95	1.09

Source: Angus Maddison, "The Productivity Slowdown in Historical and Comparative Perspective" (University of Groningen, the Netherlands, 1985), table A-5 as reproduced in Martin Neil Baily and Alok K. Chakrabarti, *Innovation and the Productivity Crisis* (Washington, D.C.: Brookings Institution, 1988), table 1–2, p. 5.

Germany's industrial efficiency has slipped under 2 percent a year, its rate of increase still outruns that of the United States by a ratio of 1.7 to 1. Of the five largest economies in the world, the French produced the best efficiency growth performance of all.

Looking for a silver lining, some have taken comfort in recent productivity statistics suggesting that overall efficiency in the U.S. manufacturing sector began to rebound following the 1981–82 recession. Indeed, in such durable-goods manufacturing industries as auto, steel, aircraft, computers, and the like, productivity growth actually achieved record levels. From 1979 through 1986, the growth rate in output per hour averaged across all durable-goods factories was 3.0 percent— triple the rate for the 1973–79 period, and even 25 percent better than the 2.4 percent growth rate during the glory days of 1948–73.[6]

In a few industries, the productivity gains were nothing short of phenomenal. The nearly complete automation of radio and TV set manufacture—led by Sony, one of the first of the Japanese "transplants" operating within the United States—sparked productivity improvement of nearly 15 percent per year between 1979 and 1986. Also doing particularly well were semiconductor manufacture, cement, sawmills, nonwool yarn mills, steel, and aluminum. Each of these averaged better than a 5 percent annual increase in output per hour during this period.[7] Productivity improvements provided the grounds for price competitiveness in at least some of these goods, notably cement, lumber, and, for a time, semiconductors.[8] Still, for the nation as a whole, the unfavorable U.S. trade balance remained high—in the $100 billion and higher range—until the end of the decade, when economic recession with its attendant decline in consumption caused a sharp drop in imports.[9]

Unfortunately, even the rebound in factory efficiency during the mid-1980s was a lot less encouraging than one might wish. Baily and Chakrabarti caution that the improvement in factory productivity was partly a statistical illusion. A disproportionate amount of the average productivity gain in manufacturing was tied to a single industry—computers; much of the growth in output per worker was accomplished simply by closing inefficient factories rather than opening up efficient ones;[10] and the government's method of compiling the raw data for the productivity measure may itself have led to an overestimate.[11] Moreover, by the end of the 1980s, U.S. factory productivity growth was once again slipping behind world competition. In 1989, factory output per hour grew by less than 2 percent compared with 2.6 percent in Italy, 4.1 percent in Germany, 4.2 percent in France, 4.7 percent in England, and 5.3 percent in Japan.[12] The United States did no better than 2.8 percent in 1990.[13]

Lamentably, America's poor productivity performance will be compromised even further in the decade to come as a result of the growth in globally traded services. Transportation, construction, insurance, communications, and banking, along with other services, are increasingly subject to international trade. This is an ominous trend, for it is precisely in the service sector—the division of the U.S. economy experiencing the most rapid growth—where America lags the most in productivity. With the major exceptions of communications (which introduced computerized telephone switching) and wholesale trade (which took advantage of computerized inventory control), overall non-manufacturing productivity advanced at only 0.6 percent a year between 1979 and 1986. The only solace one can take in this performance is that it was virtually double the 0.3 percent recorded during most of the 1970s. Construction productivity actually *fell* by 2.2 percent a year during the 1980s, while the booming finance, insurance, and real estate industries saw a yearly *decline* in output per hour of nearly 1 percent, despite the introduction of program trading in the securities markets and computer-linked multiple-listing operations in real estate.[14] As a consequence, overall U.S. productivity in the middle of 1990 was lower than in the middle of 1988, despite positive growth in factory efficiency.[15] This weak performance is of our own making.

WHY IS PRODUCTIVITY GROWTH SO WEAK?

Within the arcane world of economics, a small cottage industry has materialized to study the sources of the productivity slowdown. By all accounts, Edward Denison of the Brookings Institution is the CEO of this minisector. Although he has been studying the ups and downs of productivity since the late 1950s, when asked what has caused the sharp decline in U.S. productivity growth since 1973 he candidly admits that he doesn't know.[16] His original list of suspects included:

Too little capital investment
The shift from manufacturing to services
Changes in the age and sex composition of the labor force
Sluggish growth in education and training
Government regulation
Oil price shocks and rising energy costs
Pollution abatement expenditures
Increased security spending to deter crime
Investments in worker health and safety
Changing weather conditions for farming
Increased labor disputes.[17]

After studying each one, Denison finds that most of the slowdown after 1973—as much as 60 percent—is left unaccounted for, no matter how many "measurable" factors are thrown into the model.[18]

The special MIT Commission on Industrial Productivity made up of distinguished engineers and economists was as frustrated as Denison in its attempt to find the culprits for the productivity collapse. It ended its long, detailed study by suggesting that "outdated competitive strategies," "short-time horizons," "technological weaknesses," "neglect of human resources," "failures of cooperation," and "government and industry working at cross purposes" had to be culpable.[19] All of these fall into Denison's "residual," the 60 percent of the productivity conundrum left unexplained.

While there is no way to parcel out the specific impact of any one of these culprits, Alicia Munnell, senior vice president of the Boston Federal Reserve Bank, provides a clue to the magnitude of their collective potential impact. Her work relies on a comparison of two different measures of economic efficiency: labor productivity growth rates and changes in the rate of multifactor productivity. *Labor productivity* is measured as the value of output per hour of employee work time; *multifactor productivity* is calculated as the ratio of output to a weighted average of inputs, including *both* capital and labor. The difference turns out to be important. Unlike labor productivity, which can be boosted simply by adding more capital to the production process, multifactor productivity separates out the contribution to growth that results from the introduction of new technology and from the better utilization of management methods.[20]

According to Munnell's calculations, the slowdown in labor productivity growth since the late 1960s appears to be due exclusively to a decline in multifactor productivity growth.[21] This means that capital investment grew fast enough to maintain historical capital-labor ratios. Workers had as much capital to work with in the 1980s as they did in the 1950s and 1960s. *What declined was the nation's technological edge and the productivity that normally comes from good management.* This crucial finding places the blame for poor productivity squarely on the shoulders of poor management, broadly defined.

Indeed, managers themselves recognize this. About 80 percent of the top managers at 221 companies surveyed by *Productivity* magazine in 1980 cited "poor management" as the key reason for lackluster productivity. The managers also blame federal regulations, weak capital spending, and poor work-force training—but not workers—for low output, but they place all of these well behind bad management practices as the chief culprit.[22] This is not so much an indictment of managers per se as of the management techniques used today to combine labor's input with that of technology and capital.

This weakening in technological and managerial prowess actually can be measured by answering the following question: What would it have taken in terms of additional capital spending in the 1980s to maintain the 3.8 percent GNP growth rate of the 1960s in the face of lagging technology and managerial weakness? Put another way, how much would the United States have had to invest in *additional* capital equipment in the 1980s to compensate for the decline in technology and management skill that apparently reduced GNP growth to only about 2.7 percent per year?

The answer: capital investment would have had to grow by 7.1 percent per year rather than the 4 percent growth actually experienced during the 1980s. That is, each year the United States would have had to spend 78 percent more on capital than it did! In dollar terms, private enterprise would have had to invest an additional half-trillion dollars (between 1979 and 1987) to make up for the slowdown in GNP growth due to the sad state of multifactor productivity—lagging technology, inept management, and other components of Denison's "residual."[23] That half trillion would have had to come out of consumption and ultimately out of wages and profits. Such large sums of money are obviously not easy to come by. Hence many analysts have come to the conclusion that the single most important factor that could reverse the decline in productivity is better management of existing resources— that is, better utilization of technology, capital, and labor.

One of the most overlooked of these factors is that of the nature of employer-employee relations. While many pay lip service to it, the difficulty in measuring it has kept it from being a key factor in enterprise efficiency in the typical economist's equation. As William A. Ruch and James C. Hershauer wrote in 1974, before the productivity slowdown was evident:

> it appears that technological variables are a prerequisite to determining potential productivity, but that the *human or attitudinal variables are the more powerful in determining actual productivity.* A lack of motivation can negate the effect of technologically advanced equipment more easily, more quickly, and more thoroughly than the reverse, whereas a high degree of motivation can effectively overcome a slight deficiency in technological progress.[24] [Emphasis added.]

More recently, in writing about the high-productivity "lean production" system, MIT's James P. Womack, Daniel T. Jones, and Daniel Roos have written:

> In the end, it is the dynamic work team that emerges as the heart of the lean factory. Our studies of plants trying to adopt lean production reveal that workers only respond [with higher productivity and quality] when there exists some sense of reciprocal obligation, a sense that management actually values skilled workers, will make sacrifices to retain them, and is willing to delegate responsibility to the team.[25]

The bottom line: in the modern era, with capital and technology so mobile, global competitiveness depends increasingly on the structure and quality of employer-employee relations. Getting this right in America will likely play a greater role in raising productivity than any other single factor. Essentially the engine for efficiency growth begins with retooling the relationship between labor and corporate leadership.

A LATE START IN THE QUALITY DERBY

Getting productivity right is obviously part of the answer to America's competitiveness problem, but boosting quality is every bit as important. If U.S. producers ignored quality in the 1950s or early 1960s, it barely mattered, for shoppers had little choice but to buy American. That constraint no longer holds.

The Japanese learned early in their postwar recovery just how important quality is to the successful enterprise. As one senior Japanese official explained to a delegation of Harvard Business School faculty: "A 1% defect rate means that if you sell 100,000 units of a product, 1,000 of them will be defective. In a country as small geographically and as crowded as ours is, it is simply unacceptable to have that many dissatisfied customers 'unselling' your product to their friends."[26] Inattention to quality may not affect short-term profits, but the loss in customer loyalty almost surely undermines long-run market share and long-term rates of return. Inevitably it has a devastating impact on jobs and potentially on the entire panoply of workplace contract provisions.

In terms of laggards in high-caliber production, the domestic auto industry is the U.S. consumer's favorite target. But it is unfair to single out this industry, for there are others that share its record of poor quality in manufacture and service. A long list of American products has the dubious distinction of losing market share or, worse yet, suffering extinction, as a result of perceived or real quality differences. Particularly notable are Philco televisions, Kodak 35-millimeter cameras, RCA and Westinghouse radio and TV broadcast equipment, Unimation robots, Schwinn bicycles, and, for a long time, Harley-Davidson motorcycles. The Wang Company, a pioneer in word-processing equipment and minicomputers, was ultimately forced out of the business of manufacturing its own name-brand equipment largely because of adverse buyer reaction to shoddy customer service.

Not all products of superior quality are now Japanese in origin, nor are all the tales of consumer dismay about American goods. Hewlett-Packard, Xerox, 3M, and Corning Glass have all won plaudits for their attention to quality, and their sales figures confirm it. The goal for the most outstanding of American firms is to reach Six Sigma quality. *Six Sigma* is a statistical term associated with "zero" defects—literally, no more than 3.4 defects per million units of output. Motorola conceived of the notion in 1987 and has plans to achieve this goal by the mid-1990s. If the company is ultimately successful in its quest, it will have reduced its defect rate more than a hundredfold from its already exceptional quality performance. As is, Motorola has become a favorite brand name in Japan as a result of its already exceptional record. The problem is that only a handful of companies nationwide do anywhere near as well.

LAGGING RESEARCH, DEVELOPMENT, AND INNOVATION

Modern consumers want more than a quality product at a reasonable price; they want world-class product performance at the forefront of technology. This has meant that manufacturers and service providers alike face an ever shorter "product cycle"—the time it takes for a new product to reach maturity and then obsolescence. Personal computers provide a perfect example. The first IBM PC was introduced in 1981. It was based on the Intel 8086 chip and operated at a clock speed of 4.77 megahertz (MHz). The first users were astounded by the performance of a computer that literally fit on a desktop. Yet, within three years, users would find the PC unmanageably slow and cumbersome. The "AT" class of machines was introduced in 1984, operating at 8 MHz. Once again, users were dazzled by its speed, but the dazzle wore off even faster than it did in the previous round of improvement. In just two years, the 386 chip was introduced, and then the 486 four years later, operating first at 25 MHz, then at 33 MHz, and within a year at 50 MHz. The new machines—twenty times faster than the original with sixty-four times more internal memory, and five hundred times more disk storage—not only made the original PC obsolete but threatened to completely expunge the market for the AT, while challenging minicomputers selling for literally hundreds of times more.[27] An anonymous computer expert has illustrated this trend by estimating that if the automobile business had developed as the computer business did, a Rolls-Royce would now cost $2.75 and run 3 million miles on a gallon of gas!

During the 1960s, industry-funded R&D spending in the United States rose by an inflation-adjusted annual rate of 6.2 percent. From 1969 to 1977, however, it fell sharply to 2.4 percent per year, and industrial innovation declined, at least partly as a result. Moreover, a sizable percentage of the dollars devoted to R&D is still directed to military rather than civilian product development.

In the 1980s spending rebounded, but the growth in new research and development, like that in productivity and quality, accelerated even faster in Japan and Germany.[28] Today foreigners apply to the U.S. Patent Office to gain patent protection almost as often as Americans do. The top four patent winners *in the United States* in 1990 were Hitachi, Toshiba, Canon, and Mitsubishi—all Japanese companies.[29] The number of patents granted annually to American inventors and corporations peaked back in 1972 and has declined substantially since then.[30] Moreover, according to patent data compiled by CHI Research Inc., a firm that tracks technical trends for the federal government, Fuji film surpassed Kodak in technical strength in 1984, and Hitachi passed the venerable IBM in 1985.[31] In the chemical industry, the number of "radical or major technical" innovations averaged 2.4 per year from 1967 to 1973; only 0.2 were introduced per year from 1974 through 1979, and none at all between 1980 and 1982.[32]

All of which leads us once again to the question of management. Either we find a better way to manage the enterprise or we continue to lose the global economic race. This is not just management's problem; it is also labor's. No matter how hard we might cling to the essential elements of the traditional Workplace Contract, as long as we do not boost productivity, quality, and innovation sufficiently, the road ahead spells trouble. The few who remain in high-wage, but increasingly noncompetitive industries, might be able to maintain their standard of living, but the rest will be jettisoned into jobs with lower wages and fewer benefits.

WHO'S AND WHAT'S TO BLAME?

"Mismanagement" is a pretty general indictment. To understand better what we mean by it, we need to look at the policies of business, labor, and government during the past two decades that have contributed to anemic productivity, inferior quality, and weak innovation. The first has to do with the pricing policies of myopic managers.

Sluggish productivity growth, by itself, cannot explain why so many American goods are priced out of the market. Managers are responsible under present arrangements to set prices, and their pricing strategies have often been counterproductive. In one industry after another, the MIT Commission on Industrial Productivity concluded in its 1989 report, management adopted pricing policies premised on unrealistically inflated short-term profit targets.[33] As a result, prices were too high to meet foreign competition.

The commission describes a sequence of events that almost invariably leads to lost market share. To paraphrase the MIT report, the American retreat from one global market to another follows a stylized pattern. First, American firms set high goals for return on investment. Second, foreign firms select a market segment and, by aggressive pricing, force down the return on investment while building market share. Third, within a short period of time, American firms retreat from the market segment. Finally, foreign firms move on to set aggressive prices in other segments, and the Americans retreat again.[34] These strategies may sometimes be criticized as being unfair, but usually the foreign companies are simply following market incentives, not breaking the rules of accepted international practice.

Take recent pricing strategies by Japanese and American firms. When Toyota debuted its all-new 1991 Tercel, it maintained the price on its basic model at $6,488, precisely the same as the older model. "We hope to get kids straight out of college with this car," explained John Hoenig, Toyota's U.S. product manager.[35] Facing a mounting recession, Mazda announced only weeks later a 5.5 percent *reduction* in its base price.

How did the Big Three U.S. auto producers respond to such aggressive price setting? General Motors *increased* the price of its 1991 models 4.4 percent over 1990 model prices; Chrysler boosted its sticker price by 2.9 percent; and Ford, by 2.7 percent. The average price hike for the Big Three was $503. The average for all Japanese cars was $49.[36] By the end of the year no one should have been surprised that the Japanese had increased their market share once again.[37]

Management's preference for short-term goals in an increasingly competitive marketplace is not surprising or altogether indefensible given Wall Street pressures. Quarterly profit reports are highly visible to investors who follow every blip in a firm's performance. Companies that invest for the long run, but fail to keep their short-term balance sheets in the black, will not infrequently see their stock prices tumble. In the extreme, stockholders will look to new management to boost the asset value of their securities or to assure a steady stream of dividends. Caught between the demands of Wall Street and the exigencies of long-term investment, managers almost invariably work to satisfy the former. They will keep prices high to maintain short-term profit margins, even at the expense of sacrificing long-term market share. They will shortchange productivity-enhancing investment to maintain "good-looking" quarterly balance sheets. Taken to excess, this behavior has led thousands of firms from a rosy present to a rusty future. With the traditional Workplace Contract's management-rights clause, labor has stood by helplessly while management pursues pricing policies that directly harm workers' and the nation's interests.

Part of the problem is that U.S. managers, unlike the Japanese, tend to rise through the ranks by hopping from one company to another rather than by moving up within the company's own hierarchy. Top managers—those who produce super quarterly profits—become, in baseball parlance, free agents. They can double or triple their salaries simply by moving from one company to another. W. Edwards Deming, the ninety-one-year-old champion of quality production, has attacked this management trend in his own irascible style: "A new president comes in to raise the quarterly dividend, then moves along to destroy some other company. . . . A better indicator than short-term profit is the [manager's] effect on production. Unfortunately, the president's right-hand man is in many companies his Minister of Finance."[38]

CORPORATE BULIMIA

A company with short-term planning horizons will do more than adversely affect price. The thrust for a quick return on assets can compromise innovation through either the licensing of technology to potential competitors or the substitution of paper asset transfers for real investment in research and development. In both cases, the company and certainly its workers are frequently placed at risk.

Selling technology to potential competitors, particularly foreign ones, has a rich history in America going back to the glory days. In one of the most remarkable cases, Western Electric licensed its newly invented solid-state transistor to Sony in 1953—for the grand sum of $25,000. Sony went on to capture a major share of the world's consumer electronics market. Along the same lines, U.S. color-television technology was acquired by the Japanese from RCA for a small fee. And in 1968, a now-defunct American company, Unimation, licensed Kawasaki Heavy Industries to make industrial robots. The Japanese now supply over half the world's demand for robotic devices. Ampex corporation passed along the basics of VCR technology for a fee and today no one owns a VCR stamped "Made in America."[39]

The Japanese no longer have the luxury of buying technology licenses for $25,000 a piece. Still, between 1956 and 1978, Japan paid some $9 billion for U.S. technology—pure profit to the American firms. Even with this price tag, the acquisitions still proved lucrative to the purchasers. George Gilder, one of the conservative gurus of the Reagan era, estimates that the Japanese would have had to spend between $500 billion and $1 trillion to develop these technologies on their own.[40] In many of these cases, the American firm added to its short-term profit while the foreign firm added to its long-term market share. The ultimate consequence was a gigantic loss in American jobs. Again, labor had no organized input over such matters.

Short-term planning horizons have also contributed to management's apparent addiction to the merger and acquisition game. "We have a societywide value problem," President Bush's budget director, Richard Darman, grumbles. "The energy of our best people is going into financial paper-shuffling."[41] Harvard University's Robert Reich coined the term *paper entrepreneurialism* for this distressing trend in the early 1980s, even before it reached full bloom.[42] In the polite company of the typical business school, it is called portfolio management.

For individuals, portfolio management involves buying and selling assets such as individual stocks and bonds in order to maximize individual or family wealth. For the paper-entrepreneurial corporation, it involves buying and selling individual company divisions and product lines, instead of improving the asset position of the firm by investing and innovating in its existing units. Portfolio management, according to *Fortune* magazine's Thomas Stewart, is fertile ground for two kinds of mistakes.[43] First, as a firm's individual operating units are each treated as expendable, salable properties, walls arise between them, inhibiting the sharing of technology, sales forces, and management wisdom. Second, a highly diversified company will eventually have to match the capital investments of less diversified rivals or lose market share. Often unable to do this across the whole range of divisions such a company might control, acquisition almost invariably leads to divestment. Mergers and acquisitions thus become habit forming. Companies begin to practice a corporate form of bulimia—bingeing and purging divisions—when they might otherwise concentrate on the basics of producing a world-class product or service.

In 1986, there were over four thousand completed mergers and acquisitions worth over $190 billion—up from a total of less than 1,600 in 1980 with a gross value of less than $33 billion.[44] The Japanese have watched these activities with amazement. According to Yamaichi Securities, the value of merger and acquisition deals in the United States in 1989 equaled 41.3 percent of *all* capital investment during the year. In Japan, the comparable figure was just 4 percent.[45]

By no means do all U.S. firms display price myopia, sell off their best technologies to the highest bidder, or spend valuable resources playing the merger and acquisition game. But there are enough cases of this behavior to suggest that past management practice has not been particularly profitable for the long-term investor or for the lifetime employee. In few cases has it been profitable for the U.S. economy.

The important point is that the traditional Workplace Contract has been essentially helpless in protecting workers who suffer loss of jobs and income as a result of management's prerogative to set prices or engage in paper entrepreneurialism. The best contract in the world might provide hefty wage increases and a cornucopia of benefits, but all of this can disappear in an instant as the result of a unilaterally fostered merger or divestiture. Employees, suppliers, the government, and the surrounding community are often the victims of attendant layoffs, reduced wages, abrogated contracts, and lost tax revenue.[46]

One grievous but hardly exceptional example involves one of America's leading conglomerates. Two years after acquiring Republic Steel in a bid to be the nation's number-two steel producer, LTV found itself in Chapter 11. It laid off thousands of employees, defaulted on $2.6 billion in debt, and attempted to dump $2 billion in unfunded pension liabilities on the U.S. government.[47] Workers saw their jobs destroyed and their retirement security threatened. Needless to say, LTV stockholders did not fare very well either.

LABOR AND THE PROBLEM OF PRICE COMPETITION

While engineers like Deming and organizational analysts like Hayes and Abernathy criticize management for the ailments of the U.S. economy, others place the blame for America's economic problems on the doorstep of organized labor. While the details may differ, the main argument of union critics is based on a set of alleged linkages that begin with union wage demands and end with U.S. firms being forced out of business. Wage increases won through collective bargaining, they argue, inevitably lead to increases in labor costs. These lead to increases in the overall costs of production, squeezing profits. Since firms cannot survive for long unprofitably, managers are forced, reluctantly, to pass along their higher labor costs in steeper prices. Consumers then switch to lower-priced alternatives, often imports. Eventually, burdened with wages that cannot be reduced because of union resistance, firms are forced to settle for ever smaller market shares. Over time, once-dominant American companies are reduced to minor roles in the global economy or drop out of the economic race altogether.[48] Obviously, if what this logic suggests is true in practice, labor has either wittingly or unwittingly contributed to its own undoing.

The theoretical integrity of this argument is not in dispute, but in practice a number of the logically necessary links from higher wages to crippled companies simply did not exist for *most* of the postwar period. For at least a quarter of a century following World War II, higher wages did not automatically lead to higher prices, driving consumers into the arms of foreign merchants. Instead a great deal of research

demonstrates that high productivity offset some—and, in many instances, all—of the wage gains. In other cases, wage increases were
paid out of existing, above normal, monopoly profits rather than passed
along in higher prices.[49] Thus the wage/price/profit/productivity nexus
yielded only slowly rising "unit labor costs"—wage gains minus productivity improvements—permitting increases in employee compensation while maintaining reasonable profit levels with no serious price
inflation. Since this is hardly the conventional wisdom, it is useful to
plumb this argument further.

First off, no one denies that unions have won higher wages for their
members. Most estimates place the average union premium somewhere between 15 and 20 percent above nonunion wages.[50] This differential is generally believed to have held in most manufacturing
sectors, at least before widespread wage and benefit concessions in the
1980s. How could such a wage premium *not* have priced unionized
companies out of the market? The answer, as just explained, is that for
much of the postwar period unionized firms paid higher wages, but
these companies received higher productivity in return.

One of the first studies to demonstrate this, by the labor economists Charles Brown and James Medoff, found that organized establishments in the manufacturing sector were on average 24 percent
more productive than equivalent nonunion firms.[51] Case studies of
various industries including cement, construction, hospital care, and
mining subsequently showed union-productivity premiums ranging
from 6 percent (cement) to 22 percent (construction).[52] In general,
the few studies indicating lower productivity levels were conducted
in industries where union-management relations were inordinately
conflictual.[53]

As for productivity *growth*—changes in productivity over time—the
data indicate that unions have generally not prevented improvements
in operating efficiency. That is, productivity growth historically has
been as rapid in unionized shops as in union-free companies. Overall,
then, unionized firms traditionally have had higher productivity levels,
and the efficiency differential between the organized and unorganized
sectors has remained roughly constant over time.[54]

To those surprised by this finding, there are genuinely good reasons
why unionized firms generally turn out to be more, not less, productive.
In their classic study *What Do Unions Do?* Richard Freeman and James
Medoff suggest three of them.[55] First, unionized firms have much lower

employee turnover than nonunionized, accounting, according to their estimates, for one-fifth of the union productivity effect. When firms do not have to replace workers continually, they save enormous resources in the hiring and training of replacements. A second factor has to do with the cost of supervision. A number of studies indicate that unionized workers need less.[56] The third reason, and perhaps the most compelling, is that managers are forced by higher wages and job benefits to pay close attention to the efficiency of their operations. The nonunion firm under competitive pressure can more easily cut costs by pressuring its labor force to speed up or by unilaterally lowering wages and job benefits. Managers in organized firms are forced to be diligent in finding other ways to lower costs. This has often led to important improvements in technology and better management of resources.

That higher wages do not automatically mean higher consumer prices is also due to the fact that in industries enjoying monopoly advantage of some type, unions take some of their gains out of monopoly profits rather than out of consumer pockets. Freeman and Medoff have estimated that between 1958 and 1976, unions reduced "price-cost margins" by an average of 17 percent in highly concentrated manufacturing industries. Other estimates run as high as 32 and 37 percent.[57] The combination of higher productivity and reduced price-cost margins meant that for much of the postwar period, the Workplace Contract in unionized firms was fully compatible with higher wages *and* reasonable prices. Part of the typical unionized worker's pay premium was covered by higher efficiency; part came out of the excess monopoly profits that otherwise would have gone to managers and stockholders. Not surprisingly, then, the antipathy directed at unions by corporate investors during the glory days stemmed not from unions affecting prices and market share but from the fact that, in the absence of the negotiated workplace contract, stockholders would have enjoyed even higher dividends.

All of this, however, does not mean that labor was free of responsibility for the economic losses the U.S. suffered in the *late* postwar period. Labor, along with management, did not commonly take into account the imperatives of a changing economic environment. When imports first began to replace domestically produced goods in the U.S. consumer's marketbasket, management failed to redouble efforts to boost efficiency or invest for the long term. Similarly labor, with an eye fixed on fulfilling workers' expectations of continued advances in living standards, paid insufficient attention to the resurgence in foreign economic prowess. The old adversarial ways of dealing with labor-management issues prevailed on both sides of the negotiating table as labor pressed to gain what it saw as its fair share of the economic pie. In certain key industries, the need to grapple with improving the rate of productivity growth all too often did not enter into the collective-bargaining discussions as an urgent or vital matter. In these industries, there was a general failure to focus attention on the continuing downward trend in productivity which, in retrospect, can be illustrated by table 4.3 and figure 4.1. In the transportation equipment industry—including motor vehicles, aircraft, and ships—productivity growth slipped from a healthy 3.5 percent during the glory days to an annual rate of only 0.1 percent during the 1970s. In rubber products, particularly tires, and in primary metals, mostly steel, it was actually negative.

Nevertheless, in an effort to hold workers harmless in the face of rising prices caused in large measure by the inflation associated with the Vietnam War and the first of the two oil crises, annual average wage growth accelerated as productivity fell. As figure 4.2 demonstrates, annual average weekly earnings of production workers grew by

TABLE 4.3

Productivity Growth in Key Industries
1948–1979

Industry	Average Annual Percentage Change in Multifactor Productivity		
	1948–65	1965–73	1973–79
Mining	3.1	2.0	-6.0
Construction	2.9	-3.9	-2.2
Manufacturing	2.5	1.8	0.6
Rubber products	2.2	1.7	-0.8
Primary metals	1.0	0.7	-2.8
Fabricated metals	1.8	1.3	0.0
Transportation equipment	3.5	1.2	0.1
Public utilities	5.8	3.0	-0.6

Source: American Productivity Center, *Multiple Input Productivity Indexes* 6 (December 1986), as reported in Martin Neil Baily and Alok K. Chakrabarti, *Innovation and the Productivity Crisis* (Washington, D.C.: Brookings Institution, 1988), table 1–3, p. 6.

FIGURE 4.1
Productivity Growth in Key Industries
(Multifactor Productivity)

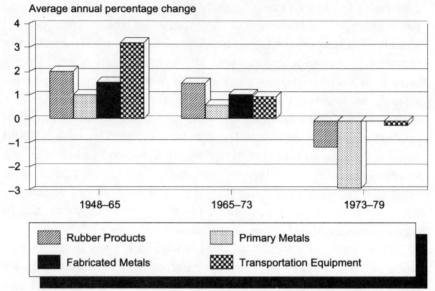

Source: See table 4.3.

FIGURE 4.2
*Nominal Average Weekly Earnings Growth
in Key Industries, 1947–1979*

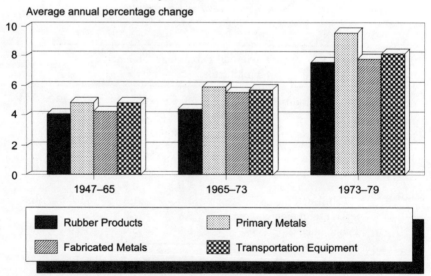

Source: Calculated from U.S. Department of Labor, Bureau of Labor Statistics, *Handbook of Labor Statistics,* Bulletin 2217, June 1985, table 80, pp. 202–203.

approximately 5 percent per year in key industries during the first two and a half decades of high productivity growth following World War II. Yet in the productivity-starved 1970s, nominal wage increases ranged from 7.5 to 9.7 percent. As productivity plummeted, wages were increased without much thought being given to finding mutually agreeable ways to boost workplace efficiency.

In most, but certainly not all, labor circles, workers continued to adhere to the traditional Workplace Contract that firmly placed worries over productivity within the realm of management's prerogatives. Such concerns were not in the workers' or the union's "job description" (unless, of course, managers tried to rectify low productivity through worker speed up). Management did not try to disabuse labor of this interpretation of the contract; it jealously guarded against any encroachment upon the stipulations of authority guaranteed by the management-rights clause. This went so far that, in 1973, when the director of the General Motors department of the UAW asked GM local unions to post on their in-plant union bulletin boards a notice QUALITY PRODUCTS ARE OUR CONCERN TOO, a corporate executive called him to complain that quality is solely management's responsibility. He demanded that the bulletins be taken down. The UAW won the battle, and the notices remained posted—but the dispute underscores the problem.

Inevitably, this approach proved counterproductive. As the price/wage/profit/productivity relation stipulates, if nominal wage growth exceeds productivity growth for any length of time, prices must rise. And rise they did, in a futile attempt by businesses to maintain profit rates in the face of cumulatively rising unit labor costs throughout the economy. At first the impact on market share was minimal. But the more American firms raised prices, the less competitive they became relative to foreign enterprise. Inevitably the price/wage or wage/price spiral led to enormous incentives for Americans to buy cheap imports and extraordinary disincentives for foreigners to buy goods made in the United States. Deeply eroded market shares in one industry after another were practically preordained.

John Hoerr, a senior writer for *Business Week*, has summarized how this occurred in the steel industry:

The steel companies and the United Steelworkers (USW) negotiated excessive wage increases in the 1970s, when for several years wages rose faster than productivity. The problem began right after World War II, when both sides started to engage in wage-price bargaining. The USW directed its negotiating efforts at forcing government approval of steel price increases to cover wage boosts. The steel companies focused on the same goal, while claiming to hold the line on wage inflation. The union played a real role in setting prices but had no comparable role in creating conditions that would allow the companies to grant wage increases without raising prices—in short, no role in increasing productivity.[58]

With wage boosts exceeding productivity gains, a serious deterioration in the competitive position of the American steel industry was set in motion, and with it the loss of almost 340,000 steel jobs between 1974 and 1986. By the mid-1980s, job losses were also enormous in the auto industry, fabricated metals, the machine tool industry, agricultural implements, and a host of other industries.

The relationship between productivity and wage growth reversed again in the 1980s. Because of wage concessions or small wage increases negotiated in industries hard hit by import competition, productivity growth in the goods-producing sector actually exceeded wage gains by a wide margin. While manufacturing productivity was on the ascent during the 1980s, the growth rate for hourly compensation in that sector was a mere 0.32 percent per year. In fact, among nonsupervisory production workers, real hourly wage growth was negative (−0.41 percent per year). The overall average was positive only because compensation growth among managers and supervisors remained strong.[59]

In retrospect, it seems easy to blame unions for the "excesses" during the 1970s that led to widespread job loss during the 1980s. But we must take into account that the traditional Workplace Contract agreed to by *both* labor and management set up a labor-management environment in purely adversarial terms. Management's goal was to strive to protect the company's stockholders from an erosion in the real value of their dividends and capital gains by maintaining strict control over all strategic decisions in the firm, including those involving productivity, quality, and innovation. Within the limits placed on them by management rights, unions understandably settled into the role of striving to safeguard their workers from job loss and of making improvements in wages and benefits without great regard in the short term to the imperatives of the productivity-wage relation. In this game of musical chairs, each *stake*holder wants to make sure he has an assured, if not a comfortable, seat when the music stops.

What added to the problem in the 1970s was a combination of "pattern bargaining" and the lack of a national consensus on a rational "incomes policy" in the face of significant differences in productivity growth across industries. Because each collectively bargained contract is influenced more by the financial status of the individual firm than by national averages, profits and productivity growth may be on a downward slide nationally while wages rise rapidly in particular firms where profits and productivity remain buoyant. The union bargaining team and management will direct their attention to these particular circumstances, and their negotiated settlement will reflect the give and take of the bargaining process. Thus, during the decade of the 1970s, while key national economic indicators began to spell trouble ahead, many firms were still reporting high earnings and their productivity growth remained in reasonably high gear. Unions targeted these successful firms and won collectively bargained wage settlements that reflected the company's good fortunes.

In firms where higher wages were ratified by higher productivity, there was no problem. But as unions strove to win settlements that followed the pattern set in the most prosperous firms, there was a tendency for overall wage growth to exceed gains in efficiency. The result was inflationary pressure beginning in firms where productivity was lagging.

Indeed, the problem is not in pattern bargaining per se. If all firms and unions had agreed on wage and benefit settlements that reflected national productivity growth, it would theoretically have been possible to keep overall inflation under control. Firms experiencing higher than average productivity growth would have been in a position to reduce their prices to consumers, offsetting the somewhat higher prices charged by those with a poor productivity record. This is more or less what went on during the 1960s and 1970s in Sweden, where unions representing virtually all workers sat down with corporate representatives of most employers and set wage patterns that reflected national productivity growth. This did not happen in the United States because unionization is much less universal here, and there is little coordinated bargaining based on a consensus about a productivity-driven national incomes "policy."

Without a way to set wages across industries through some form of nationwide collective bargaining, there is a tendency at times for the sum total of wage gains across *all* groups of workers to exceed the level consistent with stable prices. When this occurs, as it did during the 1970s, success at the bargaining table can contribute to a weaker competitive position in world markets.

LABOR AND WORK RULES

Work rules and lines of job demarcation and job jurisdiction pose another problem. Higher wages do not cause lower productivity and indeed, as we have seen, can even contribute to improved efficiency. However, under the nagging threat of unemployment, unions have frequently bargained for work rules and employee jurisdictions not only to guard against arbitrary and capricious workplace actions by management or to protect health and safety but to retain as many jobs as possible for their members. The problem is that rapid increases in productivity can adversely affect employment security.

The classic case involves "featherbedding." When the railroads moved from steam locomotives to diesel, the rail unions were successful for a time at maintaining a now unnecessary "fireman" as part of the engine crew, as mentioned in the introduction. To protect employment for long-haul truckers, the Teamsters Union won an agreement on work rules that limited what cargo could be carried by truckers on return trips from distant depots. As a consequence trucks often returned empty, at a cost to shippers and customers. For many years the Teamsters also opposed "trailer on flat car" technology (TOFC), in which trailers are latched down to railroad cars to cover long-distance routes. Preservation of jobs was also why longshoremen on the East Coast fought "containerization"—the mechanized loading and unloading of transport containers as a substitute for bulk product handling.

In the public sector, job preservation has led in some cases to union demands for larger crews on maintenance trucks and strict jurisdictional lines in teaching and nursing. In a recent case, fearing continued "privatization" of public transportation, the MBTA union representing workers on Boston's mass transit system vehemently opposed a plan to permit local doughnut shops to sell subway tokens along with morning coffee. A convenience to public transit riders, the seemingly innocuous plan would not reduce employment within MBTA's jurisdiction by even one worker. Nonetheless, the union feared that it was one more step toward moving vital mass transit functions from the public sector, where it does have jurisdiction, to the private sector, where it does not.

These types of work rules and job classifications are harmful to American competitiveness, but during the glory days their import appeared to be of little consequence. Unfortunately, the "tried and true" can be difficult to dislodge even when it is no longer "true." As Machiavelli noted four hundred years ago in *The Prince:* "It must be considered that there is nothing more difficult to carry out, nor more doubtful of success, nor more dangerous to handle, than to initiate a new order of things. For the reformer has enemies in all those who profit by the old order, and only lukewarm defenders in all those who would profit by the new."[60]

It would take time for the drag such rules placed on the economy to be recognized. Still, under the pressure of global competition, deregulation, and sometimes public outrage, labor is awakening along with management to the realization that certain work rules and job classification systems that seem to preserve jobs can be counterproductive—leading to less employment security, not more. Truckers finally accepted TOFC; the longshoremen worked out an acceptable agreement on handling containers; and, in some industries, "modern operating agreements" are being negotiated that alter existing practices, give recognition to the importance of productivity improvement, and provide for sweeping structural change aimed at economic survival.[61]

Without the pressure of global competition, it is likely that neither labor nor management would have come to grips with the need for productivity improvement and structural change. As late as 1971, when Katzell and Yankelovich surveyed union leaders about productivity, they found that only 39 percent thought that increasing efficiency was essential to ensure a high standard of living; only 46 percent believed that productivity improvement included concern for customer or client satisfaction; and a majority (52 percent) felt that productivity was management's responsibility, not theirs.[62] Today, in education programs across the country, unions are singing a much more positive tune when it comes to matters of productivity and product quality. Organized labor has always been sensitive about improvements in efficiency that lead to a reduced demand for labor, but unions are rapidly becoming aware that in an open global economy paying no attention to productivity or quality can be even worse.

THE GOVERNMENT'S ROLE IN THE ECONOMIC DOWNTURN

Having placed a good deal of the blame for lagging efficiency, quality, and innovation on management practice, and having duly noted the role of organized labor in this sphere, we must emphasize that government also bears substantial responsibility for the decline in the American economy. The Federal Reserve Board for one has played a significant role at critical junctures in pricing U.S. goods out of foreign markets and provoking the import flood. Likewise, the White House and Congress share the blame for failing to provide adequate investment in public "infrastructure" needed to assure efficient, high-quality, innovative production in the private sector.

The Federal Reserve Bank's impact on investment, prices, and imports, particularly at the beginning of the 1980s, is not well understood outside of economics circles. With inflation running at 13.3 percent in 1979 and 12.5 percent in 1980, with a Congress unable to come to grips with what at that time seemed unacceptable deficits, and with a president paralyzed by the hostage crisis in Teheran, the Fed Board, under its new chairman, Paul Volcker, moved decisively to raise interest rates in a desperate effort to choke off further price escalation. Ultimately, the Board's actions would prove "too" successful. By 1982, annual increases in the Consumer Price Index would be brought under 4 percent and would remain low for the next seven years. In the process, however, interest rates would soar to the highest level in modern U.S. history, provoking the worst recession since the 1930s.

Ultimately, the high interest rates would strike the economy, particularly the manufacturing sector, a triple whammy. First, high interest rates reduced capital investment. In 1986, Japanese companies like Fujitsu were able to go to their own credit markets and borrow at 4.5 percent interest. U.S. firms, attempting to compete with Fujitsu, were forced to pay nearly twice that for comparable loans.[63] Thus it was less likely that American companies would invest in new plants and equipment and more likely that their managers would pursue short-term objectives. The higher the interest rate, the more quickly a given investment must return a profit to be financially worthwhile. With less investment during the high-interest period, productivity advance was crippled.

The second whammy was the direct decline in consumer sales, particularly consumer "durables": homes, furniture, and cars. Doubling the interest rate has almost no effect on a household's food purchases, but it raises the effective price of anything bought on credit. With mortgage rates at 15 percent, as they were in 1982, few bought new homes. Construction firms went bankrupt and construction workers lost their jobs.[64] With auto-loan rates at 18 percent or better, the car market went into sharp decline.

High interest rates had a third impact, often overlooked, yet perhaps even more powerful than the first two. With a growing disparity between U.S. interest rates and those available abroad, foreign investors discovered one American product they wanted to import: American assets, including government bonds and bank-offered certificates of deposit. A shrewd Japanese investor could convert a billion yen into dollars and, on the interest rate differential alone, double the return on his money. Then, when the dollar appreciated in value the capital gain from buying dollars when they were cheap, earning high interest, and then trading them back for yen when the dollar was dear could mean a total rate of return of over 25 percent a year.

So many foreign investors wished to take advantage of the artificially high U.S. interest rates that the inflated demand for dollars drove the exchange rate to all-time highs. The multilateral trade-weighted exchange rate index rose from 83.2 in 1979 to 132.0 in 1985, an increase of nearly 60 percent. Against the Belgian franc, the French franc, and the Italian lire, the dollar more than doubled in value; against the German mark, it rose by 61 percent, against British sterling by 39 percent, and against the yen by 9 percent.[65]

The newfound "strength" of the dollar essentially decimated U.S. industry. Those sectors already exposed to import competition took a direct hit. The price of imports plummeted almost overnight, knocking down domestic market share to new lows. Meanwhile, U.S.-led export drives shriveled as the landed price of American-made products put them out of the reach of foreigners. No industries were more stricken than autos, consumer electronics, and household appliances. General Electric bailed out of the home-appliance market altogether. The triple whammy, a direct derivative of the Federal Reserve high-interest-rate policy, took industries already in difficulty and pushed them over the edge. It nearly finished off an already ailing Chrysler Corporation.

Interest rates began to come down in the mid-1980s and the dollar was devalued following the Plaza Accord in 1985, under which the major trading nations agreed to coordinate their central bank policies to realign the relative values of their respective currencies. But the damage had been done. Markets that had been sacrificed to imports were hard to regain. As Berkeley's Laura Tyson dolefully notes, "In short, our macro policy choices superimposed a short-term erosion in U.S. competitiveness on a more fundamental long-term erosion."[66] Instead of helping to rebuild American competitiveness, the Fed policy hurried along its descent.

TOO LITTLE INVESTMENT IN INFRASTRUCTURE

Faulting the Fed for its role in reducing productivity-enhancing investment and pricing American goods out of global competition does not free the rest of the federal government from culpability. The White House and Congress also played a role in the demise of private-sector productivity by its neglect of public-sector infrastructure. Crowded airports, poor rail transportation, insufficient sewer capacity in many cities and towns, and highways and bridges in disrepair turn out to be more than just nuisances or even dangers to health and safety. David Aschauer, an economist now at Bates College and formerly at the Federal Reserve Bank of Chicago, has discovered a striking correlation between the slowdown in the nation's productivity and a deficiency in public capital investment.[67] Simply put, poor transportation links add to the cost of producing and delivering a product.

International comparisons confirm the domestic correlation. Among the seven most powerful developed countries, the United States had the slowest rate of productivity growth at the same time that it had the lowest ratio of public investment to GNP. Japan was tops on both.[68] Aschauer's general conclusions have been confirmed in more recent research by Alicia Munnell, the economist who had measured the difference in labor and multifactor productivity. Munnell finds that a 1 percent decline in public capital reduces labor productivity by up to

0.39 percent.[69] The MIT Commission adds that to regain the competitive edge, "the nation needs to rebuild its technological infrastructure—broadly defined to include public laboratories and facilities, communication links, intellectual property laws, technical standards, and other aspects of the environment within which the private sector moves to commercialize new technology."[70]

Productivity in the private sector, certainly in the long run, is similarly affected by investments in "social infrastructure," in particular, education. According to a raft of reports, the American school system, especially K through 12, is in dire straits. Trends in Scholastic Aptitude Test (SAT) scores furnish just one indication of how far and fast schooling as one component of social infrastructure has deteriorated. The average verbal SAT score in 1967 was 466; by 1981 it had plunged to 421. Nearly a decade of agonizing over the decay in primary and secondary schools has done little to improve student performance. By 1990 the average verbal SAT had gained a mere three points. The same pattern was true of math SATs.[71]

The Cornell University economist John Bishop has demonstrated a close link between the downturn in student test scores and the slowdown in productivity growth and GNP:

> The test score decline's major impact on productivity growth has come in the 1980s. During a period in which falling oil prices, lowered marginal tax rates, scaled-back regulations, and an aging work force were expected to cause productivity growth to rebound, the test score decline has been an important drag on productivity growth.[72]

Bishop calculates that the reduction in the growth of "labor quality" among youth, reflected in the ebbing of test scores, will contribute to a 0.19 percent-per-year deficit in productivity in the 1990s and will continue to mean a 0.12 percent-per-year decline right through the first decade of the twenty-first century.[73]

The problem is not merely that the United States has suffered failing academic skills. It is turning out the wrong skills. Each year America produces too few scientifically and technically trained people. Only 6 percent of U.S. baccalaureates are taken in engineering versus 20 percent in Japan and 37 percent in Germany.[74] Instead of scientists and engineers who could design products to compete in global markets, the

United States has a penchant for schooling lawyers. As Robert Reich (a lawyer himself!) reports, between 1940 and 1960, only about 1 American in 600 was a lawyer; between 1971 and 1981, that number jumped by 64 percent. In contrast, during the same period, the number of U.S. engineers increased only 15 percent. In Japan, only 1 out of every 10,000 citizens is trained in law, while 1 in 25 is trained in science or engineering.[75] Moreover, while Germany and other European countries have developed far-reaching apprenticeship and vocational programs for young workers and placed emphasis on building polytechnics, "the American system of on-the-job training is called 'following Joe around' "—and, according to the MIT Commission, "it does not work."[76]

GOVERNMENT'S INACTION ON QUALITY AND INNOVATION

One might expect the government to play a constructive role in aiding the private sector with productivity-enhancing physical infrastructure. But in a number of ways, the federal government could also help the private sector to improve quality and spur innovation. Yet, time after time, Washington's resolute practice of laissez-faire has cost U.S. firms competitive advantage.[77] In each round of the GATT talks—the international General Agreement on Tariffs and Trade—U.S. delegates have pressed for the elimination of tariffs and nontariff barriers, quotas, and government subsidies. In the so-called Uruguay Round completed in 1990, America was so insistent on winning an unpopular global agreement that would bar tariffs and quotas on agricultural products that the entire round of talks came to naught despite hundreds of other more important items on the agenda.

In theory, free trade is supposed to benefit everyone by producing "allocative efficiency." Barring barriers to trade, each country will specialize in those products or services in which they have comparative advantage. As a result, every traded commodity will be produced at lowest cost, and customers will benefit by paying the lowest possible price. In contrast, if there are barriers to trade, customers are forced to pay a premium to subsidize relative inefficiency. In theory, one can hardly quarrel with this logic.[78]

In practice, however, the world does not work this way. Every nation has in place a vast repertoire of policies to "protect" its industries either directly or indirectly. Tariffs, quotas, "local content laws," financial subsidies, and outright dumping are the most obvious of these. In the early days of the electronics revolution, the Japanese protected their own fledgling enterprises from foreign competition by setting domestic prices well below the break-even point of foreign manufacturers. They permitted their own firms to "dump" products—that is, to sell them in foreign nations below the price prevailing in their own country—in order to gain a toehold in global markets. While such a practice is explicitly prohibited under GATT, the U.S. often failed to file dumping charges except in the most blatant of cases. Within a decade or less, a toehold turned into absolute market domination.

Developed and developing countries alike have used other schemes to tip the scales of trade in their favor. Mexico has "encouraged" all three U.S. automakers to establish plants in their country by legislating that they produce in Mexico the equivalent of 80 percent of the value of the cars they market in that country. Along with such local content laws, Mexico has established duty-free and tax-free zones that have helped induce such firms as Kodak, IBM, Whirlpool, and Caterpillar to set up modern production facilities south of the Rio Grande. With the possibility of unrestricted free trade with Mexico on the horizon, literally hundreds of American firms are pulling up stakes in the United States and moving across the border to take advantage of low-cost labor and local tax havens.[79]

Even if the United States were to convince the rest of a wary world to eliminate all tariffs, quotas, and local content laws, the absence of an "industrial policy" could keep America behind the competition. While the U.S. subsidizes its defense industries, making them the most productive on earth, the rest of the world has focused its government-backed industrial strategy on commercial products. European R&D subsidies to Airbus Industries, the developer of the European competitor to Boeing and McDonnell-Douglas, is one case in point. Airbus received close to $10 billion in government aid for its first three models and another $4 billion to $5 billion for development work on the A330/340 program.[80] As of 1991, Airbus had eclipsed McDonnell-Douglas in aircraft sales and even threatens Boeing in key market segments.[81]

To remain competitive, the Japanese government funds half of both the development and production costs of its aviation consortia in both airframes and engines. In the machine tool industry, Japan's Ministry of International Trade and Industry (MITI) tapped pools of cash from legalized gambling on bicycle and motorbike racing to provide up to $100 million a year to its machine tool industry. The list goes on, covering semiconductors, supercomputers, high-definition television, and industrial materials. MITI does not always "guess right" on what sectors to subsidize, but it has by all accounts assisted in developing globally competitive industries once dominated by Europe and the United States. The United States has lost out, in part by eschewing a government role in maintaining an edge in innovation.

Clearly, when it comes to America's competitiveness problem, there is more than enough blame to go around. But the $64,000 question is how can we rebuild the essential elements needed to compete successfully in world markets? Getting government policy right is important. But it is our contention, shared with many organizational experts, that the *sine qua non* for an American economic renaissance lies primarily in a restructuring of labor-management relations. As we shall argue, such a restructuring is needed to expand the planning horizons of both labor and management and to ensure the total and effective utilization of the American work force.

Whatever its strengths, the traditional Workplace Contract is now obsolete, and something must be developed to take its place. It is to this matter that we now turn our attention. We begin in the next section by examining key elements in the history of labor-management relations.

PART III

FROM THE ADVERSARIAL WORKPLACE TO EMPLOYEE INVOLVEMENT

CHAPTER 5

Management Rights and Union Demands

The rights and interests of the laboring man will be protected and cared for—not by the labor agitators but by the Christian gentlemen to whom God has given control of the property rights of the country.

—*George F. Baer (1842–1914), Industrialist*

Unions are, first and foremost, organizations seeking to improve the lives of those they represent by improving their conditions of work. . . . Since its earliest days, the labor movement has sought to improve the quality of work life, create work place democracy and participate in joint employer-employee decision-making.

—*"The Changing Situation of Workers and Their Unions," Report by the AFL-CIO Committee on the Evolution of Work (1985)*

The guru of modern conservative economics, Milton Friedman, once remarked that the drive for profit in a competitive economy is so compelling that any firm engaged in philanthropic activity should be the first target for federal antitrust action. Only a firm with monopoly power can escape the iron logic of the competitive market, he argued. A dollar given to charity was a dollar that could not be reinvested in the firm to assure that its technology and the quality of its products would be second to none.[1]

For those who find this argument callous in the extreme, the iron law comes in a more malleable version: the more strenuous the competition, the greater the pressure on management to do everything in its power to maximize revenue and minimize cost. "Business management," Peter Drucker has stressed over the years, "must always, *in every decision and action,* put economic performance first. . . . This, whatever the economic or political structure or ideology of a society, means responsibility for profitability."[2] More than a century ago, William Henry Vanderbilt, one of America's most colorful early railroad magnates, put it even more bluntly: "The public be damned. I am working for my stockholders."[3]

MANAGEMENT'S STRUGGLE TO CONTROL THE WORKPLACE

It is precisely this unvarnished profit motive that has historically motivated managers to develop strategies to control as much of their economic environment as possible. Executives aspire to a world where they can have control over the prices they pay for raw materials, control over the prices they can charge for their products, and control over the stream of inputs into the production system—free of interference from labor and government. Ironically, if the economic world were this certain and risk-free, it is likely that top managers would not command anywhere near the salaries they do, for corporate managers are paid for one service: to steer their firms profitably in a world that is often wildly unpredictable.

To cope with the economic environment within which they must function, managers have historically resisted the encroachment of both labor and government into what they have seen as their managerial prerogatives. No matter how socially desirable government regulation might be, management's reaction is based on its reticence to face even one more restriction or one more barrier to running its business in as unencumbered a way as possible. It is not surprising, therefore, that throughout the years, the National Association of Manufacturers (NAM) and other business associations have opposed socially desirable legislation that is nearly universal today: child-labor laws, compulsory free education, the eight-hour day, workers' compensation, unemployment compensation, social security, "truth in packaging" laws, pure food and drug statutes, antidiscrimination rules, and environmental protection measures.

For precisely the same reason, management has traditionally been in conflict with its own employees when they have attempted to organize. This is due to the practical consideration that, out of enlightened self-interest, labor seeks control of much the same work environment over which management already lays claim. The goals of managers and workers, at least at one critical level, are incompatible. Those who manage corporations would like to pay the lowest possible wage *for a given quality of labor;* workers obviously would like to have the largest paycheck and the most extensive set of job benefits consistent with a modicum of employment security. The adversarial relations between worker and boss stem from this basic conflict of interest.

Managers and workers also have divergent objectives when it comes to the most fundamental issue of all for the firm: what the enterprise should strive to maximize. The competitive marketplace, as noted earlier, demands that managers continuously attempt to earn the highest immediate profit even at the expense of other plausible goals. Workers concerned with employment security are usually better served if the firm's objective is to maximize total sales or its market share. Before the historic 1945–46 auto industry negotiations, the UAW's Walter Reuther penned a pamphlet that spoke directly to this issue. He suggested there were two routes the industry could pursue in the postwar period. One he called Low Gear Production, a strategy in which companies would sell at high prices, pay low wages, and yield a high profit on each sale. The better alternative, Reuther argued, was High Gear Production, with low prices, high wages, and smaller per-unit profits applied to a large market share. In both cases, the companies would be assured a high volume of earnings, but the national interest, according to Reuther, would be better served by the latter.[4]

Unfortunately, at least in the short run, the *highest* possible profit and the *largest* market share are incompatible. A price that provides the greatest market share may not be high enough to leave a satisfactory level of profit to the firm. An interim position dubbed "profit satisficing" can potentially appease both labor and management.[5] Under profit satisficing, the firm sets a profit target and then attempts to capture as much market share as possible through lower prices while maintaining profits at this level. In a market where a firm does not have to contend with intense competition, profit satisficing may even lead to higher long-term corporate earnings—good for the stockholder, the manager, and the worker. Lower prices than those consistent with short-term profitability may increase customer loyalty, inhibit new firms from entering the industry, and provide the firm with "economies of scale" in production. In highly competitive markets, however, management seldom has the maneuvering room to profit-satisfice, its efforts constantly focused on simply remaining financially solvent. In this case, management and labor are typically reduced to dueling over such fundamental issues as employment security and the pace of work.

THE END OF A "GUILDED" AGE

Despite management's desire for total control, it has not always had its way. At one time, skilled workers ruled the "factory" floor. In the medieval period of the guilds, the master craftsman who built the great cathedrals and turreted castles of Europe exercised total authority over the economic and working conditions under which the journeymen and apprentices worked and lived.[6] As the centuries passed, however, and "modern" technologies fashioned the basis for an altogether different national economy, the guilds gradually withered away. By 1789, they had disappeared entirely in France.[7] Still, in the basic manufacturing industries, including textiles and steel, much of the control of the factory floor remained with the craft worker. Before the development of the automatic loom and the open-hearth furnace, the master weaver and the skilled steelmaker were invaluable to the employer. The same dominance of the skilled worker held true when shoes and hats, "horseless carriages," and steam engines were built by hand. Acknowledging this, "employers ceded to senior workers considerable control over the shop-floor division of labor as well as the operation and maintenance of machinery."[8]

With the emergence of the Machine Age in the nineteenth century, control over the job gradually shifted from the worker to the employer as managers moved to appropriate the craftsmen's considerable skill and incorporate it into the machine. According to the labor historian William Lazonick, during the first half of the nineteenth century a scarcity of skilled labor in America provided a strong inducement for employers to develop "skill-displacing" technologies. "Capitalists found that highly mobile skilled labor could demand wages that were, from the point of view of profitability, too high in exchange for effort that was too low."[9] Waves of eastern and southern European immigrants provided the unskilled masses while new technologies provided the tools that permitted American employers to attack the craft control that workers had staked out in the early post–Civil War era.

As control shifted away from the worker, twelve- and fourteen-hour workdays became commonplace—as did the six-day workweek and the use of child labor. Whether in the mill or the mine, workers were effectively compelled to make their purchases at company stores at inflated prices. In this way, the employer made a double profit, from depressed wages paid to the worker as worker and from the company store through the prices extracted from the worker as consumer. Those employees who expressed their independence from employer arbitrariness by refusing to shop at the company store risked their jobs and their livelihoods. Health and safety practices were largely ignored by the employer, and injuries and deaths soared among those who toiled in the unregulated mills, mines, and factories of the time. In some cases, employers went so far as to instruct their employees to vote for particular candidates in general elections—a clear manifestation of the "boss's" control beyond the confines of the normal employer-employee relationship.

According to Professor George Lodge of the Harvard Business School, in the early days of the Industrial Revolution such detailed control of employee behavior was considered completely legitimate, resting upon

> an ideology derived from the British social philosopher John Locke. Lockean ideology placed primary emphasis on ownership of private property (a gift from God) and the unquestioned right of the property owners to exercise authority over how that property was used. The authority of managers, then, was bestowed down the hierarchical ranks from above, ultimately from property owners.[10]

Not much had changed by the early part of the twentieth century. In 1915, the elder Henry Ford introduced the Ford Motor Company profit-sharing plan and accompanied it with a booklet sent to all Ford employees. In many ways it was a remarkable document, couched in the "enlightened" paternalistic mode. Most of the booklet's contents comprised instructions relating directly to the deportment of the employee and family outside the workplace. "The sole aim," the booklet explained, "is to better the financial and moral standing of each employee and those of his household; to instill men with courage and a desire for health, happiness and prosperity." Toward this end, the booklet covered an entire gamut of do's and don'ts covering home comforts and sanitation (no boarders, use plenty of soap and water, bathe frequently, keep the premises and backyard clean, cover garbage cans at all times, cultivate a vegetable garden or flowerbed, and so on); the proper care of children and their education; the maintenance of sound health practices (including sleeping with the window open and not sleeping in the same room with more than one other person); the importance of being thrifty, spending wisely and putting aside savings for emergencies and old age, investment advice, and even "suggestions" for the kind of life and fire insurance to purchase.[11] The booklet's title was "Helpful Hints and Advice to Employees," but the "hints" were reinforced by a staff of investigators who went into workers' homes to make certain they were following Ford's "advice." Those who were not were barred from participating in Ford's profit-sharing plan. Those who did not change their ways were subject to discipline and ultimately dismissal. Thus the company exercised a substantial measure of control over its employees and their families, reaching far beyond the workplace and into the privacy of the home.

THE MANY FACES OF MANAGEMENT CONTROL IN THE TWENTIETH CENTURY

Managing is clearly one of the most imprecise terms in the dictionary, reflecting the schizophrenic meaning we attach to it. At one end of a continuum, to manage means "to make obedient" or "to 'boss.' " Both of these definitions refer to a form of control that is strictly hierarchical and highly autocratic. But *managing* can also mean "to guide" or "to coordinate," implying a more cooperative and even democratic mode of control. The search for the most suitable approach to management has captured the imagination of tyrants and democrats alike, particularly because power is almost always distributed unequally, and, as a result, relationships are forever punctuated by some degree of conflict.

The central question of management "science" is not *whether* to control, but *how* to control. Richard Edwards, an economist at the University of Kentucky, suggests in his insightful treatise, *Contested*

Terrain, that no matter the specific nature of the system, managerial control can always be analyzed in terms of three basic elements: (1) the mechanism or method used by employers to direct the work of employees; (2) the evaluation procedures used to assess employee performance; and (3) the disciplinary apparatus used by employers to elicit cooperation or enforce compliance with the wishes of management.[12]

What has changed over time and what varies among firms are the particular mechanisms used to control the work force to meet the goals of the firm. Changes in technology, in the size of establishments, in the power relations between workers and their supervisors, and in government regulations all have had an impact on what types of controls will be adopted by management. In the nineteenth century, for example, most businesses were small and highly competitive. The foreman was king in the typical firm, and reigned over what was the "foreman's empire." As a gang boss on the factory floor, the foreman "had almost all the powers now held by a far greater number of managers— personnel directors, research and development scientists, engineers, efficiency experts, inventory controllers . . . timekeepers, bookkeepers, and other white-collar workers."[13] The foreman was largely responsible

> for making decisions having to do with the hiring, firing, training, motivating, and disciplining of workers; decisions bearing on wage rates, work sharing, the manner and pace of production, the cost and quality of the work, and the levels of inventory; and decisions pertaining to the ordering of materials and the scheduling of deliveries.[14]

This system of "simple" control survives today only in the small business sector of the economy, although some of its worst excesses have been tamed by government regulation and, in good economic times, by workers exercising their power to quit.

In the late nineteenth century, with the growth of mass industry— first in the colossal textile mills in New England and later in the mighty steel mills along the Allegheny and the Monongahela rivers, and later still in the auto, rubber, chemicals, and electrical equipment industries—the sheer size of the enterprise undermined simple control. In 1916, for example, International Harvester employed fifteen thousand workers at its giant McCormick Works alone.[15] Multiplying the number of foremen and supervisors directly under the entrepreneur in a "flat" hierarchy failed to provide the "social planning" necessary to control such a massive work force.

As a consequence, a new system of "hierarchical" control gradually began to replace the earlier method of simple control. A direct chain of command was instituted, patterned after the military, where each level of supervision reported to a higher level, right on up to the top officials of the corporation. At each level, each supervisor had control over the workers under him. He could direct production, evaluate performance, and discipline his "troops." What was new about hierarchical control was the organizational chart and the giant pyramid; what was old was the preservation of direct personal control over each worker in the plant.

Over time, resistance arose against the arbitrary nature of personal control within the strict hierarchical system. One method used by management in dealing with the growing militancy of industrial workers was brute force. When workers tried to organize into unions, management hired private "goon squads" to smash the union, often by cracking the heads or breaking the legs of its organizers. The brutality of management in the Pullman Strike in 1894 and at "Little Steel" in 1919 are today the stuff of legend and folk song. What has gone generally unrecognized are the countless episodes of physical violence, intimidation, and outright murder committed in the course of management's attempt to retain control of the workplace during the "robber baron" days of the last part of the nineteenth and the early decades of the twentieth centuries.

Such brutal repression of the work force inevitably had its price, which increasingly became evident to cost-conscious employers. Assault victims became martyrs, seldom forgotten by those who were forced back to work. Sabotage and "soldiering"—malingering on the job out of sight of the foremen—could be countered only by adding to the already bloated numbers of foremen, "inspectors," and "detectives" whose direct contribution to output and profit was zero. Eventually, management recognized that less violent forms of control were needed.

WELFARE CAPITALISM AND THE "SOULFUL" CORPORATION

By the 1920s, many of the most powerful corporate leaders in America were adopting a more "enlightened" attitude toward their workers, particularly in response to the growing hostility in America toward the captains of industry who by their excesses had brought on the Progressive Era, Teddy Roosevelt's "trust-busting," muckraking journalism, and a growing coalition of farmers, workers, and consumers aligned against big business. Charles M. Schwab, the venerable president of Bethlehem Steel, warned an audience of mechanical engineers in December 1927:

> Our job primarily is to make steel, but it is being made under a system which must be justified. If . . . this system does not enable men to live on an increasingly higher plane, if it does not allow them to fulfill their desires and satisfy their reasonable wants, then it is natural that the system itself should fail.[16]

The president of General Electric, Owen D. Young, translated Schwab's warning into a motto: "The Golden Rule supplies all that a man of business needs."[17] To gain cooperation from its workers, management was reluctantly coming to the conclusion that it had to provide better treatment to its employees. Judge Gary, the legendary chairman of U.S. Steel, tried to convince his subsidiary presidents in 1919, the same year as the pitched battle at Little Steel, that "there is nothing we can do better than to be sure we are liberal in the protection of our workmen and their families. . . . Make the Steel Corporation a good place for them to work and live [and there will be] no just ground for criticism on the part of those who are connected with the movement of unrest."[18]

Schwab, Young, and Gary had, by no means, relinquished their shared belief that profitable operations required subservient loyalty from the work force. What the times demanded, however, to borrow a more contemporary expression, was a kinder, gentler approach to workers, one hearkening back to an earlier time when benevolent entrepreneurs took an interest in the personal lives of their employees. The emerging, short-lived era of welfare capitalism saw a growing number of firms, including many of the industrial Goliaths, supply their workers with recreational services, health care and clinics, pensions, stock-ownership plans, housing, education, and a host of social services, all in the hope of retaining the allegiance of an increasingly disaffected work force.[19] Armstrong Industries, the world's leading supplier of linoleum flooring, provided paid dental care for its employees as early as 1909. The company added extra pay for overtime in 1913, paid vacations in 1924, and group life insurance in 1931.[20] Some firms adopted plans providing their employees with financial aid and technical assistance toward the purchase of first homes. By the end of the 1920s, more than three hundred of the nation's largest firms were offering stock-ownership plans and pensions.[21] While the practice peaked in the mid-1920s, it continued for a time during the Great Depression. In 1933 nearly half of all workers in mining and manufacturing worked in firms that experimented with at least one such unilaterally imposed "fringe" benefit.[22]

But this primordial form of welfare capitalism did not succeed for long in securing the loyalty of workers or in soothing fractious labor-management relations. For one thing, unlike many of today's expensive and valuable benefit packages, the benefits in the 1920s and 1930s were usually meager. One study estimates that the average yearly welfare expenditure was approximately $27 per worker, about 2 percent of the typical worker's annual income.[23] But, more important, welfare capitalism did not get to the root of what was behind worker discontent: the absence of any employee control over the job, the continued arbitrary treatment by foremen and supervisors, and the inhumane pace of the work. Workers were not hoodwinked by managers who bribed them through small and inexpensive acts of paternalism, but who ceded no control over the workplace and still forced them to work ten hours a day six days a week at a breakneck pace. By the 1930s, welfare capitalism, as a faintly disguised attempt to resist union-organizing drives, had failed. When the Great Depression ultimately forced industry to cut workers *and* wages, the era of welfare capitalism was over.

TAYLORISM, FORDISM, AND SCIENTIFIC MANAGEMENT

While paternalistic welfare capitalism was explicitly encouraging worker loyalty and hence performance, a second movement was already well under way. Its implicit purpose was to assure that workers could not interfere with the production process. "Taylorism" or "scientific management" was established on the principle that modern scientific methods could be used to rationalize every job on the factory floor, in the office suite, or in the retail establishment, so as to assure management's full control over every aspect of the production process. For this to be realized, management had to master the expertise of each and every worker, avoiding dependence on any individual worker's own judgment of what constituted the most effective process of production and "a fair day's work for a fair day's pay."

It was Frederick Winslow Taylor, in *Scientific Management*, published in 1911, who laid out the rationale, the ground rules, and the implementation process underlying this boss/worker control system. Taylor endorsed monetary incentives for workers who perform effectively and are therefore more productive. In his "scientific" approach to managing the workplace, however, he asserted that management alone has the intelligence and knowledge to organize the work process to obtain maximum productivity. By extension, employees gain financially only by obeying in precise military style the instructions they are given.

Taylor carefully outlined management's responsibilities and rights in the application of "scientific management" and set forth the following "principles":

First Principle:
The managers assume . . . the burden of gathering together all of the traditional knowledge which in the past has been processed by the workmen and then of classifying, tabulating, and reducing this knowledge to rules, laws, and formulae. . . .

Second Principle:
All possible brain work should be removed from the shop and centered in the planning or laying-out department. . . .

Third Principle:
The most prominent single element in modern scientific management is the task idea. The work of every workman is fully planned out by the management at least one day in advance, and each man receives in most cases complete written instructions, describing in detail the task which he is to accomplish, as well as the means to be used in doing the work. . . . This task specifies not only what is to be done, but how it is to be done and the exact time allowed for doing it.[24]

The effective implementation of these principles and processes was aimed at one supreme objective: to make each worker's job "idiot proof."

Underlying this production system is the notion that workers are mere adjuncts to the tools they use, extensions of a machine. Managers, engineers, and other trained specialists do the thinking and planning while workers are assigned a single, simple set of tasks. Each task comprises certain designated elements of work, requiring minimal training at minimal cost, minimal intellect, minimal education and knowledge, and maximum obedience. The French dramatist Jean Giraudoux captured the spirit of Taylorism in his much-acclaimed *The Madwoman of Chaillot:* "the only safeguard of order and discipline in the modern world is a standardized worker with interchangeable parts. That would solve the entire problem of management."[25]

One of Taylor's most productive disciples, Frank B. Gilbreth, operationalized scientific management by studying, identifying, and classifying all of the motions involved in manual work—"lifting," "moving," "putting down."[26] Gilbreth named his smallest unit of manual effort a *therblig*—a close approximation of his own name spelled backward. Using Gilbreth's measurements, supervisors could disassemble every manual operation in the plant into a series of minuscule individual motions—therbligs—in an attempt to save a hundredth of a second on this operation, or two-hundredths on another. Another Taylor disciple, Henry Gantt, is credited with developing an additional component of scientific management—the Gantt, or organizational chart. Gantt addressed himself to the actual organization of production by working backward from the goals of the enterprise to every step in the production process needed to attain them. But nowhere was scientific management put more to the test than in the factories of Henry Ford. Indeed, *Fordism* is now used to define the epitome of managerial control of a work force and the assembly-line production process.

Ironically, Taylor did not begin his research solely to improve the efficiency and profitability of the corporation. As Peter Drucker notes, "Taylor's aim from the beginning was strictly in accord with the most humanist approach to working."[27] Taylor ardently believed that by organizing work in such a way as to eliminate wasted manual motion, the worker would be less exhausted at the end of the day, both physically and mentally. It therefore was no accident that one of Taylor's earliest and strongest supporters was Louis D. Brandeis, later a Supreme Court justice known to this day for his progressive stands on behalf of human rights and human dignity. Indeed, according to Drucker, it was Brandeis himself who coined the term *scientific management* to describe Taylor's method.

Notwithstanding the liberal endorsement of Taylor's theories, what was the real effect on the worker? Adam Smith had a premonition of it nearly a century and a half before it took hold. Even as he extolled the productivity virtues of a factory's minute division of labor, he recognized the woeful impact it would have on the worker. With keen perception and foreboding insight, he wrote: "The man whose life is spent in performing a few simple operations has no occasion to exert his understanding. . . . he naturally loses, therefore, the habit of such exertion, and generally becomes as stupid and ignorant as it is possible for a human creature to become."[28] Even when Taylor himself explained his concept of scientific management, he described the prototypical worker as one who is required to be "so stupid and so phlegmatic that he more nearly resembles in his mental make-up the ox than any other type."[29]

As scientific management evolved, refinements made robots of workers, removing from them, to the greatest degree possible, the need for education, knowledge, skill, creativity, and intelligence. Workers were expected to check their brains and their freedom at the plant gate when they went to work in the factory.

The imposition of scientific management remains to this day a major responsibility for line management. The complete Taylor system involved a time-and-motion study of every single job in the enterprise and monitoring of the training of each worker to make sure that the best practice techniques were strictly followed. For most companies, the system was too complicated, too costly, and too time consuming to implement.[30] In any event, its most extreme forms were often successfully resisted by workers through work slowdowns and strikes when the "time-and-motion men" showed up on the factory floor. Absenteeism, shabby workmanship, and high turnover plagued one factory after another. Impersonal science turned out to be no substitute for good social relations.

Still, Taylorism survives in the modern era and is no longer confined to production operations per se. Indeed, as electronic technology has become increasingly sophisticated, the precepts of scientific management have been applied to service work as well. With the advance of computer technology, management has been able to divide the mind from the hand among the service work force toward the same objective it achieved with the production worker: to create a work organization composed of order givers and order takers. One need only take note of how the theories of Frederick Taylor are used today in the fast-food business:

> By combining twentieth century computer technology with nineteenth century time and motion studies, the McDonald's corporation has broken the jobs of griddleman, waitress, cashier and even manager down into small, simple steps. Historically these have been service jobs involving a lot of flexibility and personal flair. But the corporation has systematically extracted the decision making elements from filling french fry boxes or scheduling staff. They've siphoned the know how from the employees into the programs. They relentlessly weed out all variables that might make it necessary to make a decision at the store level, whether on pickles or cleaning procedures.[31]

According to Carl Botan and Maureen McCreadie, experts on information technology, by the late 1980s 5 to 7 million clerical, professional, technical and retail sales workers were being continuously monitored in the electronic workplace. An estimated 350,000 communication employees work daily at monitored video data terminals. At Northwest Airlines in Minneapolis, the acceptable data-entry pace of travel agents is recorded for the three fastest operators. The keystroke output of other operators is continuously monitored and is expected to come within at least 70 percent of this pace. Even long-distance truckers, "long thought to be independent and freewheeling, now frequently travel in the company of Tripmaster, a black box that records average speeds, the number and length of stops, mileage, and even shifting patterns."[32]

Not surprisingly, what goes around comes around. Taylorism in modern dress has now reached up into the ranks of middle management. According to Botan and McCreadie: "Even the freedom of executives to make judgments is being altered by new information technology as more and more middle managers who use computers [are] monitored on how many appointments they have and how many hours they spend on various activities."[33]

CONTROL WITH A VELVET GLOVE: THE HUMAN RELATIONS APPROACH

Welfare capitalism was loosely premised on the theory of economic bribery, and Taylorism on the principle of the technological fix. Over time, both proved inadequate as methods for controlling workers in the interest of efficiency and profitability. Despite the appearance of concern for the worker's welfare under both systems, neither paid satisfactory attention to the "human relations" aspects of production. Workers were still being treated as cogs in the machinery or mere badge numbers when times were good. When times were bad, layoffs and wage cuts led to even greater discontent. General foremen in the factory were trapped in the worst of all possible positions, caught between top management, which ordered them to meet output targets set according to "scientific" principles, and an increasingly rebellious work force who would have none of it.

One variant on the human relations theme was management's creation of "company unions." To stem the growth in industrial unionism toward the end of World War I, some of the largest companies in the United States experimented with "works councils" or "shop committees." The Lynn Plan of Representation at the GE works in Massachusetts, for example, provided for workers to elect their own employee representatives to a committee that had an equal number of management appointees.[34] Subcommittees for grievances and safety were established. The principal function of the plan was to provide grievance machinery that workers could invoke to solve disputes with the company. In GE's case, the plan worked reasonably well, if success can be measured by the fact that its plants were not organized by independent unions until the mid-1930s.

In the end, however, company unions did not prove successful for a simple reason. What management unilaterally provides, it can just as easily annul. Insofar as these "representative" bodies gave little direct control to the worker, and decisions over working conditions could be reversed by management at any time, the establishment of company unions seldom assured a productive and effective work environment. As Drucker made abundantly clear more than forty years ago:

A plant government that rests on management's good intentions alone will be unable to oppose management. It will be like that Russian parliament called by an absolute Czar that was dissolved the first time its vote went contrary to the Czar's wishes. At best it will be an advisory body; it cannot have any real authority or enjoy any real respect.[35]

Workers found that the grievance procedures established under company unions allowed them to air their complaints about how they were treated under plant rules, but did not give them much opportunity to establish or change the rules under which they worked nor to assure them fairness in the disposition of their grievances. As the number of complaints accumulated, the cracks in the human relations machinery that management had conceived became more evident. Finally, under the pressure of the Great Depression, the system buckled. It was replaced by a wave of independent unions organized in the mass-production industries. Company unions were finally outlawed by the federal government in the sweeping labor legislation of the 1930s.

BUREAUCRATIC CONTROL

Experiments with Taylorism, human relations approaches, and company unions taught management one lasting lesson: complex organizations are best governed by laws or rules rather than by the often arbitrary judgments and edicts of line foremen and supervisors. If the control mechanism could be submerged in the structure of the work itself, the appearance of raw personal power on the part of management could be made largely invisible.

Bureaucratic control rests on two pillars. The first is the intricately detailed codification of conduct within the firm. Explicit seniority ladders within the firm's own "internal" labor market assure that employees who abide by the rules will eventually better their occupational status. Each job has a tightly prescribed description and defined standards of performance. The second pillar is the bureaucratic hierarchy. The great mass of workers in an enterprise is divided into finely graded divisions and strata with multiple levels of supervision. Lines of communication are clearly designated and the chain of command is explicit.

The combination of technical control of each job and bureaucratic control of the enterprise seemed finally to assure management a governing mechanism free of the shortcomings of strict Taylorism. But ultimately this proved illusory, for bureaucratic control has two monumental defects that haunt the modern corporation.

One is the proliferation of layers of bureaucracy and supervision. Earlier forms of technical control had been quite parsimonious in their use of foremen. The assembly line eliminated "obtrusive foremanship"—the close supervision of each worker. Ford, for example, according to a 1915 study, employed just 255 department foremen, job foremen, assistant foremen, and "straw bosses" to supervise 15,000 workers—a ratio of just 1 foreman for each 58 workers.[36] In the early post–World War II era, before the full-scale emergence of bureaucratic control, there were on average 2 to 3 foremen per 100 workers in manufacturing companies. By 1970, with full bureaucratic control in the ascendancy, the number approached 5 per 100.[37] As a result, firms were paying relatively fewer people to produce things and more to oversee their operations.

The second problem, stemming from the extravagant proliferation of administrative structure, is the bureaucracy's ponderously long reaction time to any change in the environment. Bureaucratic control *may* work reasonably well under stable conditions where change is slow and market competition is weak. But in an economy where competition is rampant and technological change is abrupt, bureaucracies tend to trip over their own feet. Thus, while bureaucratic control was not inconsistent with efficiency and profitability in the immediate post–World War II era when firms enjoyed monopoly advantage and the threat of imports was essentially nonexistent, by the beginning of the 1970s, and surely by the 1980s, bureaucratic firms were too bloated with middle-level managers to be efficient and much too burdened by rules and regulations to dance fast enough to keep up with foreign competition. More and more companies began to realize that top-down bureaucratic control was antithetical to productivity, quality, and innovation.

THE MOVE TOWARD "MANAGERIALISM"

As a result, for the past decade or more, American firms have been experimenting with new systems of control and new methods of organizing production. One of these has been dubbed *managerialism*.[38] It refers to a limited system of worker participation in decision making, as opposed to strict bureaucratic control and Taylorism. Practiced explicitly in *nonunion* settings, it "proposes that *every* employee be a manager, involved in decisions and contributing intelligently to the goals of the corporation."[39]

Managerialism often begins with "job-enlargement" and "job-enrichment" programs aimed at providing workers with greater on-the-job responsibilities and a wider variety of work. It tends to use "problem-solving groups" and, recently, "semi-autonomous work teams," in which groups of workers have direct responsibility for organizing their own work settings and work schedules. Since workers supervise themselves collectively, the need for the traditional line or area foreman is acutely diminished. Interestingly, the structure of semi-autonomous work teams bears a striking resemblance to the craft control of the steel industry before the turn of the century—a real-life case of "back to the future."

The rise of managerialism in the postwar era is consistent with the distinction made by Douglas McGregor more than thirty years ago between what he called Theory X and Theory Y.[40] Theory X, the traditional approach to the worker, assumes that people are innately lazy, dislike and shun work, and have to be driven by the carrot and stick to accomplish anything. It rests on the assumption that most people—at least most employees—are incapable of taking responsibility for themselves and have to be carefully and persistently monitored. By contrast, Theory Y assumes people have a psychological need to work and will strive to perform admirably if given the chance. Theory X conceives of men and women as immature children; Theory Y postulates that people want to be treated as adults.

There can be little doubt from several hundred years' experience with Theory X that, while it appeared to be successful for a time, it contains an inherent fatal flaw. People who are treated like children begin to act like children. They are not particularly productive, and whatever creative tendencies they begin with are quickly smothered. Recall that Frederick Taylor himself recognized this propensity when he wrote that the prototypical worker was required to have the mental makeup of an ox. For this reason, more and more firms are treating their employees according to the precepts of Theory Y, permitting them to help set goals and manage their own work.

In practice, managerialism is different things to different people. In its most benign form, it provides for an expansion of channels by which employees can voice their concerns. But in many cases, as the labor relations expert Charles Heckscher has suggested, "a great deal of fakery passes under the banner of reform."[41] Reform then becomes merely a manipulative tool used cynically to benefit management to the disadvantage of labor. Too often, it is attempted simply as a device to avoid unionism—a growing practice among American firms.[42] Paid labor consultants and industrial psychologists ply their trade of teaching employers how to avoid unions through the use of positive rein-forcement, employee value systems, problem-solving orientations, and "performance through motivation." One union-avoidance expert, Dr. Charles L. Hughes, explains to his clients unabashedly how the tech-niques of managerialism can be used to defuse a union drive. Good communications with your employees, the establishment of employee "committees," the substitution of job titles "that have some good strokes" (such as "petrochemical technician" for oil-tank cleaner), and "constant attention to the attitudes and personality of your employees" are all part of the process.[43]

Firms may establish managerialist structures, but their own paternal-istic drives and the overarching demand to control often leads to an abuse of corporate power under the guise of employee empowerment. In the absence of an independent union with the legal right to represent workers, it is not unusual for even the most benevolent management to misuse its power, especially when outside pressures reduce profitability or otherwise threaten the economic security of the firm. In short, managerialism appears to work best when the firm is economically secure and unthreatened—perhaps precisely when, from manage-ment's perspective, it is needed least.

LABOR'S STRUGGLE FOR WORKERS' RIGHTS

Regardless of the mechanism of managerial control, there is bound to be some level of conflict between labor and management since the objectives of workers and owners are never perfectly congruent. This is simply in the natural scheme of things. The problem is to figure out how to distribute power between labor and corporate management in such a way that all the stakeholders in the enterprise—workers, owners, and managers themselves—forge the best collective outcome possible within an economic and social environment riddled with constraints.

Historically, workers have turned both to their unions and to the government in their striving to circumscribe the power of management. Gaining recognition for their own organizations, winning seniority rights and better pay and benefits, improving occupational safety and health, controlling against speedup, and establishing contractual rights over dozens of areas regarding the conditions of work have all become part of the American labor-management landscape. In the twentieth century, labor has countered welfare capitalism, Taylorism, the human relations approach, bureaucratic control, and managerialism with ideas of its own.

GOVERNMENT REGULATION OF THE WORKPLACE

Workers have used two institutions to protect themselves from the unfettered power of employers: the government and the trade union. Beyond circumscribing management prerogatives to protect consumers, the environment, and public health—a movement that began early in the century—there arose a parallel movement to safeguard workers from exploitation and discrimination in the workplace. One of the early legislative struggles concerned the prohibition of child labor. In the period immediately following the Revolutionary War, nine- and ten-year-old children "constituted the principal labor supply in the textile mills." Textile mill owners proudly argued that these children, working twelve and thirteen hours a day, "were serving God as well as aiding their families."[44]

With the federal government remaining largely on the sidelines, it was not until the end of the nineteenth century that individual states, spurred on by the labor movement, passed the first laws restricting the use of child labor and the number of hours women could work. They also began to regulate industrial safety and the methods of wage payment (for example, outlawing payment in scrip redeemable only at company stores) and to establish limited machinery for the mediation of labor disputes. In 1912 and 1913, the first state minimum-wage laws were authorized—initially applying solely to women and children—and spread to seventeen states in the span of ten years.[45] From the beginning, management complained bitterly that government was trampling on their prerogatives.

To provide workers with some income when their employers laid them off, a coalition of progressive reformers in 1916 induced Massachusetts to propose the first "unemployment-compensation" law, patterned after a system adopted in Great Britain five years earlier.[46] Conservative legislators mustered enough votes to forestall passage of the bill, which would have compelled employers to pay into an unemployment fund. Wisconsin was actually the first to ratify such a statute, but not until 1932. A workers' compensation law, providing cash benefits to workers who became injured on the job, was first passed in New York in 1909. By 1948 every state had enacted some form of this legislation.[47] Later, the workers' compensation system was extended to cover occupation-related diseases as well as injury.

As might have been expected, most of these state laws were enacted over the strenuous objection of business. In 1923, for example, the Associated Industries of Massachusetts—the leading trade organization in the commonwealth—published as the main article in a 1923 issue of its official magazine, *Industry,* "What Can We Do to Prevent Unwise Social Legislation?" The "unwise" legislation they were referring to included minimum wages, workers' compensation, and prohibitions on child labor.[48]

With the major exception of the 1926 Railway Labor Act, which gave national legislative recognition to collective bargaining in the railroad industry, it was only after the election of FDR that the federal government began to play a more central role in protecting workers through legislative restrictions on management prerogatives. The monumental Social Security Act of 1935 not only established what today has become the bedrock Old Age, Survivors, Disability, and Health Insurance program (OASDHI) but also created the modern federal/state unemployment compensation system. After enactment of the national law, every state promptly adopted an approved insurance scheme for the unemployed.[49] The 1938 Fair Labor Standards Act mandated the first federal minimum wage, established the standard workweek, and strengthened child-labor laws. At twenty-five cents an hour, the statutory wage floor hardly kept workers from poverty. Requiring time-and-a-half pay for work exceeding forty-four hours a week (now forty hours) did not bar firms from requiring mandatory overtime. Still, these represented momentous gains for workers, not only in terms of improved income but, more important, in institutionalizing principles to protect them from unfair practices.

In the 1960s and 1970s, the federal government once again expanded restrictions on business to protect workers at the work site. The Federal Coal Mine Health and Safety Act, passed in 1969, provided tougher health and safety standards in the mines and provided cash benefits to miners who suffered pneumoconiosis—black lung disease.[50] The very next year, Congress passed the historic Occupational Safety and Health Act, designed to help prevent injury and disease on the job. Under the law, a newly created Occupational Safety and Health Administration (OSHA) was given the power to establish mandatory standards for conditions of work and the legal clout to order employers to take corrective and preventive measures to ensure worker safety. Employers were also compelled by a formidable new civil rights law—Title VII of the Civil Rights Act of 1964—to follow nondiscriminatory guidelines in their hiring practices and in the terms and conditions of employment. In practice, firms were required by the law to follow "affirmative action" guidelines in hiring and firing in order to reverse past discrimination.

Other federal and state laws that protect workers at the expense of what managers often see as their inviolable rights include the Davis-Bacon Act, first passed in 1931, stipulating that workers employed on federal construction projects must be paid "prevailing wages."[51] Management's hands also have been partly bound when it comes to their retired employees. Under the 1974 Employment Retirement Income Security Act (ERISA), employee pension funds must be invested in a "prudent" manner—prudence not always being in strict accord with management's own investment priorities.

THE UNION CHALLENGE TO MANAGEMENT RIGHTS

Legislated protection is available to workers regardless of whether they belong to a recognized union. The other form of protection, and in the United States a more potent intruder into managerial authority, is the trade or industrial union. As with government regulation of the workplace, it was only in the twentieth century, and not really until the 1930s, that unions gained the power to challenge successfully what had been the ironclad prerogatives of management in many of the powerful manufacturing sectors of the economy. And it took government action to help make that possible.

Until 1935, the federal government provided only meager protection to the trade union movement. At the behest of big business and corporate lobbyists, the federal courts were openly hostile. In 1805, when the shoeworkers in Philadelphia demanded an increase in their wages, they were indicted and brought to trial on the charge of "forming a combination and conspiring to raise wages." The prosecution relied on a parliamentary act that had been passed in England in 1349, the Statute of Laborers, to argue that workers had no right under the law to join together in demanding higher pay. The jury in the case found the workers "guilty of a combination to raise wages." The defendants were fined eight dollars each as the penalty for their illegal act.[52] Thus it was held to be a crime for "an association of workers" even to try to negotiate the wage they would be paid by the employer. Property rights and, by extension, managerial rights won out over labor's demands. Between 1806 and 1842, there were more than fifteen applications of the "conspiracy law," which "put a chill on virtually any form of labor organization that went beyond a mere social club and sought to influence wages and conditions of work."[53]

Matters improved marginally for organized labor after 1842 in the wake of a subtle shift in judicial interpretation of the conspiracy law. In *Commonwealth v. Hunt*, heard before the highest court in Massachusetts, the court ruled that union activities per se were not illegal, but rather that their legality rested on the objectives they were striving to attain.[54] Still, in some states affairs had hardly changed by 1875, when miners on strike over wage scales in Pennsylvania were found guilty of conspiracy. The union's elected leaders were sentenced to jail.[55] It is noteworthy that the hue and cry raised by this trial and its outcome persuaded the Pennsylvania legislature to pass legislation exempting unions from the charge of conspiracy, something the federal government failed to do until the passage of the Clayton Act nearly forty years later.

For nearly a century, from *Commonwealth v. Hunt* to the Norris-LaGuardia Act of 1932, unions existed more or less as legal organizations, but the government did little to protect their rights to organize and to bargain collectively. Often local authorities, and not uncommonly state and federal government officials, openly sided with employers, using local police and even in some instances federal troops to drive organizers out of town and disrupt union meetings. At the request of employers, the courts regularly imposed injunctions on strike activity and brought contempt citations against union organizers. Employers were not required to recognize the existence of unions, nor forced by law to negotiate with them; rather, "they were legally free to interfere with, obstruct, or combat the development and activities of unions as they saw fit, within the broad confines of criminal law."[56] Union organizers were routinely fired, union members were blacklisted from jobs, labor spies and strikebreakers were hired to disrupt embryonic organizing drives, and workers were forced as a condition of employment to sign "yellow-dog" contracts pledging not to join a union.

Not until the Clayton Act of 1914 did labor gain any recognition from federal authorities—and even then the federal courts failed to provide appropriate enforcement. Section 6 of the act forbade the use of the Sherman Antitrust Act against labor while Section 20 was designed to prevent the wholesale use of the court injunction against strikes, boycotts, and picketing. Union drives were thwarted, however, as judicial interpretation of the law made it practically useless.[57]

Only with the onset of the Great Depression did labor finally win a true legislative victory. The Norris-LaGuardia Act of 1932 explicitly prohibited the enforcement of yellow-dog contracts and deprived the federal judiciary of issuing labor injunctions. After nearly a century and a half, the national government was moving toward a policy of "neutrality" toward labor and management. Labor relations experts Herbert Northrup and Gordon Bloom assert that Norris-LaGuardia reflected a brand new philosophy: "The disputants should be left to their own resources to work out their own problems. Both labor and business would now be free to promote their own interests in the field of labor policy through self-help without interference of the courts."[58] Labor did not have a friend in government in its challenge to management, but it no longer had a mortal enemy.

LABOR'S MAGNA CARTA

As the depression deepened and more Americans came to blame big business for their economic plight, FDR and Congress moved from strict neutrality in labor-management matters to active support of trade union activity. President Roosevelt expressed his personal sentiments concerning the union movement when he stated, much to the chagrin of the business establishment: "I believe now as I have all my life in the right of workers to join unions and to protect their unions."[59]

Until the early 1930s the American Federation of Labor's position regarding broad social issues—establishing laws regarding hours of work or providing Social Security benefits, for instance—was that these benefits should be won through collective bargaining, not through legislation. But with the desperate decline in the economy, the AFL reversed its position on these issues at its 1932 convention. It lobbied hard for sweeping new labor legislation that would promote unionism. In keeping with its past practice, the National Association of Manufacturers, the chief lobbying agency for big business, mounted a multifaceted campaign to dissuade the president and Congress from enacting new labor legislation, relying on radio, personal letters, telegrams, public speeches, and the news media to make its point. It pressed its members to join the congressional battle. But in the end this effort proved futile. The passage of the National Labor Relations Act (NLRA) only three years after Norris-LaGuardia established for the very first time the inalienable right of workers to join unions free of management interference.

To make this guarantee effective, the law—popularly known as the Wagner Act, after its leading sponsor, Senator Robert Wagner of New York—prohibited a number of "unfair employer practices." It forbade employers from interfering with their employees' rights to organize and bargain collectively. It banned "company unions"—internal organizations of employees initiated and controlled by management. It barred firms from discriminating against workers who are or become union members. It prohibited employers from discharging or discriminating against workers who file charges under the act. Finally, it compelled employers to bargain collectively and in good faith with unions selected by employees in federally sanctioned "certification" elections.[60]

An independent agency, the National Labor Relations Board (NLRB), was established to oversee the law, to investigate and hold hearings on unfair labor practice complaints, to issue cease-and-desist orders against employers found guilty of unfair practices, to determine the composition of appropriate individual employee bargaining units, and to oversee union certification and decertification secret ballot elections.

Labor's struggles for recognition of the rights of workers came in response to employment conditions dramatically described by Walter Reuther, then a young officer in the fledgling United Auto Workers. He wrote poignantly about life in the factory before the new growth of unionism, spurred by the passage of the Wagner Act:

> Injustice was as commonplace as streetcars. When men walked into their jobs, they left their dignity, their citizenship and their humanity outside. They were required to report for duty whether there was work or not. While they waited on the convenience of supervisors and foremen they were unpaid. They could be fired without the necessity for a pretext. They were subjected to arbitrary, senseless rules. . . . Men were tortured by regulations that made difficult even

going to the toilet. Favoritism was endemic to the factory. Men were fired to make way for supervisors' nephews, foremen's brothers-in-law, college chums. Long years of employment entitled workers to nothing. When men slowed down at forty or forty-five they were laid off without hope of recall. After layoffs there was never assurance that a man would get his job back if work started up again, or if he did get his job that he would return to work at his old pay. The millions of unemployed outside the plant gates were used to frighten workers into subservience.

Despite grandiloquent statements from the presidents of huge corporations, declaring their door was open to any worker with a complaint, there was no one and no agency to which a worker could appeal if he were wronged. The very idea that a worker could be wronged seemed absurd to the employer.[61]

With the NLRA and the NLRB, workers finally possessed an instrument to counter Taylorism, welfarism, and managerialism: legally enforceable collective bargaining.

Union organizing drives blossomed as the Wagner Act took effect. Business challenged the constitutionality of the law, but the U.S. Supreme Court upheld its validity. With the founding of the Committee of Industrial Organization (later the Congress of Industrial Organizations—the CIO) under the leadership of John L. Lewis, the president of the Coal Miners Union, unionization spread rapidly.

The thrust of industrial unionism, with its credo of organizing all the production and craft workers in a given enterprise, captured the imagination and loyalty of industrial workers throughout the country. In industry after industry, in steel, auto, electrical goods, rubber, chemicals, and glass, national and international unions were established. The United Steel Workers (USW), the United Auto Workers (UAW), the United Electrical Workers (UE), and other unions grew rapidly as organizing the unorganized became the rallying cry of the day. Workers flocked to the new union movement, in many instances knocking on the door of the CIO, anxious and prepared to join a union and take advantage of the now fully legalized collective-bargaining process. In just three years following the enactment of the Wagner Act, trade union membership doubled.[62]

The nascent philosophy now undergirding labor-management relations was that of "countervailing power." Before the growth of industrial unions, large employers were seen as exercising a type of monopoly power over the purchase of labor. In the absence of unions, bosses unilaterally determined wage scales, the level of job benefits, and what working conditions would prevail. This was particularly true in company towns where the employer had control over every lock, stock, and barrel. Even outside the company town, workers were often trapped in their jobs largely by the fear of unemployment or of being blacklisted. Whatever the reason for entrapment, workers were hardly in a position to bargain as "free agents."

In this context, government-sanctioned unions were seen as the vehicle to provide workers with a "monopoly" of their own to countervail the power of management.[63] With the federal government as overseer, the Wagner Act "created three power bases—management, unions, and government—which would now act as countervailing forces. Management would speak for the interests of shareholders, unions would protect organized workers, and the government would attempt to seek a balance between the two on behalf of the 'common good.' "[64]

On a more level playing field, battles over sharing the proceeds of the economic pie would be determined ultimately by the ability of a union to prolong a strike versus the company's financial strength to weather it. In an era of limited import competition, expanding productivity, and oligopolistic industry, the system was expected to work reasonably well.

Later would come a conservative backlash to the liberal NLRA. By 1946, long after the depression and soon after the war, many states, particularly in the South, surrendered to pressure from local business groups and passed their own laws to limit the provisions of the Wagner Act. Sixteen had laws either circumscribing or prohibiting the "closed shop"—whereby no one can be hired who is not already a member of a specific trade union. Eleven states regulated picketing, twelve outlawed certain types of labor-backed boycotts, and twenty-one placed restrictions on strike activity.[65]

Eventually the business community found sympathy in the House and the Senate, claiming that the original 1935 act went too far by restricting the activities of employers while doing nothing to curb the "socially irresponsible" behavior of unions. A majority in Congress was influenced by labor dispute statistics emanating from the Department of Labor. The agency counted nearly five thousand individual strikes in 1946. Fully one-tenth of the American labor force was on strike at sometime during the year—the result of pent-up grievances and economic demands unresolved during the period of wartime wage controls.[66] Over the veto of President Truman, Congress passed the Taft-Hartley Amendments to the Wagner Act.

Taft-Hartley, officially known as the Labor-Management Relations Act of 1947, outlawed secondary boycotts and jurisdictional strikes, made illegal the closed shop, permitted states under its Paragraph 14b to outlaw the union shop, and made it possible for employers to bring unfair practice claims of their own against union representatives.[67]

These amendments made it more difficult for unions to organize and restricted the tactics they could use in the course of collective bargaining. Nonetheless, much of the labor-management relations system put in place as a result of the original Wagner Act prevailed, and union organizing activities flourished during the 1950s. By 1955, the AFL had 10.6 million members, the CIO had 4.6 million, and another 1.8 million workers belonged to unions not affiliated with either—primarily the Teamsters.[68] More than one-third of the nonagricultural labor force in the United States had become dues-paying union members.

FIGHTING FOR CONTROL OF THE WORKPLACE

The introduction of unions into the business enterprise immediately raised the issue of managerial control, for the essential thrust of unionism is to bring to the workplace the basic democratic values that workers enjoy as citizens in a free society. Peter Drucker recognized the problems managers face when a union enters the scene:

> Every single area of union activity is inevitably a management area, whether it be working hours or working conditions, job definitions, job assignments, hiring and firing policies, supervisory authority or seniority provisions. . . . Hence the union is always a part of the governmental structure of the enterprise. . . . It is shortsighted to the point of folly for any management to deny that the union necessarily concerns itself with problems which are "properly management's prerogatives."

So as not to leave the point in doubt, Drucker metaphorically nailed his message to the corporate boardroom wall: "Any concern of the union is with matters which are properly management's prerogatives; in fact it is precisely because of this 'prerogative' that the union exists" at all.[69]

Yale University's Neil Chamberlain, arguably the foremost student of industrial relations at the end of the war, noted just how far labor had come in making inroads into management prerogatives. At the National Labor-Management Conference held at President Truman's behest in Washington in the fall of 1945, he noted that management "sought to secure union compliance with the jurisdictional areas which they had delimited for their sole exercise of the management function." This effort on the part of the managers to obtain recognition from the unions, he wrote, "is as significant a social struggle as the earlier effort of unions to obtain recognition from the managers."[70]

Labor had found a voice through its unions. In the organized sector of the economy, management could no longer rule unilaterally. Workers were fulfilling a pledge that Sidney Hillman, the president of the Amalgamated Clothing Workers Union had made in 1918: "What labor is demanding all over the world today is not a few material things like more dollars and fewer hours of work but a right to a voice in the conduct of industry."[71]

WHAT WORKERS HAVE WON

By definition, union-won provisions always squeeze the perimeter of managerial prerogatives, but unions—regardless of management's worst fears—have traditionally limited their demands well short of controlling the enterprise. Wages and other economic benefits are the perennial subjects over which the parties negotiate. Establishing processes and procedures guaranteeing decent working conditions are of equal significance. Workplace issues have dominated the bargaining table as negotiated seniority rules covering layoff and recall, transfers and promotions, shift preference, and job selection replaced the exclusive management right of making decisions about who would be laid off or recalled, or who would be transferred or promoted. The grievance procedure with binding arbitration as the final step, the right to contest, and, in some cases, even the right to strike during the contract period over what the union views as an inhumane work pace, over health and safety issues, and over the establishment of wage rates for newly created job classifications—these and a host of other conditions of work issues added an ever-increasing number of clauses to labor contracts. Nearly every added provision in the negotiated agreement signaled a further encroachment on the employer's control of the workplace.

Yet what labor unions have learned, as global competition has intensified, is that trying to protect their members' jobs and living standards through traditional contract language is no longer sufficient. Leaving decisions on productivity, quality, and innovation in management's exclusive control allows for the possibility that decisions made at higher levels of the firm will have the consequence of eliminating thousands of jobs while the contract provisions save a mere handful. As a result, labor has begun to see the need to develop a new relationship with management based on co-responsibility for seeing that what is produced in the workplace meets world standards for efficiency and quality.

Indeed, despite the real confrontational factors inherent in the relationship between management and labor, it is evident that between them lies a plenitude of common concerns and mutual interests. The problem facing management and labor is to find the methods and means to accomplish common goals and to distribute the gains of market success equitably.

In the continuing drama of collective bargaining, the adversarial system will no doubt endure as a centerpiece of labor-management relations. In the decades to come, union and management representatives will still be involved in the tough bargaining process of resolving wages, benefits, and conditions of work. Concurrently, however, an added dimension to the union-management relationship is taking form—and, indeed, has been for more than two decades. This is the system of employee involvement typified not by the adversarial struggle between labor and management but by a commitment to building a partnership or accord that can provide for employment security and enhanced job satisfaction while rebuilding the economic competitiveness of American enterprise. It is to this new participatory system that we now turn.

CHAPTER 6

Employee Involvement in Action

We must create a company in which the skills, intelligence, and ideas of each person are valued and utilized. To me, employee participation means that everyone must have the opportunity to identify and help solve real problems where they work. I look forward to an organization where people come to work every day thinking about how they can make things better—and knowing that they will have the opportunity to have their ideas heard and implemented.

—Herbert Elish, CEO and President, Weirton Steel Corporation (1990)

Even before the 1980s, rising inflation, growing unemployment, lackluster profits, and stagnating incomes were already making it clear that America was falling behind in the global economic race. As we have argued in previous chapters, mediocre productivity growth, consumer suspicion about the quality of American-made goods, and lagging innovation were all critical in bringing on the economy's ill health. In many industries, both corporate management and labor fell prey to the illusion that the traditional ways of doing business would continue to serve the interests of stockholders and workers alike, despite sea changes in the structure of international economic relations. In the organized sector of the economy, the traditional adversarial model remained dominant, even as membership declined in a broad array of seriously affected industries. When profits fell sufficiently to raise the anger of stockholders, companies turned to tried, if not true, ways to cut costs. In unionized settings they demanded, and in nonunion settings they unilaterally imposed, wage and benefit concessions. They moved operations abroad to obtain low wages and a docile work force. They closed operations to try to compete in sectors not subject to import competition.

PRODUCTIVITY THROUGH PEOPLE

"Lean and mean" became the order of the day, but not universally. By the early 1970s, before the massive import surge, there were those who recognized the need for change as the global challenge accelerated. It would not do simply to run away from American workers or their unions. Instead, it would be necessary to maintain on a continuing basis world-class standards of human relations to achieve world-class standards of productivity growth, quality, and innovation with the physical plant and labor already being utilized. By 1982, there were enough firms experimenting with a new "corporate culture" to provide Tom Peters and Robert Waterman with sufficient raw material to complete *In Search of Excellence,* which lauded the success of what they termed "America's best-run companies."[1] Peters and Waterman spent years studying U.S. companies, particularly those that had outdistanced the competition, both domestic and foreign. In studying such firms as Boeing Aircraft, 3M, Procter & Gamble, IBM, Maytag, Digital Equipment Corporation, and Frito-Lay, they documented what they considered to be the characteristics of successful enterprise in the brave-new-world economy.[2] What they found, somewhat to their surprise, is that the content of the corporate culture in all the firms they studied was invariably limited to a handful of themes: "Whether bending tin, frying hamburgers, or providing rooms for rent, virtually all of the excellent companies had, it seemed, defined themselves as de facto service businesses. Customers reign supreme."[3]

But Peters and Waterman went farther than simply identifying quality and service as the hallmarks of the successful company. The secret, they argued, is "productivity through people." The success of America's best-managed companies came from "treating people decently and asking them to shine, and from producing things that work." In virtually all of the firms that they judged to be excellently managed, "a numbing focus on cost [had given] way to an enhancing focus on quality. Hierarchy and three-piece suits gave way to first names, shirt-sleeves, hoopla, and project-based flexibility. Working according to fat rule books was replaced by everyone's contributing."[4]

Beneath the authors' *own* hoopla was a commonsense lesson: to win the productivity, quality, and innovation game, workers must be satisfied in their jobs and enjoy confidence in their personal employment security. Peters and Waterman, of course, did not invent this formula, nor did they take credit for it. They merely documented it by analyzing specific firms in considerable depth and explained it in simple-to-understand terms.

Indeed, throughout the 1970s and 1980s, in the public as well as the private sector, in service industries as well as manufacturing, in union and nonunion sectors alike, thousands of experiments in employee participation were initiated with no two exactly alike. A 1987 survey by the U.S. General Accounting Office found that 70 percent of nearly five hundred large companies had some kind of employee involvement program.[5] An earlier U.S. Department of Labor survey found that by 1983, eighty-five national unions were involved in employee participation "joint action" experiments in companies where they had collective-bargaining agreements.[6]

Some of these experiments were influenced by the Japanese model of motivating workers through lifetime employment security and organizing employees into "quality circles." In Japan, where about one-third of the labor force is affiliated with a national union and about the same proportion benefits from lifetime employment security, union-management cooperation is fostered through a joint consultation system *(roshi kyogisei)*. This approach provides union leaders with the opportunity to consult with management on the general direction of the enterprise and negotiate working conditions, wages, hours, and benefits.[7] The customary issues of collective bargaining familiar in the American system are resolved through the joint consultation system. But on the shop floor, beyond these traditional Workplace Contract issues, union members work closely with management through quality circles, pursuing the mutual goal of improving organizational performance.

Contrary to some media coverage, this approach does not automatically ensure that Japan is a nation of happy workers. Workers there have many of the same complaints as workers in the United States: production speedup, unhealthy working conditions, stern supervisors. Still, the Japanese penchant for quality production and their obvious success in world markets have spurred a growing number of American firms to experiment with variations on what managers here take to be the two key Japanese principles of industrial relations: (1) guaranteed employment security and (2) team production.

"GUARANTEED" EMPLOYMENT SECURITY

Traditionally, the American experience of "rugged individualism" has its parallel in labor relations circles: the worker is expendable. When a company no longer needs as many workers, it simply gets rid of the excess. As *Fortune* magazine's Bill Saporito puts it: "Like the captain of a dirigible that is fast losing altitude . . . the typical response from corporate commanders . . . is to throw the crew overboard, or at least a substantial fraction of it."[8]

The problem, he notes, is that while to the outsider this strategy seems to pay off in terms of short-term gains in both earnings and stock price, "the experience tends to give almost everyone left aboard a powerful set of the shakes, in ways that may end up as a drag on the enterprise."[9] For this reason, many of the companies reputed to be the best managed are those that have rejected the notion of the expendable worker.

Among large American firms, the one that perhaps has come closest to the ideal of the Japanese "permanent employment" policy is Hallmark, the nation's leading greeting-card designer and manufacturer. Hallmark's chairman, Irvine O. Hockaday, Jr., has time and time again reaffirmed that shutting down plants and terminating employees are absolutely anathema at his company—and the company is true to its word. Hallmark has never imposed a layoff since its founding in 1910.

According to Hockaday, there are two qualities that are essential to his company's success: a commitment to excellence and "a commitment to brotherhood."[10] Other firms—including Advanced Micro Devices, a maker of silicon computer chips; Worthington Industries, a producer of steel and plastic parts; Johnson Wax; and Delta Airlines—have also been noted for placing employment security at the center of their industrial relations systems.[11] Hallmark maintains a no-layoff policy by constantly retraining its work force; by rotating its production employees to any vacant job, including in the company cafeteria (at factory wages); and by reskilling production workers as clerical employees. Lincoln Electric, as well-regarded as Hallmark for its employment security record, refuses to submit to the boom-bust cycle in its industry by limiting new orders and customers so that it can maintain full employment without causing violent fluctuations in the personnel required.

"DE-TAYLORIZED" TEAM PRODUCTION

The second principle borrowed from the Japanese involves the use of production "teams" rather than having each worker do his or her own routine job under the direction of a supervisor. Executives at many companies have reevaluated Taylorism and become convinced that its methods have a stultifying effect upon the worker as a thinking, creative human being; in an "information age," such methods hinder efficient operations. "De-Taylorizing" the workplace involves job enlargement and job enrichment, affording employees the opportunity to make decisions on the job.

With the goal of improving job satisfaction and unleashing creativity within the work force, various structures of employee involvement have evolved. The oldest and most common is the suggestion box, with monetary rewards offered for good ideas.[12] This represents the mini-malist approach to employee involvement. The team concept that has come on the scene more recently assumes a vast array of forms. In some cases, teams have permanent status, meeting regularly to examine problems and devise solutions. Workers in these teams have the right to implement these solutions, or at least to submit proposals to a higher authority for implementation approval. A one-shot special team may be organized to examine and find the solution to a particular problem. Once the problem is solved, the team disbands. Some teams comprise a small group of employees performing common functions. Other teams may involve employees performing different functions that are interrelated in the production process. There are teams that operate on a continuing basis as self-managing groups without supervision; others carry out their missions under specially trained supervisors.

Team members can learn all the tasks within their group and rotate from job to job. In some cases, these teams take over such functions as work and vacation scheduling, ordering materials, and rearranging the means and methods of production. The traditional role of supervisor may be transformed into coordinator or facilitator. At Ford Motor

Company, ten different kinds of teams operate simultaneously (see table 6.1) Underlying them all, to one extent or another, is the practical application of the employee involvement principle.

A veritable flood of titles and accompanying acronyms is associated with the generic label employee involvement (EI). Quality circles (QC), adopted from the production methods advocated early on by W. Edwards Deming and Joseph Juran, refers to employee groups that are organized to find solutions to problems of poor quality. Some other groups go by the names Work Improvement Program (WIP), Quality of Worklife Improvement (QWL), Participative Management (PM), Cost Study Team (CST), Competitive Action Team (CAT), and simply Employee Involvement Team (EIT), as well as Autonomous or Semi-Autonomous Work Groups, Parallel Organization Structures, Special Task Forces, and Business Teams.

While some of these new approaches to employee relations are narrowly targeted or restricted in scope of operation, others are afforded license to focus on a broad range of workplace issues—with decision making and follow-through resting within the general control of the employee groups themselves. In each case, to a greater or lesser extent, there is a shift away from the strict Taylorist managerial-control system to a more democratized system of decision making, generally confined, however, to the immediate employee work environment.

The well-documented story of the cultural and operational changes at the Shell Oil Company plant in Sarnia in Ontario, Canada, reveals many of the practices that reflect a rejection of the miniaturization, specialization, and trivialization of job tasks under "scientific management." The workers at the Shell facility take direct responsibility for their operations, determining among themselves in small groups who will perform which functions and how the tasks will be rotated among themselves each day. The functions cover a variety of skills including warehousing and shipping as well as janitorial and other maintenance work.[13] Traditional lines of job demarcation have gone by the wayside.

JOINT ACTION

Guaranteed employment security and team forms of production are only two of the three major types of experiments in new management techniques in the United States. The third, often referred to as joint action, exists only where there is a recognized union. Only in such a

TABLE 6.1

Types of Employee Involvement Teams
Ford Motor Company

Problem-solving teams
A form of teamwork in which immediate groups deal with their own job-related concerns.

Special project teams
Teams usually formed around an important issue or event, such as process improvement, concept-to-customer, and total quality excellence.

Opportunity teams
Teams formed on an ad hoc basis as needs and opportunities are identified, often because of upcoming work-related changes.

Linking teams
Teams usually made up of representatives where a need exists for interdepartmental, intershift, or cross-functional cooperation.

Launch teams
Teams formed to participate in final stages of product and process development, bringing together representatives of various functions including production, process, and design.

Vendor, dealer, and customer quality teams
Teams that meet with vendors, dealers, and customers to develop solutions to problems, to initiate problem prevention strategies, and to seek new business opportunities.

Line-staff project teams
Teams that are formed to combine the knowledge of line and staff personnel in the creation of improvement and other types of projects with potentially wide application.

Cross-functional teams
Teams that work on complex issues requiring a range of knowledge and experience not normally found in any one function.

Joint company-union committees
Teams comprised of company and union representatives who focus on mutual interests.

Hybrid teams
In practice, teams are combinations of the preceding forms, which should not be seen as "pure" types. The key is to fashion and use teams appropriate to the situation and the goals being pursued.

Source: Adapted from Ernest J. Savoie, director of Ford's Employee Development Office, "We Are a Team" Program as reported in *Work in America* 14, no. 4 (April 1989): p. 1.

setting do workers have the legal standing to ensure that contractual matters cannot be unilaterally contravened by management. As Charles Heckscher, an organizational specialist at Harvard University, has argued, the nonunion setting associated with modern "managerialism" (discussed in the last chapter) is invariably prone to the abuse of power, if not by current management, then by those who take its place upon retirement. Thus a system of union representation is needed "that can stand up to misuse of power and that does not rely on an extraordinary level of managerial enlightenment."[14] He notes that the failure to replace the unions' function as a "security base" against illegitimate coercion is one major weakness of the new nonunion managerialist system.

"Democratizing" of decision making under joint action goes well beyond teams, but does not depend on the existence of teams for implementation. In a joint action enterprise, union representatives and management representatives form problem-solving task forces, as well as planning and implementation committees, to carry out joint projects. Under the expanded joint action Workplace Contract, rights and responsibilities within the firm are reassigned. Labor participates with management in fashioning and administering programs that traditionally have fallen within management's exclusive domain.

LINKING EMPLOYEE INVOLVEMENT TO AMERICAN COMPETITIVENESS

Guaranteed employment security, de-Taylorization, and workplace democracy can, and often do, exist independently of one another in individual companies. A majority of firms practice at most one of these. It is the rare enterprise that has implemented all three. What they have in common, however, at least from management's perspective, is that all are put into practice to help the company operate efficiently with world-class quality. A simple model of what management strives for is found in figure 6.1.

Implementation of guaranteed employment security or a job enrichment program, or democratization of the work setting is supposed to improve job satisfaction and employee morale, and unleash company-

FIGURE 6.1
*Links Between Employee Involvement
and Market Competitiveness*

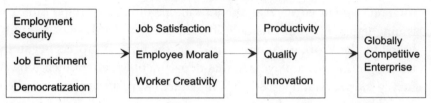

Employment Security	Job Satisfaction	Productivity	
Job Enrichment	Employee Morale	Quality	Globally Competitive Enterprise
Democratization	Worker Creativity	Innovation	

wide employee creativity. This, in turn, should lead to a work force that is motivated to boost productivity, improve product or service quality, and implement innovations in both the firm's product and in the processes used in its manufacture or provision. From labor's perspective, a satisfactory introduction of such programs occurs if workers experience enhanced job satisfaction, with the added benefit that if the system improves the market position of the firm, their own employment and standard of living may be more secure. Success becomes a win-win situation.

EMPLOYEE INVOLVEMENT IN THE NONUNION SETTING

The focus of attention in the nonunion setting has overwhelmingly been on job restructuring and job enrichment—de-Taylorization—as a means to improve employee satisfaction. One firm that has been repeatedly referenced as being among the more successful in this regard is Hewlett-Packard. Its Manufacturing Council, composed of a corporate vice president and senior manufacturing managers from its various business groups, set forth as early as 1975 a code of operation that, in many respects, underlies Hewlett-Packard's success in the computer industry. Among its nine basic guidelines are specific references to employing people at all levels who are "generalists with broad skills, concerns, and involvement," who share "knowledge and commitment to the emerging basics of operations excellence," and who have "rising performance expectations of self and others." Particular reference is made to "flexibility as a means to improve performance, not an end in itself."[15]

This increased attention to flexibility is hardly restricted to the man-ufacturing sector or standard production-type functions. The First Na-tional Bank of Chicago, for instance, undertook in the mid-1980s a total redesign of virtually all the jobs in one of its units responsible for issuing letters of credit. As described in the *World of Work Report* pub-lished by the Work in America Institute, the change process began by learning how the employees in that department felt about their jobs. A survey showed that up to 80 percent of them were dissatisfied with their jobs. The 20 percent who were satisfied were all professionals—manag-ers and technicians.[16]

An analysis of the survey results led to expansive alterations in the design of the work system and consequently of all employee functions. Goals were set and a three-point strategy was adopted: (1) abolishing the assembly line used in the credit operation, (2) creating whole jobs, and (3) giving individuals customer responsibility. Paraphrasing the *World of Work Report,* under the new system each employee became a "documentary products professional," performing customer-contact work with added responsibility for research, writing, costing, and other implementation tasks formerly distributed along the assembly line. Much of the routine clerical work disappeared into a computer system the department already had but never utilized.[17]

The program at the First National Bank of Chicago is not atypical of the examples to be found in many industries. The efforts at Affiliated Medical Enterprises (AME) in southern California to redesign its work practices around employee involvement brings the concept into an-other service-sector organization. With management approval, the em-ployees, in this instance in a hospital setting, developed "work redesign models"—changing each job to make it more efficient.

In the nonunion setting, the introduction of these experiments stems invariably from a management initiative, and the format, structure, administration, and general functioning of the process remain a pre-rogative of management, as is true of all other policies and programs concerning the work system. More enlightened management may open up wider parameters within which the employee involvement process operates. But these are always subject to ultimate managerial control.

Hence companies in the nonunion sector can do a great deal to ensure employment security and to de-Taylorize jobs. What they can-not do, however, no matter how hard they try, is democratize the workplace—that is, provide workers with true contractual empowerment. The underlying weakness of the nonunion work force lies in its total dependence on the goodwill and the personal philosophy of the managers. The enterprise remains essentially under authoritarian control, no matter how benevolent its management at any given moment. Once again, Peter Drucker had it right. As he noted more than forty years ago, benevolence often lasts only so long as the sky is blue:

> A management might be as solicitous of the worker's welfare, as genuinely concerned with his interests and purposes, as it can possibly be. It still must put the economic responsibility of the enterprise to society and the survival of the enterprise as an economic producer before anything else, including the interests of the worker. At best, the maxim that management always puts the worker's interests first can work in fair weather. As soon as hard times come management must reverse its policy. No matter how sincerely management believes in its paternalistic slogans, they must appear to the worker as hypocritical and as an insidious attempt on the part of the "bosses" to gain control over him.[18]

In 1990 the Harvard labor law professor Paul Weiler put a modern spin on Drucker's views:

> In recent years, the limits of participatory management have become vividly apparent in friendly mergers, hostile takeovers, and leveraged buyouts. Firms engaged in such major "restructuring" often increase the value of the shareholders' equity at considerable cost to the stake that the employees have built up. When put to the test in these cases, even the most open, participatory style of management has been of little help in defending vital employee interests.[19]

EMPLOYEE INVOLVEMENT IN THE UNION SETTING: THE THREE-TRACK SYSTEM

In the union setting, the process, while appearing the same, actually rests on a very different premise: joint action by mutual agreement between management and the chosen representatives of the employees within the bounds of the established bargaining unit. While employment security and de-Taylorizing jobs are often major agenda items in the union setting, democratizing decision making beyond the confines of the traditional Workplace Contract takes on central importance. *Democratization* in this case means further encroachment upon management prerogatives.

In analyzing the unfolding scene of union-management relations from early times to the current period, we find it useful to refer to a taxonomy we have termed the three-track system. It captures the many and varied manifestations of the process of democratization that has evolved within the collective-bargaining arena since early in the century. Each of the tracks addresses the issue of the degree of union/ employee participation in the decisions governing the management of the enterprise, but the instruments or mechanisms employed to accomplish a particular goal vary, as table 6.2 indicates. Taken together, the three tracks cover a broad spectrum of decision-making power, ranging from the governance of day-to-day administrative operations at the work site to certain policy decisions that are usually made only at the highest executive level.

TABLE 6.2

The Three-Track System of Labor–Management Relations

Track 1: *Representative* employee involvement over traditional issues of:
- union recognition
- wages and job benefits
- seniority provisions
- grievance machinery
- work rules

Track 2: *Direct* employee involvement over issues of:
- productivity
- product quality
- innovation

Track 3: *Representative* employee involvement over such workplace isssues as:
- product quality
- in-plant communications
- training programs
- technology introduction
- employee assistance programs

TRACK 1

Track 1 applies to the traditional unionized environment. It is represented by the conventional confrontation between union and management over controversial issues and worked out in an adversarial mode. In both the private and the public sectors, wages and salaries, job benefits, and the general conditions of work are subject to the tough bargaining of the negotiating table. These subjects will occasionally flare up into crises and will be resolved, as they have been historically, in the heat of collective bargaining, sometimes by strikes, occasionally by the use of arbitration. When the issues on the bargaining table are settled, the usual practice is for the union to monitor diligently management's implementation of the negotiated contract provisions as they relate to each individual worker and to the work force as a whole, and to protect against violations of the contract through an established negotiated procedure—usually involving formal grievance machinery, including final and binding grievance arbitration. Track 1 remains to this day the central instrument of labor and management relations in the union setting.

TRACK 2

Anchored likewise within the framework of collective bargaining, Track 2 establishes a far different format from Track 1. It customarily concerns subjects of common and mutual interest but defines them in the labor agreement in general terms. Its key element is the *direct* involvement of employees in making decisions related to their work, usually in groups of employees or teams, on matters related to:

- Quality improvement
- Methods, means, and processes of manufacture or service delivery
- In-process inspection
- Material flow within the plant
- Plant and equipment layout
- Redesign of individual jobs
- Job layout and operation sequencing
- Ergonomical design

- Introduction of statistical process control (SPC)
- Cost-reduction techniques
- Production scheduling
- Visits to vendors
- Customer contacts
- In-plant "creature comforts"
- Reduction of paperwork
- Reduction of material waste and conservation of supplies
- Design and redesign of specific tools
- Preventive maintenance
- Energy conservation
- Determination of personnel requirements

The contract language, more often than not, will point to the objective of enhancing the quality of the employees' work life, with the anticipation of improving efficiency and product quality. The difference in the union setting is that direct employee involvement is codified in the contract, and the union acts as a partner with management in planning, designing, implementing, and receiving feedback concerning the process. As opposed to the unilateral action in the nonunion setting, employee involvement becomes bilateral in the presence of organized labor.

Where employee involvement is in place, it is reasonable to ask about the kinds of issues teams actually handle in the normal course of their work. Our review of scores of case studies suggests that it covers practically every aspect related to performing their jobs. It may be a matter of finding ways to make operations more efficient or ergonomically acceptable or more comfortable, or maintaining quality and making certain that the product meets specification requirements.

Through team work, employees develop new tools that make the job easier to perform. Teams design and implement new methods that reduce scrap and repair. At the same time they take responsibility for in-process inspection instead of relying on a cadre of inspectors to catch quality defects. Skilled trades personnel devise preventive maintenance programs to forestall the frequent equipment breakdowns that belabor the production process. Employee teams review the process of material flow established by engineers or office managers and make alterations calculated to assist production more efficiently. They are involved in helping to design plant and equipment layout, again to ensure more effective operations. Workers in teams undertake the task of refashioning and redesigning their jobs, individually or as a team engaged in the same or similar activities. Ways and means of saving energy and the costs attendant to the use of electric power occasionally enter team discussions. Close examination of machinery and equipment leads to alterations in design so as to take into account the ergonomics or human mechanics of operation. Implementing statistical process control (SPC) to help resolve production or quality problems is often part of a team's function.

Added to these activities, employee involvement is used in setting production schedules, devising departmental budgets, and developing new products as existing ones become obsolete. Employees' direct knowledge of operations often enables teams to discover ways of reducing paperwork and eliminating waste of materials and supplies, both effective ways to reduce overall cost.

Employee teams have even taken on the responsibility of performing tasks outside the workplace. The quality of parts received from suppliers, for instance, may not be up to specification. Employees who work with these supplies will visit the vendor's facility, then discuss the problems with management and the vendor's employees in an effort to explore possible solutions. Similarly, teams will visit facilities that manufacture new equipment their firm has ordered and lend their ideas to the design of the equipment, which may make it easier for them to operate it once installed. Then there are the customer-contact programs. Employees have been used to maintain contact with customers, to discuss the quality of their products or services, and to arrange for appropriate response to customer complaints.

The essence of all of these and thousands of other employee involvement efforts is to challenge the old-line management slogan: "If it ain't broke, don't fix it." Instead they direct the spotlight on a newer concept: "Even if it ain't broke, make it better."

TRACK 3

Track 3 is symbolized by the creation, through the collective-bargaining process, of union-management joint committees whose function is to develop and administer designated activities of mutual interest and concern to both parties. Such committees are by no means a new phenomenon. They were fashioned during World War I as productivity committees, sponsored by the National War Labor Board. Soon after the war ended, they were dissolved, presumably their mission accomplished, not to reappear until America's entry into World War II. Before the end of that conflict, approximately five thousand joint committees were operating. History promptly repeated itself at the end of the war: the government-sanctioned joint labor-management committees vanished from the scene, and management reverted to exercising the sole prerogative to guide the enterprise and the workplace.

Even then, in key industries, programs such as skilled-trades apprenticeship training had a decades-long history of joint union-management administration. And in some instances, union representatives have been assigned to and been involved in monitoring occupational health and safety problems in accordance with negotiated labor contract provisions. Today Track 3 joint action has expanded well beyond apprenticeship training and occupational health.

Its structure is simple. A committee of union and management representatives is formed for each subject area the parties have determined will be jointly managed. Each committee is responsible for planning, designing, implementing, and monitoring specific programs to deal with the issue. Thus a joint committee on health and safety will not only monitor and implement safe practices among the workers but might also discuss the major considerations in preparing educational and instructional material concerning detailed health and safety issues. It would then follow up with a comprehensive educational program among the employees, including, of course, appropriate management personnel.

One of the most prominent and significant Track 3 developments lies in the arena of improving the quality of the product or service. Joint Quality Network Committees have been organized under union contract, comprising labor and management representatives and devoted to the single objective of producing a well-designed, well-engineered, zero-defect product. Ford's commitment to its joint "Quality is Job 1" program was instrumental in that firm's recovery from desperate straits in the early 1980s. Cadillac's successful bid to win the Malcolm Baldrige Quality Award in 1990 is also testimony to its joint efforts. Other joint union-management committees have been established to deal with the introduction of advanced technology.

Track 3 developments also include jointly administered communications systems designed to help build trust, confidence, and higher morale. Companies and unions have been experimenting with a wide array of joint action programs, including:

- Meetings to discuss production schedules, production difficulties, purchase orders, shipping schedules, supplier and customer problems, and other topics necessary to managing the workplace
- Joint publication of newsletters or monthly newspapers bearing the logo of both the company and the union, keeping the work force apprised of ongoing developments of importance to the enterprise.

In some instances television screens in various locations of the facility, made available by a joint union-management committee, provide up-to-date information. Even items of general interest may float across the screen: World Series baseball or championship basketball scores. At Weirton Steel Corporation in West Virginia, where the employees enjoy majority ownership of the firm, information is imparted through the usual channel of the printed word, informal in-plant meetings, and the TV screen network.

Jointly administered education programs have a similar purpose.[20] With the recent epidemic of substance abuse both in and outside the workplace, management has become a willing partner in joint Employee Assistance Programs (EAP) designed to help those whose addiction or emotional state interferes with their health, job performance, and personal well-being. Long experience with such programs has proven that sympathetic intervention and counseling can save lives, keep families intact, and allow the skills and abilities of those helped to continue to contribute to the well-being of the company.[21]

Still other joint union-management activities include dislocated employee programs to train and assist employees in the search for new employment after a permanent layoff, attendance programs to reduce the rate of absenteeism, joint new-hire orientation sessions, joint preretirement planning programs, and the provision of child care. Typical Track 3 issues include:

- Quality improvement through Joint Quality Networks
- Joint apprenticeship training
- Co-sponsored communications systems
- Enhanced education programs

- Introduction of new technology
- Skill-development programs
- Jointly administered college tuition assistance
- Employee Assistance Programs
- Joint health and safety committees
- Dislocated employee programs
- Attendance programs
- New-hire orientation
- Health-care cost containment
- Child care
- Pension fund investment policy
- Fringe benefit administration
- New joint business ventures
- Contract bidding

In recent years the subject of providing health-care coverage has raised the hackles of negotiators as have few other collective-bargaining issues. Health-care costs have been rising at rates of inflation as high as 20 percent annually, far exceeding the rise in the Consumer Price Index. Strikes over the issue of employee co-payment and/or reducing benefits have littered the collective-bargaining scene. In an effort to stem the tide, unions and management have been cooperating to explore ways to slow down the inflationary push without watering down the benefit structure.[22] Some companies have gone so far as to join with their unions to look into legislation that could establish national medical-care standards or national health insurance.[23]

As the sheer magnitude of employee pension funds increases, Track 3 administrative structures are likewise coming into existence to formulate a joint union-management retirement fund investment policy. Customarily, the selection of pension fund trustees is in the hands of management. But the AFL-CIO has taken a forceful position on the subject of pension funds, arguing that pensions are workers' deferred wages and thus should be placed in joint trusteeship.[24]

To round out this list, we might add that some companies and unions have relied for decades on joint administration of fringe benefit programs such as pensions, health and life insurance, and supplemental unemployment benefits.[25] But it can require special expertise to understand all the nooks and crannies of the legalese used in the contract language governing these benefit programs. As one union representative described it to us: "Between learning to understand the technicalities of health care and the SUB (supplemental unemployment benefits) contract language, I now know how we broke the Japanese naval code in World War II!" Despite the difficulty, workers are learning the intricacies of these programs and often develop as good a working knowledge of them as do the program managers themselves.[26]

Decades ago most of the joint action programs that make up Track 3 either did not exist at all or, as in the case of welfare capitalism, were run strictly by management. Today that is changing dramatically. According to a random survey of nearly two hundred unionized companies recently conducted by Professor William Cooke of Wayne State University, nearly half (48 percent) had joint health and safety committees, more than a fifth (21 percent) had established joint substance-abuse programs, and approximately the same proportion (19 percent) had begun QWL or Employee Involvement plans.[27] A 1983 Conference Board survey of approximately four hundred large companies suggests that 56 percent of unionized business units have established programs wherein "employees meet in small groups to discuss productivity and quality."[28]

Naturally differences may arise as union and management representatives attempt to discover the best way to meet a particular objective or to implement a specific procedure. The negotiated contract language covering a given subject will not necessarily be precise, leaving it to the joint committee to flesh out. The goal is not to create confrontation but rather to strive jointly and through consensus to fulfill the stated objective. Where it is implemented conscientiously, labor and management are finding it much better to use Track 3 than to adhere strictly to the old adversarial approach of Track 1.

The result is a climate in which partnership replaces controversy in the work setting; in which resolution by joint action replaces grievance mills; in which the employees reap the benefit of a more democratized process in the fulfillment of contractual obligation; and in which management and the union learn to work together as co-partners with co-equal status and responsibility.

As noted, the number of working-condition issues subject to the joint implementation process has grown quite remarkably and promises to expand even more in the years ahead. To be sure, the attempts at joint action are not a panacea that obliterates every disagreement between labor and management, nor do they—or should they—eliminate every confrontation. They do, however, help create an atmosphere within the workplace that is conducive to positive achievement and enhanced organizational effectiveness.

At its core, the introduction and expansion of the joint action process rest on the fundamental precept of bringing democratic values into the workplace. Given this, we may then ask: Does democratization lead as well to the fulfillment of economic goals for the employees, management, the organization, and, finally, society? Do firms in which new workplace institutions are in effect find themselves better able to meet the exigencies of the global marketplace, and have workers gained more employment security and greater job fulfillment as a result? In the next chapter we will examine the answers to these questions.

CHAPTER 7

Does Participation Work?

An economy may have two equilibria: a superior one with participation, and an inferior one without.

—*Alan Blinder,* Paying for Productivity *(1990)*

We must not ignore the systematic and, in some cases, surreptitious efforts to implement team concept programs in our workplaces. These programs must be challenged; they must be resisted.

—*International Association of Machinists' policy on "team concept" programs (1990)*

Physicists maintain that theoretically bumblebees cannot fly. In the real world, of course, they do. In theory, employee participation properly implemented should work. What happens when theory is put into practice may be another matter. Do the links in the job satisfaction/ competitiveness model hold when subjected to the real world? Does productivity improve? What happens to quality? Is innovation enhanced? In the final analysis, if new forms of employer-employee cooperation and joint action are to survive and disseminate throughout the economy, they must succeed here. They must work to the advantage of employees *and* management, and ultimately society.

THE POTENTIAL BENEFITS OF EMPLOYEE PARTICIPATION

From management's perspective, there are a number of benefits that should be expected when a firm adopts employee participation.[1] These include a significant number we have already identified: increased productivity, improved quality of product, and improved customer relations and service.[2] Management can also benefit as a result of reduced waste and duplication, lower overhead and material handling costs, and reductions in absenteeism, tardiness, and turnover.

There are potential benefits from the employee's perspective as well. Improved working conditions, enhanced employment security, and financial rewards are by no means the least of these. Also high on the list are dignity, self-esteem, pride, and the intrinsic rewards that come from participating in the involvement process itself. Where a union is present, the specific interests of union leaders are promoted as a result of greater appreciation by their own members of the improvements within the workplace, including more direct participation in management decisions, fewer time-consuming contract administration problems, and in some cases increased membership participation in union activities and policies.

THE POTENTIAL COSTS OF EMPLOYEE PARTICIPATION

With such a battery of potential benefits, we must ask why participatory management has not taken the country by storm.

One answer, some argue, is that it doesn't work, all of its celebratory publicity notwithstanding. Another is that even when it does succeed in some measurable way, it carries baggage that is unacceptable to management, workers, or their union representatives. Indeed, as with major departures from past practice, there are potential costs to each of these groups. Employee involvement does not come for free. From management's perspective, it adds to the direct cost of the firm as a consequence of the necessary investment in reorientation and training programs for staff and employees, not to mention the possible waste of valuable time in what Gene Shalit, the movie critic, once called the bane of all human existence—meetings. There is also the prospect that first-line supervisors and middle managers will become expendable if workers can supervise themselves.

For their part, employees are justifiably anxious that participation may mean not working smarter, but working harder. If teamwork boosts productivity, there is the tangible fear that the company will eventually use the efficiency gains to reduce the size of the work force. There is also a more subtle concern: the introduction of employee involvement systems might create unwanted peer pressure from advocates to become involved and equal pressure from critics to abstain.

In fact, the reluctance among managers to undertake employee participation goes much deeper than any of these trepidations, calling on traditional beliefs about the "proper" roles of management and labor in a free enterprise system (as discussed in chapter 5). Sharing power with labor runs the risk of having worker demands collide head-on with the stockholders' demand for higher profits. Also, management is often skeptical of labor's ability to co-manage the workplace. After all, as one manager asked us, "Isn't my M.B.A. worth something?"[3]

Worker and union opposition to participation may seem less warranted, for genuine employee involvement entails a partial shift in workplace authority and power from management to labor. Still, some labor representatives' objections to team concept and joint action are as impassioned as those of management. Such criticism by union officials is by no means a recent phenomenon. In 1943, the United Electrical, Radio and Machine Workers union (UE) distributed to all of its members a pamphlet revealing its strong opposition to participatory schemes. The leadership of the union argued that "the union has abandoned its rightful function—that of protecting the worker—when it participates in management's function."[4] Nearly a decade earlier, in the preamble to the 1935 UAW Constitution, the auto industry's labor leaders attempted to mollify both management and union critics by pledging that "the automobile worker does not ask for a place on the Board of Directors of the automobile industry. He merely asks for his rights."[5] Not until 1980 did the UAW amend its constitution with respect to management prerogatives. The new preamble deleted these phrases, declaring that "workers must have a voice in their own destiny and the right to participate in making decisions that affect their lives before such decisions are made."[6]

A few in the labor movement fear that unions run the risk of cooptation by management whenever they agree to joint action within the enterprise. Others worry that participating in these experiments inevitably dilutes the militancy of union leaders and robs the membership of a strong independent voice committed exclusively to serving workers' interests.[7] Cooperation with management, the argument goes, subtly but inevitably turns into competition with one's fellow workers. By assuming even modest co-responsibility for productivity and quality, the union unwittingly collaborates with management in pitting department against department, worker against worker. The consequence, say critics, is an undermining of union solidarity.[8]

Adding fuel to union opposition is the way employee involvement has been used as an effective anti-union tactic. According to Charles Heckscher, firms as prestigious as IBM have warded off union-organizing drives by making extensive use of worker participation programs. Even those who support EI within the union movement are conscious of surveys showing that the nonunion worker who enjoys authentic autonomy and responsibility on the job is significantly less likely to vote for union representation.[9]

In theory, employee involvement leads to greater job satisfaction, but critics worry that in the wrong hands it results in "management-by-stress": speedup, cutting the number of workers assigned to a particular set of operations, and assigning workers additional tasks.[10] QWL "feels good," according to critic Mike Parker, because it builds on workers' natural desire to identify with the product they produce, because it reflects their desire to do a good job, and because it expands on their opportunity to make a real contribution rather than simply being a cog in the machine. In the end, however, say the critics, it simply caters to management's true objectives: access to workers' knowledge about the work process, cooperation from employees in introducing new technology, and increased flexibility in the workplace. QWL, in practice, they argue, leads to less shop-floor power and job protection for workers, not more.[11]

For all these reasons, instead of universal support from organized labor there remains a strong undercurrent of ambivalence over the desirability of moving affirmatively on team concept, quality of work life programs, and other forms of joint action.[12]

ASSESSING EMPLOYEE INVOLVEMENT IN PRACTICE

Most analysts, as well as a fair number of managers and pro-EI union leaders themselves, readily admit that the team concept, QWL, and other forms of employee participation can go in either of two directions: they can empower workers as supporters contend or weaken them as the critics warn; they can increase productivity, quality, and innovation or, as the skeptics surmise, do little for a firm's competitive position. The only way to judge the "new" industrial relations is to examine these programs in action. In doing so, one can examine three types of evidence: opinion surveys, statistical results, and case studies.

OPINION SURVEYS

One of the earlier attempts at measuring manager and employee opinion about a specific EI program was conducted in seven Ford Motor Company plants throughout the country in 1982.[13] The survey was conducted two years after employee involvement activities were put in place by the UAW and the company. Each worker was asked to compare the nature of activities in the plant before and after EI programs were implemented. Approximately 33 percent of the EI participants indicated that they had had an opportunity to work with others in solving job-related problems *before* EI teams were initiated in their plant. *After* EI began, 83 percent were working in such problem-solving groups. By large margins, those interviewed suggested that after EI started, in-plant communications, job satisfaction, and job commitment all improved. Opinions about such "outputs" as quality production also appeared to be supportive of EI. Slightly more than half (54 percent) of EI participants rated their department's quality as having been excellent before EI; after the introduction of EI, that proportion increased to 81 percent. The survey also indicated that the EI process increased cost consciousness among workers—while simultaneously boosting job satisfaction among EI participants from 27 to 82 percent.[14]

Support for quality circles at Boeing Aircraft has been less enthusiastic.[15] There fewer than 20 percent of production employees were in QCs at the time they were interviewed, and fewer than half of the remaining nonparticipants expressed any interest in joining one.

Arrayed alongside individual company opinion surveys is a massive study carried out in 1987 by the General Accounting Office of the U.S. Government (GAO). The GAO surveyed the Fortune 1000 companies—virtually all the largest firms in America.[16] About half (47.6 percent) agreed to participate in the government study. In their evaluation of the GAO data, labor studies professor Adrienne E. Eaton and economist Paula B. Voos found that the typical corporate executive believes that EI programs provide only moderate improvements in company functioning.

But "typical," like any average, tells only part of the story. The survey uncovered a large minority of executives who believed that such programs are extremely valuable. Within unionized firms, for example, more than 40 percent of corporate executives questioned reported that they detected "great" or "very great" improvements in the implementation of technology; 45 percent believed EI improved employee trust in management; and nearly half, 48.7 percent, suggested increased or much increased information flow throughout their companies (see table 7.1).

There was somewhat less enthusiasm in the nonunion sector, but even there more than one-third of executives surveyed suggested great or very great improvements in communications, in implementation of technology, and in overall organizational processes and procedures.[17] A paucity of information on the intensity of the EI experience in each of these firms makes it difficult to judge whether executive support varies on the basis of how far employee participation has proceeded or the method by which it has been implemented.

A 1986 survey by William Cooke, the industrial relations expert at Wayne State University mentioned earlier, also provides some information about the opinions of union leaders toward EI.[18] Roughly half of Cooke's sample of 350 large unionized manufacturing facilities had some form of joint labor-management program at the plant level at the time of interview, mostly quality circles, work teams, or union-management committees. Cooke interviewed both plant managers and local union officials in each of these firms. What he found among both was general agreement that productivity and product quality had improved and scrappage and waste had declined as a result of the EI process. His results indicate that quality is what most improves as a result of joint action on the factory floor. In only a few cases did individuals report a negative outcome on any output measure (see table 7.2).

TABLE 7.1

Managers' Evaluations of the Influence of Employee
Involvement Programs on Business Environment

	"Great" or "Very Great"		Scaled Mean	
	Union	Nonunion	Union	Nonunion
Improved implementation of technology	40.3%	35.1%	2.49	2.66
Broadened skill development at lower organizational levels	44.1	36.5	2.65	2.64
Increased information flow throughout the organization	48.7	44.0	2.75	2.86
Increased employee trust in management	45.2	31.3	2.65	2.61
Improved organizational processes and procedures	38.0	37.3	2.50	2.69
Improved union-management relations	22.9	na	2.09	na

Source: GAO data as analyzed by Adrienne E. Eaton and Paula B. Voos, "Unions and Contemporary Innovations in Work Organization, Compensation, and Employee Participation," in *Unions and Competitiveness,* ed. Larry Mishel and Paula Voos (Armonk, N.Y.: M. E. Sharpe, 1991), table 6, p. 201.

Scaling: Very great = 5, Great = 4, Moderate = 3, Some = 2, Little or none = 1

STATISTICAL ANALYSIS

The GAO and Cooke surveys appear to provide strong evidence for the efficacy of EI programs. But given the personal stake that participants have in any social process, particularly one within the workplace, the results of opinion surveys are never definitive. Those who have played an affirmative role in establishing an employee involvement program obviously have at least some interest in viewing the outcomes in a positive light. Those who opposed EI from the beginning may be subject to the opposite bias—a tendency to downplay any success.

For this reason, it is useful to consult studies that measure outcomes independent of participant observation or opinion. To date there have

TABLE 7.2

*Perceived Changes in Performance
Since Joint Programs Began*

Outcome	Management Response	Union Response
Worker productivity		
Much higher	14%	8%
Modestly higher	50	60
About the same	29	28
Worse	7	4
Product quality		
Much higher	20	16
Modestly higher	51	55
About the same	28	25
Worse	2	4
Scrappage/Waste		
Much lower	10	10
Modestly lower	47	42
About the same	39	30
Higher	4	18

Source: William N. Cooke, *Labor Management Cooperation* (Kalamazoo, Mich.: W. E. Upjohn Institute, 1990), charts 4.1 and 4.2, p. 83.

been only a few such studies, but the results are intriguing, particularly as a balance to the opinion surveys. One of the best known was carried out in the auto industry by Harry Katz of Cornell, Thomas Kochan of MIT, and Jeffrey Keefe of Rutgers.[19] Using various standard statistical techniques, the three discovered, somewhat to their surprise, that the use of teams had a *negative* impact on productivity.[20] In plants where teams were utilized, the ratio of supervisors to production workers was actually higher, not lower, and, on average, it took some seven and a half hours longer to assemble each car.

But there is an interesting twist to this story. The researchers found that while teams per se (Track 2) did not improve measured perform-ance, representative union participation in decision making (Track 3) did. In plants where the *union* played a greater role through joint action committees, the supervisor/worker ratio was lower, and it took, on average, almost five hours less to build a car. The same phenomenon held for product quality. Team-oriented plants with no direct union role had somewhat higher defect rates than average; joint action plants had somewhat lower.[21]

The critical importance of the union role in participatory schemes is corroborated in new research by Maryellen Kelley and Bennett Harrison of Carnegie Mellon University.[22] Their study, involving a random sample of over one thousand large and small establishments in a wide variety of U.S. metal-working and machinery sectors, found that nonunion firms that had adopted employee involvement plans were, on average, significantly *less* productive than firms without such experiments. Unionized firms adopting participatory schemes had no such loss in efficiency, although unionized firms without an employee involvement plan had the highest efficiency of all. This last result might simply reflect the fact that the Kelley-Harrison study does not explicitly differentiate between the effects of Track 2 (direct worker participation) and Track 3 (joint union-management action) programs.[23] If Track 2 and Track 3 initiatives could be statistically untangled, it is possible that union settings with joint action committees would be shown to outshine all others when it comes to productivity improvement.

On reflection, that the presence of a union improves the likelihood of EI success is not a surprising finding. There are at least six good reasons why it should, according to a 1989 U.S. Labor Department corporate/labor symposium that dealt with this issue.[24] For one, unions help weed out the bad plans up front; for another, they keep companies from reverting to old ways. In addition, they provide a mechanism for addressing a company's glitches in their EI procedures without throwing out the whole participation process, and they tend to be the only practical way to give workers a meaningful voice. Finally, unions have played a crucial role in educating workers to make informed decisions, and have provided a creative power and tension to the process that simply does not exist in a nonunion setting. Where unions do not exist and EI is promoted unilaterally by management, employee commitment is likely to be weak.

We should note for the record that the majority of employee involvement research reaches a more sanguine conclusion even where unions are not present. Analyzing nearly fifty statistical studies concerned with the productivity impact of employee participation, David I. Levine and Laura D'Andrea Tyson find that over half showed improved productivity as a result of employee involvement or worker ownership. Another ten indicated either a neutral effect or one that was salutary but short-lived. Only two out of forty-seven—not counting Kelley and Harrison's research, which appeared after their review was complete— reported negative effects.[25]

CASE STUDIES

Large surveys are useful for understanding the average response, but they can never provide the rich detail of well-conceived and well-executed individual case studies. Indeed, if there is one common thread that runs through conversations with those responsible for the day-to-day practical application of EI and joint action, it is that no two programs are identical in form, design, structure, or implementation. Some employee participation programs are just beginning to form, some are almost ripe, some have been carefully nurtured and fertilized, while others have suffered blight or a plague of exogenous forces.

No general survey that we know of has ever gauged the strength of top management's commitment to EI. None has measured what proportion of the total work force is fully participating in the EI process— and in what capacity and with regard to which functions of the organization. The type and extent of orientation and training in the EI process may be a critical factor in its success, but questions about such matters are usually not detailed enough in general surveys to provide a fine distinction. Likewise, it is the rare survey that asks any of the following questions: Were supervisors and middle managers, and union representatives in the unionized setting, provided with the necessary training to alter the traditional culture of the boss/worker relationship? How much time was given to employees to devote to problem solving? What kind of communication system existed and how effective was it? Were established work rules left intact or were changes made to accommodate the EI process? Was there any particular reward system put in place coincidental with the adoption of the participatory process, and, if so, what kind, how was it implemented, and how did employees and management respond to it? And, of course, one of the major considerations is simply the length of time the process has been in effect.

These represent only some of the factors that affect the efficacy of an EI experiment. Any one or a combination may determine success or failure. For this reason, it is necessary to consult case materials, to determine not so much the current state of success across the board but the *potential* of EI if it is implemented properly and effectively.

What follows is a brief sampling of the numerous cases suggesting that, properly implemented, EI proves its value. There are hundreds of similar examples of positive results.

Corning Glass

According to *Business Week*, Jamie Houghton, the CEO of Corning Glass, "reinvented" his company.[26] With the support of its union, Corning established teams of hourly workers to redesign their factories and decide who should work which jobs. A total of forty-seven job classifications were folded into one. Under the new system, employees rotate through jobs weekly and earn higher pay for each new skill they learn in a "pay-for-knowledge" system sanctioned and jointly coordinated with the union. Joint training programs have been organized, so that all employees spend 5 percent of their time in job-related training.

The payoffs have been impressive. Defects in the ceramic plant have been reduced from 10,000 parts per million to 3 parts per million. Corning's clinical-lab testing unit in 1990 delivered 98.5 percent of its reports to customers in twenty-four hours or less, up from 88 percent in 1986. And customer returns of optical fiber have dropped to fewer than 1,000 parts per million from 6,800. A focus on quality, on forming marketing alliances, on sharing technology, and on building a partnership with the glass workers' union lifted return on equity to 16.3 percent in 1990 from 7.3 percent in 1983.

No one would suggest that all of the progress at Corning has been the result of teamwork, joint action, and employee involvement. Nor would anyone suggest that Corning and its union have solved all of the issues that plague workers. Temporary layoffs are still common, for example. At least partly for this reason, blue-collar employees voted down a regional contract they did not find to their liking. Still, the preliminary evidence suggests that "reinventing" the company's industrial relations system had a beneficial effect on the company's bottom line and in the workers' employment security and pay envelope.

Ford

The Ford plant in Sharonville, Ohio, is one of the oldest facilities in the entire Ford system. It manufactures transmissions for both automobiles and trucks. But in the late 1970s and early 1980s it was rated as having the poorest production and quality records in a division of seven plants, and rumors were rampant that Ford's top management was on the verge of shutting down the facility. As a last-ditch effort, in August 1980 a new plant manager took over the facility's helm.[27]

The new manager analyzed the problems plaguing the operation and decided that the old-style authoritarian managerial practices amounted to a dead-end approach. Under the newly signed 1979 UAW–Ford National Agreement, which urged local parties to undertake the EI process, the plant manager sat down with local union officials to design a joint plan. Out of these meetings came a joint coordinating committee that selected two pilot areas in the plant where workers had volunteered to participate in employee involvement groups. The success of their efforts led to an expansion of the EI process throughout the plant.

Adoption of joint action is credited with saving the plant. Between 1980, when the EI concept was born at Sharonville, and 1985, the participative system had so improved the quality and production of the assembled transmissions that, far from closing down, the Sharonville plant won the internal bid for production of Ford Motor Company's newly developed transmission—a transmission that will keep the plant in operation at least through the year 2000.

Sharonville has influenced other plants in the Ford system. For example, Ford Motor Company's new engine plant in Romeo, Michigan, barely a year old in 1991, was already ranked by Ford management as building the company's best-quality engines worldwide. Romeo's 880 hourly and salary workers are currently building 2.04 engines per worker per day. According to James Harbour, a manufacturing consultant in Michigan, "that's the best there is" among Big Three engine plants. George Pfeil, the plant manager, attributes 50 percent of Romeo's improved productivity to high-tech manufacturing processes, 40 percent to innovative labor-management relations, and 10 percent to simplified engine design.[28]

Romeo's joint action program with the UAW is fashioned along team lines of eight to twenty-four workers who function as independent businesses, with team managers, coordinators, engineers, a financial analyst, and skilled trades and production workers all cooperating without a foreman. There are no inspectors or foremen, and hundreds of job classifications have been reduced to four for production workers and eleven in the skilled trades. Through 225 shop-floor computers, blue-collar workers have access to the same quality, productivity, and financial data as the plant manager.

No one would call Romeo a bed of roses. On a scale of 1 to 10, the shop chairman of the UAW Local at the plant rates teamwork now a 3, but feels it is improving. It is hard for the union to embrace the lost jobs caused by a combination of productivity increases and a recession in the industry. Still, as one senior blue-collar worker put it, "there's been 'a little bit of conflict' in recent months because high-seniority workers" in his team don't want to rotate jobs. "But most workers are happy, and most are working hard to improve quality and output."[29]

Campbell Soup

At the Campbell Soup plant in Maxton, North Carolina, virtually every employee was first trained in statistical process control and the quality techniques of W. Edwards Deming.[30] Then, according to the manufacturing vice president at the plant, "we turned the business over to them." Self-managed teams took the place of most supervisors, met with vendors, and set their own schedules. They even proposed capital expenditures, complete with calculations of the internal rate of return. A new machine suggested by one work team is so productive that it provides the company a 30 percent return on its investment. In a single year, the plant as a whole set a record 16 percent increase in productivity.

Northern Telecom

Northern Telecom's 420-employee digital telephone switching equipment-repair facility in Morrisville, North Carolina, began moving toward a team-directed work force in 1988. In this nonunion plant, employees are organized into eight "cells," or teams, that control their own share of the business. The cells set their own goals for meeting common objectives ranging from manufacturing efficiency to turn-around times. Cell members also may conduct performance peer reviews, interview job applicants, and adopt flexible working schedules. In its first three years, revenues at the facility are up 83 percent, earnings per employee have increased by 93 percent, and the company notes a 51 percent increase in quality and a 65 percent improvement in customer service.[31]

Reports on Northern Telecom do not include information about how production workers view their jobs, but it appears that middle management has been encouraged by the gains at this facility.

A. O. Smith

A Milwaukee-based manufacturer of auto vehicle frames for the Big Three, A. O. Smith began adopting quality circles as early as 1981.[32] Joint union-management problem-solving committees began being formed in 1984, and by 1989 there were work teams throughout the plant. The union and the company are involved in joint action on a host of issues, including a set of strategic plans concerning production. In the early days, employee involvement did not lead to improved quality or productivity. But in the face of massive layoffs and a fear that the plant might be forced to close, the authority of the production work teams was expanded dramatically. Elected leaders of the teams now assume many managerial duties, including scheduling production and overtime, ordering maintenance work, and stopping the line to correct defects. They even revise work standards set by engineers.

As a result of the stepped-up EI program, the company reduced the supervisor-to-worker ratio from 1:10 in 1987 to 1:34 two years later. By 1988 productivity was double its 1981 level, and defects had fallen from 20 percent to 3 percent. To be sure, problems still exist at A. O. Smith. According to management, the plant is still not "world-class" on every measure, and the union and company still clash on tough issues such as guaranteed lifetime employment. But the EI program was by all accounts a major reason for the company's being back in the black by 1989 after a number of years of red ink.

New York City Department of Sanitation

Union-management team efforts are not limited to the private sector. In rounding out this gallery of success stories, one case among a growing number in the public sector deserves mention. The New York City Sanitation Department's Bureau of Motor Equipment (BME), a public agency with the responsibility for keeping all of New York City's sanitation trucks and equipment on the road and in good working condition, has made one of the most extensive uses of joint action. Working with the twenty trade unions representing the repair workers in this facility, the deputy commissioner of BME in the late 1970s and throughout much of the 1980s, Ron Contino, completely reorganized the bureau.

Joint problem-solving teams were established throughout the facility to work under a top-level "Labor-Management Team." Each unit was set up as a separate "profit center," and workers kept track of their own progress toward improved maintenance productivity and quality. The employees devised more efficient methods. As a result, work that was being outsourced to private contractors was brought back into the bargaining unit. Moreover, additional skilled workers were hired to develop a preventive maintenance unit. One of the employee involvement teams is even credited with having designed a "robot" that completely changed the method used for repainting sanitation department equipment.[33]

The team effort begun in the Bureau of Motor Equipment has paid off handsomely for the workers and for New York City and its taxpayers. Out-of-service rates on critical equipment dropped from 50 percent to 15 percent. The Deputy Commissioner in the department argues that the resulting $16.5 million in savings is attributable in part to "labor's full support for efforts to improve productivity, with $2 million of that directly attributable to improvements generated by the Labor Team." In addition, an R&D unit within the department has implemented thirty-one of its many designs and operational improvements, yielding large savings in maintenance dollars, improvements in vehicle safety aspects, reduced vehicle damage, and decreases in vehicle downtime. In the first year of operation alone, the BME work teams increased productivity by 24 percent, providing a "shadow" profit of $2.4 million a year.[34]

THE NEED FOR CAUTIOUS OPTIMISM

Naturally, each of these cases makes only a minuscule contribution to improving productivity, quality, and innovation in the U.S. economy as a whole. But they do point to the positive outcomes that can be achieved when teams are implemented in a comprehensive way. They may not lend themselves to precise measurement in national surveys—and some outcomes may not be easily quantified at all—but the effective implementation of the participatory concept demonstrates a new way to negotiate the future. After nearly twenty years of experiments, there are enough individual success stories to urge skeptics to take another look at innovations in labor relations as a serious mechanism to enhance job satisfaction and to help rebuild national competitiveness and improve employment security.

In no way does this conclusion imply that employee involvement is easy to implement or certain of success. As Cooke reports, "the gains from cooperative efforts appear to increase initially, rising at diminishing rates, then eventually falling and leveling off." Typically there is a strong burst of enthusiasm for involvement and participation followed by a waning of interest. The identification and resolution of many production and other workplace problems are fairly easy to tackle at first, but over time the new problems become successively more difficult: "As gains are harder to accomplish, enthusiasm is harder to maintain, and hence commitment to joint activities often dwindles." Moreover, over time there is a tendency for adversarial conflicts to reemerge. If this increases distrust between the parties, the best of cooperative efforts can be undermined.[35]

Because of the difficulty of sustaining EI enthusiasm over the long run, it is estimated that the attrition or failure rate for quality circles is approximately 20 percent, even within the first year.[36] In light of such findings, and in light of his own earlier survey results, MIT's Tom Kochan concludes that "quality circles or similar forms of worker participation are useful starting points for change but standing alone do not achieve sufficient results to be sustained."[37]

Despite all of the strains and difficulties of making EI work, Harvard's Charles Heckscher sums up the case for optimism. He writes that while experiments in employee involvement have been only partially successful to date, over time a clear and curious pattern has emerged. Historically, he finds,

the repeated demise of particular efforts never slowed the *general* enthusiasm for employee involvement. Indeed, in each instance the movement arose phoenixlike, in a stronger and more inclusive form. The succession from job enlargement to job enrichment to problem-solving groups to autonomous teams has steadily increased the responsibility of workers. The latest autonomous team plants come close to completing the trend: they may have a hundred workers with only two or three "managers" per shift, whose duties are primarily advisory. Again and again apparent failure has only spurred further experimentation.[38]

This is the beginning, not the end, of a story. What it tells us is that there are "threshold effects" in EI. It may be necessary to push employee involvement and joint action well beyond current levels in order to achieve the positive results that its advocates project. In any human endeavor there are successes and there are failures. Practical experience establishes that, given the proper conditions, EI does work.

WHEN EMPLOYEE INVOLVEMENT AND JOINT ACTION WORK BEST

No single, comprehensively detailed, preset blueprint automatically assures happy results from workplace-oriented EI programs. But the evidence from hundreds of case studies we have reviewed reveals three underlying *conditions* that are absolutely indispensable to the success of participatory programs:

- full *commitment* to the concept of "involvement" throughout the organization
- attainment of an internal organization-wide relationship of *mutual trust and respect*
- genuine opportunity for broad-based direct employee involvement in decision making—in short, the *democratization of the workplace.*

The fact that general surveys often show little gain from employee involvement schemes more than likely reflects the fact that most EI efforts are put in place in a slapdash manner, without full commitment, mutual trust, or any attempt to democratize the workplace. Rhetoric is no substitute for substance. Research studies again and again have reached this conclusion. In their critically important work on how to build "lean production" systems in industries that have failed the test of global competition, James P. Womack, Daniel T. Jones, and Daniel Roos of MIT have revealed a basic principle:

Workers respond only when there exists some sense of reciprocal obligation, a sense that management actually values skilled workers, will make sacrifices to retain them, and is willing to delegate responsibility to the team. Merely changing the organization chart to show "teams" and introducing quality circles to find ways to improve production processes are unlikely to make much difference.[39]

This kind of simple commitment to trust and honest dealing may seem old-fashioned today, but the evidence suggests that, when truly practiced, it is critical to the success of employee involvement.

BEST AND WORST PRACTICES

The slogan "commitment, trust, and democracy" makes a fine bumper sticker, but putting this philosophy into practice requires hard work. Understanding the best and worst practices in the workplace can serve as a guide.

The list of "best" characteristics of a well-managed firm typically includes, for example, good communication and responsive management. "Worst" characteristics include autocratic, top-down supervision; fear; boredom; lack of teamwork; and lack of recognition. Table 7.3 provides a list of the best and worst characteristics of a work setting based on group conversations we held with white- and blue-collar workers, union leaders, and corporate executives. Of particular interest is that often no specific mention is made of the income and job benefits issue in the long list of best characteristics. When we pointed out such an omission, the respondents usually replied that such things are taken for granted.

It is evident from table 7.3 that people evaluate their gratification at work in terms of their general desire for dignity and the specific actions that enhance their feeling of self-worth. Practically every descriptive value relating to the best characteristics reflects the *antithesis* of the work climate symbolized by "scientific management."

TABLE 7.3

Characteristics of Best and Worst Organizations

BEST	WORST
• Common purpose and program to rally around; sense of belonging	• Disregard of the individual
• Spirit of camaraderie and teamwork; respect for one another; absence of internal strife	• Domineering supervision
• Opportunity to be an active participant in discussions leading to decisions; opportunity to be creative and make decisions concerning one's job	• Motivation by fear, punishment
• Enhanced sense of pride and self-worth, self-esteem, self-actualization	• Internal jealousies and friction
• Emphasis on quality rather than production	• Dissension, argumentativeness
• Open, continual two-way communication; candor and honesty in sharing information concerning the job and the organization	• No enjoyment in working with others
• Product or service fills a social need	• Unwillingness among members to cooperate; each determined to win the advantage over the other
• Excellent top leadership; not domineering or autocratic; minimal surveillance; clear chain of command; responsive management	• Leaders unable to provide a program around which to rally
• Line supervisor a resource and facilitator rather than an overbearing monitor and disciplinarian	• Layers of bureaucracy that stymie action
• Employer confidence in employees; employee confidence in management	• Lack of authority to make decisions; simply following instructions
• Mutual respect; trust	• Demand for strict conformity with protocol and orders
• Opportunity to develop abilities–to learn, to advance, and to enjoy a variety of functions	• More time spent building fences than in constructive activity
• Perceived interrelationship with the total product; clear, realistic goals	• Lack of communication

TABLE 7.3 (continued)

- Challenging and diversified work

- Responsibility that matches authority

- Recognition of achievement; feedback on job performance

- Pleasant, comfortable work environment

- Fairness in administering established policies, no discrimination

- Freedom to "bitch"

- Clarity of instructions; no ambiguity

- Opportunity to socialize with fellow members or workers

- Adequate training

- Adequate tools and resources to get the job done

- Good working hours

- Safe and healthful working conditions

- Freedom from conflicting demands

- Decent income and income protection; no wage/salary discrimination; adequate fringe benefits

- Employment security

- No interaction except at meetings; no feedback

- No meaning to the job

- High turnover rate

- Heavy absenteeism

- Low morale

- Inconsistency in motivation

- Inadequate pay and benefits

- Poor physical working conditions

- Constant uncertainty concerning employment security

THE ROLE OF THE UNION

Finally we come down to what appears to be a virtual sine qua non for EI success: a strong union presence. It simply does not suffice to rely solely on the personality, the human relations philosophy, the motivation, and the goodwill of a "good manager" to make participation work. Employees know that managers come and go. It makes good sense, therefore, that a structure and a process that will better ensure continuity and the full implementation of the "good management" philosophy is what is necessary for employee involvement to work.

Procter & Gamble, the conglomerate food and home-products giant, is putting this reasoning to the test. Long known for its cooperative labor-management relations and its genteel management style, the company recently selected a hard-nosed executive as its CEO. Almost overnight, Edwin Artzt substituted the team approach that had been successfully nurtured over many years with his "like-it-or-lump-it" approach, as *Business Week* described it.[40] Teamwork, by all accounts, had produced major savings in inventory and better service for customers. But with yearly earnings growth declining as a result of the 1991 recession, Artzt pushed through his plan for individual rather than team accountability. Without contractual language to prevent this radical departure from the teamwork approach, employees had no option but to go along with it or leave. According to critics, many of those who had been the agents for progressive change and who had produced record profits during the 1980s either have been silenced or have left the company. Whether Artzt's old-fashioned autocratic style improves P&G's bottom line remains to be seen. In the meantime, as one manager put it, the company is hardly a good place to work anymore. One executive has changed the motivating force in a billion-dollar corporation from teamwork to fear.[41]

Responsibility for continuing the teamwork approach cannot be left in the hands of a few individuals at the top of the organization. It must be the result of an agreed-upon commitment whose application is not voluntary but contractual. Of course, the individual employee does not and cannot enjoy such a contractual relationship, and that's where the union comes in—as the legal representative of the work force. The guarantee that the employee involvement mode of operation will prevail, with its proven benefit to the employees and the organization when there are no gimmicks, cooptation, or control by management, lies in the ability of the union to assume an integral role as a co-equal player in the process. Participation works best when it takes the form of Track 3 union-management joint action, as opposed to unilateral management imposition of teamwork.

Obviously, not every unionized setting is conducive to success in employee involvement. Union representatives must be thoroughly committed to the joint action process. Just as managers must be oriented to the new way of corporate life, so union representatives must undergo the necessary training. Their responsibilities to negotiate the labor contract and to protect its provisions from violations by management must remain intact while they learn to perform new roles as coordinators and facilitators in the practical application of the joint action process.

Thus we come full circle, to the key ingredient: the co-equal status with management of the employees' representative body—the union—in planning, designing, implementing, and obtaining feedback concerning all aspects of the involvement concept and process. To be sure, the joint action concept, in and of itself, does not necessarily spell success. Time and again, the hard reality of outside forces or human error converts success to failure or causes the process to falter as the parties seek collaborative ways to hurdle the barriers. For all their success at spawning joint action, General Motors workers have not been spared from mass layoffs and plant closings. Nevertheless, the positive constructive role of a union devoted to the aims and purposes of the process, with a management likewise committed, creates the most benign climate for its successful fulfillment.

In the best of worlds, management and labor organize the workplace along the lines laid out here. But why stop at managing the workplace? Why should labor be excluded from managing the enterprise itself? The key decisions that determine competitive success are often made not in the plant or the office but at the strategic level of the firm. The best productivity performance on the factory floor can be undone by inept or inappropriate design and engineering or failure to invest in world-class technology. The best quality can be undone by a pricing strategy that emphasizes short-term profits at the expense of long-term market share. Everything from the accounting system used to keep the company's books to the choice of subcontractors is vital to the interests of workers as well as stockholders.

Going well beyond current forms of workplace joint action is already on the horizon. Indeed, extremely valuable experiments in employee involvement entailing co-managing the enterprise are now under way in a small number of fascinating cases. It is to these experiments that we turn in the next chapter.

PART IV

TOWARD AN ENTERPRISE COMPACT

CHAPTER 8

From Co-Managing the Workplace to Co-Managing the Enterprise

In order to do that which has not been done, we must try that which has not been tried.

—*John Ruskin*

"There's no use trying," she said, "one can't believe impossible things." "I daresay you haven't had much practice," said the queen. "When I was your age, I did it for half-an-hour a day. Why, sometimes I've believed as many as six impossible things before breakfast."

—*Lewis Carroll*, Alice in Wonderland

Nothing we have discussed so far is considered radical or revolutionary any longer in most labor-management relations circles. Now, however, we are prepared to take a giant leap into the future. Again, we begin with some postwar history before taking a glimpse of three contemporary experiments in transcending the limitations of the traditional Workplace Contract and current approaches to employee involvement.

It is 1949. The United Auto Workers Union (UAW) has just published and distributed to its local union leadership and its staff its monthly magazine, *Ammunition*. This issue calls upon the automobile industry to produce a "low-cost, small, light car." It even gives a name to its proposed automobile: A Motor Car Named Desire—a takeoff on the title of Tennessee Williams's popular play. The auto industry turns a deaf ear to the argument that production of such a vehicle selling at a commensurately moderate price would enable lower-income families to purchase a new car. The rationale for this negative response is highlighted in an item in the magazine *Iron Age* appearing that same year:

A fact seldom discussed by the car makers is that passenger cars are really not designed for the mass purchasers as is commonly supposed. Rather, new cars are actually designed for the families in the higher income brackets, professional men, salesmen operating on expense accounts, well-to-do farmers and a few hourly paid employees. Union sources in Detroit have claimed that, even before the war, less than one-fifth of the auto workers actually bought the cars they helped to build. Under these conditions, it is not to be wondered that established car producers have hesitated to bring out a light car.[1]

In a caustic analysis of the small-car debate, *Ammunition* chides the U.S. auto industry:

It is the old story of prosperity from the top down. You see, it's easy—sell the big expensive cars to the man with money or to the man who can borrow it. When the cars begin to burn oil, need tires, clutches and paint jobs, the mass market not able to buy a low-maintenance-cost small car will be forced to buy the second-hand oil-burners on the used car lots.[2]

Years later, GM, Ford, and Chrysler would try their hands at building a small car—but would never figure out how to make one desirable. The Chevrolet Corvair came under fire as a highly unstable and dangerous vehicle; the Chevy Vega was a disaster mechanically, and the Ford Pinto had the infamous tendency to explode when struck from behind. The few small cars that became successful, such as the Ford Mustang and the Chevrolet Camaro, would invariably be made longer, heavier, and more expensive each year—leaving the small-car market to the Germans and the Japanese.

The year is 1982. Japanese imports have virtually captured the rapidly expanding and lucrative small-car market. In June, GM's vice president for engineering meets with two of his top engineers to discuss an innovative small-car project.[3] The following month, *Saturn* is chosen as the code name for the project, an appropriate reminder of the powerful rocket that launched Neil Armstrong, Buzz Aldrin, and Mike Collins toward the moon in 1969, thereby leapfrogging the Soviet Union's lead in manned space exploration. The goal of the Saturn project is "to design an American vehicle that can beat the Japanese in the current small-car race"—and to develop and build it in a brand-new way.[4]

THE SATURN PROJECT: A CULTURE OF CONSENSUS

Today Saturn is approaching full production, and a visit to the plant suggests that something extraordinary is going on there. Writing in *Automobile* magazine in November 1990 as the first Saturn rolled off the assembly line, the auto expert David E. Davis, Jr., summed up his first impressions of the plant, located in the rolling hills of rural Tennessee:

> When you walk into the Saturn plant, near Spring Hill, you half expect to find them making mountain bikes, or computer software. The factory neither looks nor feels like a traditional automobile factory. The workers don't act like automotive workers and the bosses don't boss like automotive supervisors. There is a cheerful sense of mission about the place, almost religious as if the Hare Krishna people were running things.[5]

Davis went on to suggest that: "however Roger Smith's great Saturn gamble works out, it is a strange and wonderful thing that's going on down in Tennessee, perhaps the greatest automotive adventure since the plants went back to building cars after World War II."[6]

How did this success story come about? In the eight years between its naming and the rollout of the first completed car, the Saturn project revolutionized labor-management relations in an auto company. In October 1983, following discussions initiated by GM with the UAW, the parties agreed to pursue the concept of a joint GM-UAW Study Center to explore new approaches to building small cars in the United

States. The corporation's chairman and its president publicly announced the Saturn project a month later, followed by the formal creation of the company-union center. Don Ephlin, then the UAW vice president and director of the union's General Motors department, describes what followed:

> GM's original plan was to have only two or three people from each side participate in the study. We persuaded GM to greatly expand the study to include a number of GM workers to ensure input from varied backgrounds, from diverse types of plants in various divisions of the corporation and from plants with different approaches to labor relations. Over time, some 99 individuals participated—55 from the union side and 44 from management.
>
> Aside from developing a different human relations system for the plant, the union participants used their background and expertise from the shop floor to consult with engineers designing and laying out a new system for building an automobile in the United States.[7]

The Committee of 99, with its majority from the union, came from fifty-five different plants and seventeen GM divisions. Participants chosen by top management and by the UAW's GM department began with widely varying views about union-management relationships. Thus, as its first defined mission, the Committee of 99 set out "to identify and recommend the best approaches to integrate people and the technology to competitively manufacture cars in the United States."[8] What they came up with in the end was a form of "consensus management." As Reid Rundell, GM executive vice president, noted, the committee:

> talked to peers . . . to outsiders like the authors of *In Search of Excellence* . . . and to each other. And they succeeded in not only defining the type of organizational structure and relationship that would make attainment of the objective possible . . . they really set a living example of the new Saturn culture. And obviously, they created the pattern that became the basis of our working agreement with the UAW.
>
> One of the many people systems that came out of the study center was the implementation of consensus management . . . a process that can be slow and trying, but one which creates a participatory job environment. This attitude also supports a philosophy of openness,

trust, respect and involvement which in turn can help grow that special "culture" which we must have to support the technology, business and people systems.[9]

On January 7, 1985, the Saturn Corporation was officially created as a wholly owned subsidiary of General Motors Corporation, independent of other GM divisions but with all its financial support coming from the parent corporation. Soon afterward, on July 26, the UAW and GM finalized negotiation of the separate and, in many ways, landmark UAW-Saturn labor agreement.[10]

Meanwhile, an extensive exploration for a site for the new manufacturing and assembly facility had been under way, and on July 30 the corporation announced its decision to settle in Spring Hill, Tennessee. The following year work began on the 4.4 million-square-foot complex. Discussions between the UAW and GM led to the decision to have the facility built by union construction workers. A special agreement was negotiated between the contractor, Morrison-Knudsen Company, Inc., and the AFL-CIO Building and Construction Trades Department and the Teamsters Union specifically for this project.

A NEW-STYLE LABOR CONTRACT

One of the many major decisions to come out of the deliberations of the Committee of 99 concerned the engineering technique to be used in the final assembly process. The usual practice is for workers to perform their functions as a moving assembly line passes their work station. Within limited space and time constraints, the worker must "keep up with the line," working and walking alongside it as it moves inexorably to the next station. The committee rejected this traditional approach in favor of a "skillet" or "platform" system. The platform moves but the workers stand on it, so they do not have to run alongside to keep up. When they have completed their operations on one body, they walk to the next unit in line. When necessary, the workers can stop the platform to allow corrections to be made in line with the strict emphasis placed on assuring that the job is always done right.

The decision to use this system was not made unilaterally by management. As "Skip" LeFauve, president of Saturn, has remarked, "our assembly line is really state of the art and it was developed through the [joint union-management] consensus process we use to make all of our decisions."[11]

The engineering of the Saturn automobile is ingenious, but just as imaginative is the labor agreement designed especially for the new labor-management relations culture underpinning the project. Contrary to customary practice, it contains no management-rights provision. Instead, the agreement spells out the basic guidelines governing the decision-making process. The introductory paragraph to Section 10, "Structure and Decision-Making Process," makes this patently clear:

> The structure of Saturn reflects certain basic principles, e.g., recognition of the stakes and equities of everyone in the organization; full participation by the Union; use of a consensus decision-making process; placement of authority and decision making in the most appropriate part of the organization, with emphasis on the Work Unit; and free flow of information and clear definition of the decision-making process.[12]

Unlike standard collective-bargaining agreements, the Saturn contract has no fixed termination date. It is a "living document, subject to renegotiation at any time" once a full complement of members has been hired. Either party can initiate renegotiation simply by furnishing the other party with a written "Notice of Request to Modify Agreement."[13]

The contract spells out the Consensus Guidelines that govern the joint decision-making process. Accordingly, "decisions and disagreements" are resolved through joint company-union efforts at discovering the "best solution" to any problems that arise in the conduct of the enterprise. The language compels the union and management to search jointly for solutions "within the context of Saturn's philosophy and mission while, at the same time, satisfying the status and equities of all major stakeholders."[14]

The specific language of the agreement evokes this new approach:

> The [administrative] structure is intended to make the Union a full partner.
>
> The parties agree that the consensus process, as outlined below, is the primary method for making decisions and resolving disagreements.

In the context of Saturn's philosophy and mission, decisions and disagreements will be resolved within the following guidelines:

- The solution must provide a high level of acceptance for all parties.
- Any of the parties may block a potential decision. However, the party blocking the decision must search for an alternative.
- In the event an alternative solution is not forthcoming, the blocking party must re-evaluate the position in the context of philosophy and mission.
- Voting, "trading" and compromise are not part of this process.[15]

Still other features add to the innovative labor-management relationships contained in the Saturn labor contract:

- No fewer than 80% of the employees will be covered by permanent job security. "Permanent job security" guarantees against layoff except in the case of "unforeseen or catastrophic events or severe economic conditions." Moreover, the union, through the joint "Strategic Action Council," has equal authority with management in determining the applicability of this provision.[16]
- The contract is, in fact, "based on a living document" concept, under which problems are solved as they arise through a form of ongoing negotiation which . . . includes the right to strike.[17]
- The bargaining unit comprises a single classification, "Operating Technician," covering all "nonskilled trades members" and three to five additional classifications to which all skilled trades members are assigned.[18]
- The compensation system is established on an annual salary basis paid semi-monthly. The "Compensation Level at Steady State" is established at "80% of straight time wages (base plus COLA) of the average of . . . competitive rates," plus a defined reward system.[19]

The salient feature of the Saturn management approach is encompassed in the internal structure of the corporation and its processes and procedures. The entire structure, from the office of the president of the corporation to the employee on the shop floor, is predicated on joint decision making in a partnership mode stretching from strategic policy making at one end of the spectrum to day-to-day, even hour-by-hour, problem solving at the other.

An appreciation of the depth and breadth of the mutual agreement to co-manage the enterprise emerges with the reading of the precise contract provisions that govern the structure of the Saturn Corporation. As table 8.1 indicates, union representatives serve at every level of management in the corporation from the individual plant-floor work teams, up through each business unit to the entire manufacturing complex, and finally to the Strategic Action Council, which oversees the long-range planning function of Saturn—decisions that in traditional settings are made only at the level of the CEO.

THE SATURN PROCESS IN ACTION

At the shop-floor level, our field work with members of the Work Units, Work Unit Modules, and Business Units provides strong evidence that

TABLE 8.1

Structural Elements of the Saturn Corporation

UNIT WORK MEMBER
   The individual Saturn employee.

WORK UNIT
   An integrated group of approximately 6–15 Work Unit members.

WORK UNIT MODULE
   A grouping of Work Units interrelated according to geography, product, or technology, with a common Work Unit Advisor.

BUSINESS UNITS
   An integrated group of Work Units and Work Unit Modules representing common areas such as stamping, assembly, or powertrain.

MANUFACTURING ACTION COUNCIL (MAC)
   An integrated group of Business Units comprising the entire manufacturing and assembly complex. The MAC is composed of all Business Unit Advisors, some from management, others from the union.

STRATEGIC ACTION COUNCIL (SAC)
   The top executive management of the corporation responsible for long-range goals of Saturn, with particular emphasis on planning and coordination with outside interested parties, including dealers, suppliers, communities, and stockholders. Composition of the SAC includes representatives from management and the union.

Source: UAW Saturn Corporation Memorandum of Agreement, July 23, 1985.

the Saturn theory and philosophy are, in fact, being put into practice.[20] The procedures for hiring new employees, for example, reflect the empowering language set forth in the contract. Saturn has a personnel office, but its job is not to hire new workers but to provide administrative services to individual work units.

The employee application forms were originally fashioned by the Committee of 99. When applications come into the plant, they are reviewed by members of those Work Units that have demonstrated a need for additional staff. Selected applicants are invited to Spring Hill, where they are interviewed by Work Unit members who try to explore not only the applicants' skills but something about their leadership qualities and adaptability to the Saturn culture. The team reaches consensus on which applicants are acceptable and extends offers to them. As new hires arrive, one of the Work Unit members told us, "they individually and together with their family become part of us. We go through a bonding process and help them move and become part of the community." Union representatives, moreover, serve on assessment teams concerning the hiring of management staff.

All training programs within the corporation are jointly administered. As of the spring of 1991, between sixty and seventy classes were being held each week, with local union officers participating as instructors. In 1989, nearly 400,000 hours of training were provided—the equivalent of 200 hours per Saturn "partner." Half of these hours were devoted to developing the human relations skills necessary for the democratized system.

The role that Saturn workers and their union play in hiring decisions and training is certainly a part of the employee involvement strategy. But what makes Saturn unique is that participation does not stop at the level of the workplace. Take, for example, the actual design of the Saturn automobile. The original Saturn was to be a subcompact with a 99.5-inch wheelbase. It was to weigh 1,850 pounds and focus on fuel economy even to the detriment of performance. Before proceeding beyond the clay model stage, the Committee of 99 "clinic-ed" this stripped-down version to learn what the customer reaction might be. They found, as one of our interviewees put it, that "this was not the car the customer wanted to buy." The committee turned to a new, larger design with a 102.5-inch wheelbase, a more powerful engine, and a sporty appearance. The new design took dead aim at Japan's hottest-selling models, the Honda Civic and Accord. Union representatives worked closely with corporate staff at the design studio in selecting the new concept.

Next it was necessary to decide on the suppliers and subcontractors who would produce the parts used in the car's assembly. Before soliciting bids, the parties at Spring Hill agreed upon a process for evaluating the suppliers who would bid for the work. They set four categories for evaluation: design, engineering, quality, and cost. A joint union-management committee then developed forty-seven attributes of these combined categories against which to evaluate the suppliers. This entailed assessments of the written submissions, site visits, and intensive discussions with the bidders, and then adding up the evaluation scores, selecting finalists, and making the final choice. One might think that the union representatives at Saturn would invariably select UAW-organized subcontractors. But there were cases in which non-UAW contractors and even nonunion contractors were chosen over unionized ones when the latter could not meet the quality or cost standards set jointly by the union and management.

Similar procedures were used in the selection of dealerships. A joint team evaluated written proposals from applicants and discussed them internally and then with the applicants themselves. The team established criteria against which to judge the applications and for scoring each applicant. The recommendations were then directed to the joint Strategic Action Committee (SAC) for a final decision. This process continues to be used for selecting new dealerships as the dealer network expands throughout the country. The selection criteria are by far more stringent than those used by other domestic producers. For instance, the union and management stipulate that anyone wishing to establish and operate a Saturn franchise has to agree to a dealership devoted exclusively to the Saturn. Moreover, dealers must send their staffs, particularly the mechanics, to Spring Hill for training. The union insists that the quality of the service at Saturn dealerships be second to none. Building as close to a defect-free car as possible was not to be compromised by inept or discourteous dealers.

Still another union-company joint committee was established to deal with marketing. The local union financial secretary is involved in the determination of marketing strategies. There are union-designated representatives as well who are assigned to work with management representatives on matters involving accounting, budgeting, and cost analysis. As the president of the local union put it, "No other union is more involved in and knows more about the finance end of the business." This serves the interests of the union, of course, but also, by sharing all cost information throughout the Saturn community, workers become intimately acquainted with the financial and cost tradeoffs involved in decisions over such matters as technology, work pace, and quality control. Thus, workers themselves search for productivity-enhancing and cost-saving methods, as well as taking into consideration the costs of absenteeism, inefficient work practices, and other matters that in traditional settings are mainly the concern of management and often a cause of friction between management and the union.

The car's sticker price was also discussed jointly. Together the parties determined the basis for profitability, evaluated competitive prices, and presented their pricing recommendations to the SAC. The SAC, in turn, reported these findings and proposals to GM's top executives in Detroit, who brought them to GM's Board of Directors for final adoption. The union insisted on an aggressive pricing strategy that would challenge the imports for market share. Having reviewed the first prototypes of the Saturn, trade magazines speculated that its base price would be around $9,000.[21] As it turned out, the base retail price for the Sports Sedan (SL) was a thousand dollars less, at $7,995; the base price for the top-of-the-line Sports Coupe (SC) was set at a highly competitive $11,775.[22]

Advertising, for both print media and TV, is managed in the same way. Prospective ad agency proposals were reviewed jointly, as were all marketing presentations. After the advertising agency was chosen, all of its TV spots and glossy magazine inserts were reviewed jointly by union and management representatives before being aired or appearing in print.

Even the decision to recall automobiles is made jointly. In an unfortunate incident, one supplier, Texaco, delivered defective engine coolant; contrary to its intended purpose, it all but burned out the engine. Saturn was obviously not at fault. A joint decision was made, nevertheless, not just to replace the engines but to provide brand-new identical cars to the owners. In this way Saturn turned a potential recall disaster into a customer relations coup.

One vitally important aspect of decision making in the arena of basic policy relates to the critical subject of capital investment. Final capital investment decisions continue to rest with the parent corporation, General Motors, its top executives, and its Board of Directors. As one

Saturn employee described it, "the GM Board of Directors is the bank, but how the money it allocates is spent is done jointly by management and the union here at Saturn." With Phase I of the total Saturn project now completed, a decision is awaited on the capital needed to embark on Phase II. The initial $5 billion projected investment has been trimmed to a little over $3 billion—still no small sum, to be sure. Nevertheless, in April 1991, some five months after its launch into the marketplace, the president of Saturn Corporation and Michael Bennett, president of UAW Local 1853, were able to announce the addition of a second shift and to make plans for the introduction of a two-shift system that would operate with three production crews to meet production demand resulting from increased sales.[23]

How far has Saturn traveled toward meeting these expressed processes and objectives? One evaluation brings the concept onto center stage:

Considering the external and internal forces working against Saturn, the experiment has made great strides in its departure from adversarial labor relations. Will employers be able to disempower and circumvent the UAW as some critics charge because of similar "joint" programs? If anything, Saturn comes closest to the concept of codetermination, which empowers a democratic union and its members to guide all facets of the business, including those not strictly related to manufacturing. Instead of back-end involvement in implementation of policy, the UAW at Saturn is involved in the front end, participating in strategic and leadership sessions that form and shape corporate direction. West German industry operates under this concept and the organized sector of their work force is much higher than the U.S.[24]

The success of the newly designed and engineered Saturn vehicle is being tested in the open marketplace, after having experienced a slow launch in the middle of an economic recession. With sales running ahead of production in 1992, it only remains to be seen how profitable this experiment will turn out to be.

Nothing on the American scene in the field of labor-management relations compares with the Saturn project's sharp departure from the traditional mode of collective bargaining. Among the most penetrating modern-day experiments in joint action at almost every level of managerial decision making, it represents the most far-reaching innovative development in all U.S. industry.

Whether Saturn can be duplicated in other settings is hard to discern. For one thing, it represents a "greenfield" site in more than one way. Not only has the entire enterprise been developed from scratch through the joint process, and not only is the physical plant brand-new, but all of the employees hired by Saturn have personally made the decision to work in this radical setting. Nearly all of them have come from other GM plants, either from layoff status or as active employees. In existing "brownfield" sites, of course, management and labor must work with existing employees (including supervisors), some of whom have traditional mindsets about the nature of work that are difficult to change. Whether traditional ways can be "unlearned" through intensive training and education is an open question. Indeed, whether Saturn can maintain the level of camaraderie and involvement over the long run, day in and day out, will be tested in the years ahead. Thus far all the signs look positive.

A NOVEL ATTEMPT IN A BROWNFIELD SITE: HARVARD INDUSTRIES

The first major test of full joint action in a brownfield site is already under way. A Saturn-type agreement is being tried in an older manufacturing facility with a history of extraordinarily poor labor relations. In 1985 Harvard Industries, headquartered in Farmingdale, New Jersey, completed an agreement with the Amerace Corporation to purchase one of its divisions that produces specialized components for the aerospace industry. The division, Elastic Stop Nut of America (ESNA), is located in Union, New Jersey. Workers at the ESNA plant had been organized and represented by the UAW for forty years. The labor agreement negotiated between ESNA and the UAW contained a typical successor clause provision. This provision spelled out the commitment that, should ESNA be purchased by another firm, the full terms and conditions of the labor agreement would become an integral part of the sale and bind the "successor" company to its provisions.[25]

Despite this legally binding contract clause, no sooner did the ink dry on the purchase agreement by Harvard Industries than all 252 UAW members were notified by the company that they were being summarily discharged. If they wanted a job under the new management they had to apply at a local hotel where Harvard Industries was accepting employment applications. Only a small number of the 252 workers who were released were rehired, and then only after management had carefully screened all the applicants with regard to their union views. This action triggered a struggle by the UAW and the workers that was to last six and a half years. The workers who were not rehired began picketing the plant, and those who had been rehired honored the picket line.

The new management refused to discuss its action with UAW representatives. The union promptly entered charges of unfair labor practices, and, following a hearing, the administrative law judge ruled in favor of the union's claims. The company appealed this decision to the circuit court in Washington, D.C. A decision was finally rendered years later, in the fall of 1990, again upholding the union's claim on behalf of the workers. The company decided not to appeal further to the U.S. Supreme Court. Instead, negotiations between the company and the union resulted in a back pay settlement totaling nearly $4 million, and all the discharged employees were offered reinstatement. The money for the settlement came from the then-overfunded pension plan.

Many of the UAW members who had been let go in 1985 chose not to return to the company. Most of them were at or near retirement age, and reemployment with Harvard Industries was not the most attractive proposition after six and a half years of struggling against the company. Others had found employment elsewhere and elected not to return to their previous jobs.

Then something quite amazing occurred. The management, in a total reversal of its earlier position, agreed to enter into negotiations for a new agreement with the UAW. Bill Kane, an international representative of the UAW, led the negotiations for the union. Don Bush, the newly appointed Harvard Industries' vice president for human resources, headed up negotiations for the company. Bush immediately made it clear that, as the company spokesperson, he was an advocate of the joint action approach to building a sound labor-management relationship. It also became evident that he had influenced top management to cease its anti-union battle and to seek the mutually advantageous adoption of a participative approach to the company's relations with the UAW. Kane, responding to this signal, proposed that the parties negotiate a contract along the lines that had been established at the UAW-GM Saturn plant. Bush agreed. Contract negotiations began in August 1991 and were concluded by October. The final document represented a remarkable turnaround in the relationship between the management and the union, and laid the groundwork for the introduction of an Enterprise Compact in a brownfield facility.

When the contract was finalized, there were 416 workers in the bargaining unit, including all production, nonproduction, and factory clerical employees. Since the new agreement, enthusiasm and active participation by the membership have been running high, and the contract has been overwhelmingly ratified by the work force.

Quite deliberately, many of the basic themes governing the original labor agreement at Saturn were incorporated into the new contract, most important among them the dropping of the management-rights clause. Under the terms of the agreement, the workers and their union representatives serve as equal partners with management with regard to workplace issues as well as the strategic and policy decisions of the business. The "philosophy statement" incorporated into the contract is designed to serve as the backdrop to the ongoing relationship between the parties and to guide their decisions and actions into the future. It is a remarkable statement for a union and a company that had been at loggerheads for over six years:

> The UAW and Harvard recognize that the relationship between workers and managers must undergo a fundamental change in order for American industry to maintain a viable position in the ever-changing world economy, and for American workers to achieve economic and social justice. In order to make progress toward attaining these mutually agreed upon goals, the method the parties have chosen is an employee-management partnership—a relationship of mutual respect, open communication, shared success, mutual aid, innovative problem solving, and shared decision making.
>
> The parties agree that in order for the Union to effectively represent its members, the Union must have a role in the decision-making process that affects its members.
>
> It is the intent of the UAW and Harvard Industries to create a

workplace that is governed by consensus, that recognizes the need for people to be treated with respect and dignity, and recognizes that collective bargaining is an essential and constructive force in our democratic society. All parties to this Agreement will strive to make the ESNA Division of Harvard Industries the best company of its kind in the marketplace; making the highest-quality product; a cost-effective, profitable operation; a coveted and secure place to work; and a responsible member of the community.

In establishing the internal joint structure directed toward implementing this Philosophy Statement, the contract language requires "recognition of the stakes and value of everyone in the organization; full participation by the union in all phases of the business; and use of a consensus decision-making process." It calls for the "free flow of information and clear definition of the decision-making process."

The contract specifically addresses the requirement for consensus decision making within a carefully designed administrative structure, patterned largely after the structure created under the UAW agreement at Saturn: employee work groups at the workplace level, combined into Production and Support Councils, with a Plant Council at the local plant level and a Business Council that includes representatives of the International Union and of the ESNA Division of Harvard Industries. It features, moreover, a carefully prepared description of the consensus decision-making process similar to the one in place at Saturn. Naturally, it also contains the usual and customary provisions found in the older Workplace Contract, including a pay-for-knowledge system, an array of job benefits, a description of acceptable working conditions, and a well-defined grievance and arbitration procedure. It also contains a standard successor clause that the union hopes will not be abrogated again should the division be sold.

Now the hard part begins. Will the commitment to consensual decision making prevail as tough problems arise? What will become the full scope of the duties and the authority vested in the top-level Business Council? As of this writing, the contract is just being put into effect. Five years from now we may be able to assess whether a Saturn contract can work in a brownfield site.

JOINT STRATEGIC ACTION IN THE PROFESSIONAL RANKS: THE UNIVERSITY OF HAWAII

Developing new labor-management relations that extend to strategic decision making within the enterprise is also important to white-collar service industries and professional occupations. A case in point involves the unique relationship between the University of Hawaii Professional Assembly (UHPA) and the administration of the Hawaii public higher education system.[26]

UHPA is the duly recognized union of university and community college faculty throughout the state of Hawaii. The union represents 3,350 members and is affiliated with the National Education Association. It has been the bargaining agent for faculty in Hawaii since 1974. Like other faculty unions throughout the country, UHPA has traditionally been involved in negotiating salary agreements and workload requirements with university administrators. Like unions in other sectors, it has negotiated agreements with virtually all of the provisions of the traditional Workplace Contract.

In 1985, however, as a result of a particular set of circumstances in some ways not unlike those at Harvard Industries, UHPA began to expand its role as bargaining agent at the University of Hawaii. Within six years, it had won the respect of the university's Board of Regents and was in the position of having co-responsibility for setting broad university priorities. The transformation of UHPA began with the 1985 appointment of a new university president, Albert Simone, who came to his new administrative post with strong anti-union sentiments. Simone openly challenged the role of faculty unions, suggesting that unions were inappropriate in the academic setting. He argued that unions were too egalitarian and too often protected the weak and incompetent. As a result, he felt faculty unions were inconsistent with excellence in education.

UHPA opposed Simone's selection as president, but was unable to prevent the Board of Regents from confirming his appointment. As it turned out, once in office Simone was willing to air his differences with the union leadership directly. Soon after his installation as president, he went to the union's off-campus offices for an informal dialogue with the faculty's elected executive board. What came of this first encounter was an agreement to keep meeting on a regular basis. From these meetings came a planned retreat between the president and vice president of the university and the leadership of the union. Simone was pleasantly surprised to find that the union held the same perspective about the university as he did: the university exists for the students, to be served by the faculty with the support of the administration.

During the retreat, the parties were able to agree on two thorny issues that had plagued negotiations for years: faculty evaluation and workload requirements. Simone found he was not dealing with a union that blindly stuck to tradition, but instead with an organized group of faculty who were willing to accept post-tenure review procedures aimed at encouraging improved faculty performance and discouraging faculty who were not making a full-faith effort in their teaching, research, and service to the community.

In subsequent rounds of discussions and negotiations, the union continued to bring to the bargaining table innovative proposals for salary adjustments. It argued for peer-reviewed merit pay to reward extraordinary performance; it argued for pay adjustments to account for differences in external market salary levels; it argued for equity adjustments in cases of racial or gender discrimination. This was a far cry from the traditional union position of opposition to salary differentials that reward individual merit or reflect market forces.

The union met with resistance to their salary proposals from two sources. Some public-sector unions criticized the UHPA for steering away from across-the-board wage increases. And from the other side of the bargaining table, the chairman of the Board of Regents opposed the salary plan not because he disagreed with the content, but because he felt the union had overstepped its bounds in attempting to set academic standards as a basis for remuneration. This, argued the chairman, was a management right not to be tampered with by the faculty union.

In the end the union won. It agreed to disagree respectfully with its fellow trade unionists, and it won approval of its salary package after the Board of Regents chair resigned. Simone, now a strong supporter of the union, defended the union's position before the remaining members of the governing board.

This inevitably led to the next step in joint action at the university. Each year the Board of Regents and the university administration submit to the state legislature a priority list of program expenditures.

It covers in numerical order the priorities of the university in terms of health and safety issues, essential academic program requirements, research initiatives, and hiring needs in both the academic and administrative structures. The 1992–93 budget request included 110 items that ranged from salary adjustments and funds for janitor positions to money for hazardous waste disposal and the microfilming of important library collections. Normally, the setting of these priorities is strictly a management prerogative. Under the new arrangement with the UHPA, the union obtains a preliminary list of priorities from the university administration and has the right to review it and to argue for additional items and changes in priority position. While not yet contractually bound to bargain over the setting of these priorities, the Board of Regents gives substantial weight to the union's position in its deliberations.

From a rocky beginning, the relationship between the university administration and the union has grown cordial, polite, even friendly. There is mutual respect between them. The Board of Regents, more often than not, now makes certain that the administration has shared with the union any plans for change before putting them into practice. The executive director of the UHPA now attends all meetings of the Board of Regents and planning meetings of the administration. What makes all this work is a basic agreement between the parties on the goals of the university and the nature of the working relationship among the union, the administration, and the Board of Regents.

There is a potential problem, however. The close working relationship is not formalized. Most of the procedures used by the union and management to come to agreement on budget priorities and other issues are not written down. Hence, with a change in administration— or in union leadership—the relationship could change overnight. Consequently the next step is to codify the working relationship between the parties and negotiate the terms guaranteeing the union's role in strategic planning within the university. This will not be easy, particularly as there are elements in the state government, other unions, the administration, and even the faculty that would like to see a return to the old days when strict union-management lines were drawn. Many of these critics remember the personal power they had under the old regime and only warily gave it up.

Whether the new informal arrangements between the union and the administration will result in higher productivity, better quality teaching, and more concern with educational innovation is still to be seen. But a casual walk across campus, a brief discussion with a random group of faculty, and sitting in at a meeting of the Board of Regents all suggest that something quite remarkable is happening in Hawaii that deserves a great deal of attention from labor-management experts.

A STAKE IN THE ENTERPRISE: SHARING OWNERSHIP, CORPORATE LEADERSHIP, AND PROFITS

Saturn, Harvard Industries, and the University of Hawaii represent unique departures in labor-management relations. Yet these new experiments do not by any means exhaust the list of reforms of the traditional relationship between labor and management. At various times and under quite varying circumstances, working alone or with organized labor, management has invited employees to share financial ownership of the firm, to join the corporate board, and to participate in profits—or "progress" sharing. Each represents another approach to encouraging labor to work with management toward the pursuit of higher productivity, better quality, and increased innovation.

EMPLOYEE OWNERSHIP

The first of these, employee stock ownership plans (ESOPs), received an enormous boost when Congress, at the urging of Senator Russell Long of Louisiana, passed legislation in 1974 promoting employee ownership. The idea, invented by Louis Kelso in the 1950s, is that employees should own a stake in the enterprise for which they work, since their livelihood is tied so closely to the firm's well-being. In the ensuing years, ESOPs have increased in number, taking advantage of tax breaks permitted by the legislation. The National Center for Employee Ownership estimates that, at the end of 1989, there were between 9,000 and 10,000 companies that had established employee stock ownership plans of one kind or another, governing 11.5 million employees. The most common of these are tax-qualified stock bonus plans and employee stock ownership plans used as a retirement plan or as a supplement to a company's pension plan.[27]

Indeed, in many instances, management's introduction of an ESOP is motivated not so much by wanting to institute a reward system for its employees but from a desire to reduce its pension costs, to escape from paying health-care premiums for its retirees, or to protect against an unfriendly takeover.[28] ESOPs may also create the vehicle for an employee buyout in an effort to save the company from folding and thereby save jobs. Some of the most publicized ESOPs are those in which the employees banded together to take over their company rather than sit by and see it founder. In reality, very few ESOPs involve majority employee ownership, and, since a large number of employee takeovers occur in the face of impending financial disaster, many fail. They simply are unable to overcome the deep economic crisis under which they were organized in the first place. Nonetheless, there are excellent examples of employee takeovers that have proven successful and have turned an impending shutdown into a thriving operation.

Union involvement in negotiating the creation of an ESOP is often the result of a "stock-for-wage trade," according to studies made by Joseph Blasi of the Rutgers Institute of Management and Labor Relations.[29] This phenomenon was the outgrowth of contract negotiations that took place during the wage concession era of the 1980s. In desperate times, unions like the Steelworkers (USWA) ended up giving wage concessions in return for stock ownership. Today it is estimated that about 50,000 to 60,000 members of the union own shares in their firms.[30]

Avis, the car-rental company, is said to be the largest company in the nation that is 100 percent owned by its employees. It became employee-owned in 1987. Of its approximately 12,700 employees, about 2,800 are represented either by the Teamsters Union or the International Association of Machinists (IAM). As a boost to its consumer appeal, the Work in America Institute reports, Avis "has made employee ownership a central theme in its television and print advertising, and there seems to be little doubt that the ESOP/EPG [employee participation group] combination is working in terms of service and profit."[31] In fact, the company's pretax profits increased from $14.8 million in 1987 to $41 million in the following year, while customer complaints dropped about 35 percent. By March 1989, the ESOP had paid off $90 million of its acquisition debt—all from funds generated internally.[32]

At the behest of the U.S. Economic Development Administration, the Institute for Social Research at the University of Michigan (ISR) was asked to assess the status of employee ownership at the end of the 1980s. "The overall findings," the ISR report noted, "are necessarily tentative. . . . Nevertheless, it appears that optimism would not be inappropriate, and that further study of long-term performance is warranted."[33]

In assessing employee influence on decisions, the report noted that ownership rights generally do not include the right of employees to vote their stock. Nonetheless, some control may be exercised by employees in other ways, especially through their union. This is often done by having union representatives sit on the company's corporate board. Indeed, in the ISR survey, 36 percent of the respondents in companies with ESOPs report that worker representatives sit on the Board of Directors, while 77 percent of the companies with direct ownership indicate that employees influence "important" decisions in the company. In some of the companies this influence extends to such decisions as whether to make major capital acquisitions.[34] The report goes on to suggest why ESOPs work when they do. In particular, management respondents suggested that their ESOPs produced better industrial relations, higher productivity, and higher profits.[35] In his own review of employee ownership, the Rutgers University law professor Alan Stuart Hyde concludes that case studies of the plywood collectives in the Northwest, of refuse collection in the San Francisco Bay Area, of taxicab collectives, and of various professional partnerships, including law and accounting firms and physician group practices, all suggest that employee-owned firms "have survived, often without tax subsidies, in hostile competitive conditions over long periods."[36]

A Case Study: The Weirton Steel Corporation

A case in point can be found in a small steel town in West Virginia. Old Man Weir, as the old-timers refer to him, founded Weirton Steel in the early 1900s. In the 1920s his successful operation was bought by National Steel and, as one of that corporation's subsidiaries, zipped through the period of the glory days as a highly profitable integrated steel mill. For decades it has stood as the main economic base of the town of Weirton, West Virginia, with a population of about 30,000. As is typical of company towns, the son followed the father who, in turn, had followed his father into the mill.

As the years went by, the mill's age caught up with it. By the late 1970s, National Steel substantially halted its investment in the mill and when, in the 1980s, the American steel industry felt the increasing pressures of international competition, National Steel announced its intention to reduce its operations at Weirton sharply. A shudder ran through the entire community.

The Independent Steelworkers Union had represented both production and clerical workers at Weirton for decades. Faced with the shutdown of operations, the local union and the local management formed a study committee to investigate alternatives. They contracted with McKinsey and Company and with Lazard Freres to conduct a feasibility study to determine whether an employee buyout would be a viable option. Based on the recommendations of the study, the decision was made to proceed with an ESOP. Negotiations with National Steel were concluded, and the Weirton assets were purchased at twenty-two cents on the dollar. Bank loans were negotiated to close the deal. The workers accepted substantial cuts in pay and benefits and substituted for them a profit-sharing plan that distributed to workers one-third of the total profit earned in any year when the net worth of the company reached $100 million, and 50 percent of annual profits when assets reached $250 million.[37]

From the first quarter of operation as an employee-owned company, Weirton began making a profit. In fact, in relation to sales, it soon became one of the most profitable integrated steel mills in the country. By 1989, profit sharing based on 1988 profits averaged $9,185 per employee.

In comparatively short order all employees who had been laid off by National Steel were recalled, and even those who had lost their seniority recall rights were offered the opportunity to be rehired. Productivity was enhanced, with the promise of further improvement as the Board of Directors approved capital investments in new technology designed to advance both quality and efficiency and to develop new products. By world standards, quality has remained high. As a result, the employee-owned Weirton Corporation has been able to increase its market share in its prime product, tin for canning purposes in the food industry. Even in the face of the 1990–91 recession, the workers and management at the newly revamped and modernized Weirton Steel Corporation exuded optimism concerning the company's future.[38]

With a direct ownership stake in the corporation, the workers received representation on the Board of Directors. Three seats out of a total of twelve went to the union.[39] One was filled automatically by the union president; the union's second selection was the union's attorney; the elder co-author of this book was asked to serve as the third. As Board members, this triumvirate of labor representatives was involved in all the decisions undertaken by the Board: raising the necessary capital; allocating capital expenditures; selecting and purchasing new technology; investing in research and development and in new products; pricing strategy; purchasing and accounting procedures; internal corporate administrative matters brought before the board by the CEO; changes in corporate structure; hiring executive management staff—and all other subjects for Board determination. One union-selected board member (the elder co-author of this book) served as a member of the Board's compensation committee, which oversaw compensation levels of all those in management positions, including department heads, supervisors, and technical personnel. Another union appointed Board member serves on the Board's audit committee.

Immediately following every Board meeting, the three labor Board members would meet with the elected officials of the union at the union hall and report on the subjects discussed by the Board, its decisions, and the rationale supporting these decisions.[40] At each annual and, if necessary, special shareholders (employee owners) meeting, it was customary for at least one of the three labor Board members to address the assembly.

Weirton management directs the firm on a day-to-day basis much in the traditional fashion. However, an employee involvement process is operational; training in the establishment of Employee Participation Groups (EPG) is jointly administered; and a full-fledged joint communication system is in effect, as are human resource programs that help build a climate of mutual understanding and respect. Great emphasis is placed on the term *employee owner*—and a sense of ownership generally permeates the operation. To be sure, the labor agreement remains in full force and effect, as does the grievance procedure. Contract negotiations are sometimes protracted, but new agreements have been ratified by the membership. Nevertheless, problems are never far below the surface in the competitive steel industry, and must be dealt with on an ongoing basis. In this case, having representation on the Board of Directors has proven of vital importance.

CORPORATE BOARD MEMBERSHIP

In 1987 a study by the U.S. General Accounting Office determined that "workers own a majority of stock in 1,000 to 1,500 companies, [but] union and non-union employee representatives sit on boards in only about 250, mainly small companies."[41] Still, having employee representation is by no means a strange notion even for U.S.-based corporations. Those that have subsidiaries in such European countries as Germany and Sweden have long been accustomed to having their employees elect representatives to serve on the supervisory board—the European equivalent of the Board of Directors. By law, in Germany, for instance, co-determination *(Mitbestimmung)* is a fact of life. In the coal and steel industries, the law requires 50-50 representation on the supervisory board with the chairman then elected by the shareholders. In other industries, one-third of the supervisory board is elected by the employees in firms with between five hundred and two thousand employees. In firms with a work force in excess of two thousand, the 50-50 representation system applies.

The first major industrial corporation in the United States to elect a union representative to its Board of Directors was Chrysler. Then UAW president Douglas Fraser was elected to the Board in 1980, coincident with the U.S. government's loan-guarantee legislation. Fraser and the UAW were deeply involved in the effort to persuade Congress to pass the legislation that would help save the corporation from bankruptcy. Since then, Fraser has been interviewed time and again concerning the significance of his membership on the Chrysler Board. He has consistently pointed to the need for and the desirability of having employee representation on the Board of Directors and its importance to the employees, management, stockholders, and community at large. In an interview in *Solidarity*, the official newspaper of the UAW, Fraser explained the significance of labor representation on the Board of Directors.

Q. How will a union seat on Chrysler's board benefit the average Chrysler worker?

A. I have no illusions that winning a seat on the board means that conditions at Chrysler will change overnight. But I do think that if the feelings and ideas of Chrysler workers had been made known at the board level in the past, some of the bad management decisions the company made might have been avoided.

Q. Since you are going to be just one out of 18 members of the board, how could you expect to alter Chrysler's course?

A. Well, one out of 18 is better than none out of 18. Right now there's no way for those corporate board members to get a sense of how workers feel about their decisions. I may be a lonely voice, speaking out on behalf of the Chrysler workers. But I'll be there—letting the board know first hand how workers feel and blowing the whistle whenever the company does something that harms those workers.

Q. Won't you have a conflict of interest on the Chrysler board at times?

A. Whenever there is a legitimate problem obviously I will not participate. I'll leave the room. If the board were to discuss collective bargaining, for example, I would not want to be involved because my clear responsibility, my total responsibility, is to the UAW members.

But on many important questions, there would be no conflict. If Chrysler was considering expanding its overseas operations as it did a few years ago, for example, I'd know about that and be able to argue the issue. In that case, its decision not only cost workers' jobs, it generally proved to be a financial disaster that harmed the company.[42]

An important point Fraser likes to make has to do with information. With board membership, labor is privy to all the key decisions made in the enterprise. Even though labor's voice is a minority voice, it has a chance of influencing corporate strategy—and a certainty of early notification of any changes in corporate direction affecting employee interests.

In another interview Fraser was asked whether labor representation on the Board of Directors may be called the wave of the future. He responded:

Well, I'm uncertain as to whether it's the wave of the future. I would argue that it should be. In time, labor leaders are going to reach the conclusion that it's not enough to protest management decisions that are already made, that are irreversible, and have an adverse impact upon the members you represent. I'm not saying that labor should have the controlling voice, but certainly labor should have some input before final decisions are made.[43]

For the record, Fraser's successor at the UAW, Owen Bieber, remained on the Chrysler Board until 1991, when a reorganization eliminated the labor member of the Board. We believe this to be an unfortunate setback for the company.

PROGRESS SHARING

Lurking in the background whenever joint action is implemented lies the issue of employees sharing appropriately in any resulting gains to the organization. Typically, executives are rewarded with a portion of the profits as a bonus in addition to their established salaries and benefits. Profit sharing, when applied to the general work force, represents a "fair share" of the firm's progress over and above the base wage and benefits already earned. Profit-sharing plans per se are not necessarily tied to the infusion of the joint action process. However, where profit sharing is not in effect it may well become a subject for consideration once the participatory process is introduced.

Gain-sharing programs of various kinds also reflect a sharing in the progress of the company, usually related in some fashion to the increase in productivity and/or decrease in production costs rather than profits per se. Thus financial enhancement, aside from job satisfaction and employment security, may become a tangible benefit attributable to participation in decision making.

Profit sharing has a long history in the United States. As early as the eighteenth century, a few firms had profit-sharing plans that applied to all the employees of the firm, not solely its top managers. The first such plan in the United States, as far as historians can tell, was introduced by Albert Gallatin, the owner of a glassworks in Geneva, Pennsylvania, who later served as Secretary of the Treasury under presidents Jefferson and Madison. Procter & Gamble has the oldest *continuous* profit-sharing plan in the country, initiated in 1887.[44] The 1980s saw a sizable increase in the number of companies in which an across-the-board profit-sharing plan was introduced, with some of these being union-negotiated.[45] Union contracts with profit sharing can be found in the steel, aluminum, rubber, airline, farm implement, and auto industries.

There is considerable variation in the formulas that determine the profit-sharing distribution. Customarily, profit sharing kicks in only after profits on sales exceed a prescribed percentage. In some instances, however, provision is made for profit-sharing payments to start on a "first dollar" basis. Moreover, the percent of the total profits shared may rise, tied to the percent of profits made on sales, up to a stated maximum.[46]

Unlike profit sharing, *gain-sharing plans* are anchored directly to improvement in productivity or cost of production. With wide variations in practical application, there are currently three types of nonindividual incentive gain-sharing programs in use: Scanlon, Rucker, and Improshare.

With *Scanlon,* workers receive a bonus when payroll costs per dollar of sales decline compared with a "start point" or historical norm. The operation of a Scanlon-type plan is tied to a single factor—labor costs—among the gamut of administrative and operational decisions that are made in managing an enterprise. Scanlon plans typically motivate employees to design more effective and efficient ways of performing their work.

Rucker gain-sharing plans are a variation of this approach. They pay a bonus based on a measurement of "value added," defined as sales less raw materials and services obtained from outside sources. Thus, if value is added using the same amount of, or less, labor, compared with an established historical norm, there is a payout to the employees. Rucker gives attention to savings generated in several different areas of operations, not just labor costs, but it does not automatically make adjustments for changes in technology or capital investment.

Improshare applies input/output factors (productivity) to each product produced. Standard hours of production are established; savings then relate to the comparison between actual hours utilized to produce the products and the pre-established standard. The bonus to employees is based on the percentage of hours "saved."

Each form of gain sharing offers a payout directly related to savings, either in direct cost or in reduced hours of production. The payout follows promptly, so that a close connection is felt between the personal involvement of the employees and their reward. Setting the historical norm against which to measure the progress and the payout becomes a delicate exercise, since it is this "start point" that affects the measurement of progress and, in turn, the size of the bonus. In a union setting, the details and operation of the gain-sharing program are a matter for collective bargaining. Ultimately, because the bonuses are tied to firm performance, the presence of gain sharing may induce workers to demand a role in decision making within the enterprise itself.[47]

Does "progress sharing"—either profit or gain sharing—work? According to exhaustive research, the answer seems to be yes.[48] In reviewing sixteen econometric studies on the relation between profit sharing and productivity (covering forty-two different samples of firms), Martin L. Weitzman and Douglas L. Kruse of Harvard University conclude that virtually none shows a statistically significant negative relationship between profits and productivity, and that in over 60 percent of the cases the relationship is positive. They find that, on average, firms with "average amounts of profit sharing" are 7.4 percent more productive than equivalent firms with no profit-sharing plan. The two economists conclude that "such estimates strike us as reasonable—they are neither so small as to be negligible, nor so large as to be implausible.[49]

But profit and gain sharing can have their downside. In the absence of a union such programs may breed the temptation to speed up production to an excessive pace or to forgo reasonable, protective work rules in the drive to reduce costs and make bonus payments more likely. In the unionized setting, however, the co-equal status of the parties and careful monitoring of negotiated contract provisions can serve to block such attempts at exploitation of the work force. Indeed, manipulative approaches by management will almost surely be recognized by employees and will often lead to resistance and an early demise of what otherwise could have been a mutually constructive program. Management, therefore, must play the game fairly and constructively, with no gimmickry. When it does, profit-sharing and gain-sharing plans can be used to buttress the nation's competitive position and simultaneously offer the possibility of income enhancement for the work force. But regardless of whether or not progress sharing is put into effect, it is the implementation of joint action processes such as those at Saturn that really counts.

CHAPTER 9

The Enterprise Compact

The biggest contribution the unions could make would be to perfect what they have now, stopping with the areas of authority they have already entered and setting the mind of business at rest.

—*Spokesperson for a steel company,*
President's National Labor-Management Conference (1945)

It is my opinion we are going to succeed, meanly or greatly, in the field of industrial relations, only in so far as we can widen the area of collective bargaining to include not only questions of wages but many other questions relating to management's conduct.

—*M. H. Hedges, Director of Research,*
International Brotherhood of Electrical Workers (1940)

Saturn, as pioneering and exciting a social development as any, could well be a harbinger of something even grander—regardless of whether the automobile itself succeeds in the marketplace. For this joint UAW-GM experience, along with a growing number of other employee involvement experiments in ownership, profit and gain sharing, and co-determination, teaches us how traditional management prerogatives and the old Workplace Contract can be challenged and supplanted by a labor-management system that is fully participatory. What the future holds we can only guess. But we believe the most plausible direction will be toward the development of an Enterprise Compact. At its core is the radical proposition that we should bid good riddance to the management-rights clause. In its place, the Enterprise Compact heralds joint labor-management action on *all* decisions of the firm, both workplace and strategic. It is the ultimate form of de-Taylorization.

The Enterprise Compact described here follows the natural evolutionary path that began with the "employee-at-will" concept only to be replaced by the traditional Track 1 Workplace Contract and, more recently, with the genesis of Track 2 and Track 3 developments— increased employee and union incursion into the accustomed set of management prerogatives. At each step in this evolution, there has been a fundamental rearrangement of rights and responsibilities between labor and management. The Enterprise Compact continues this process of reallocation, with the explicit goal of rebuilding American competitiveness and raising American living standards while offering greater employment security to the work force.

While there is nothing inevitable about the transformation of labor-management relations, we project that the expansion and challenge of global competition make something akin to the Enterprise Compact not only conceivable but necessary. Given what we have learned about the sources of productivity decline in the United States and the need for improved quality and enhanced innovation to compete in world markets, we contend that the Enterprise Compact can be the culmination of management's search for improved profitability as well as labor's search for employment security, better compensation, and an improved quality of work life. This chapter is devoted to outlining the fundamentals of the Enterprise Compact and enumerating its key provisions.

THE CHALLENGE TO MANAGEMENT
PREROGATIVES—AGAIN

As we noted in chapter 5, the expansion of labor's rights and—what amounts to the same thing—the contraction of management's prerogatives have always been the touchstone of employee-employer relations.

The end of World War II provided a particularly fertile period for debating the appropriate jurisdictions for both management and labor. No one better chronicled this brief era than Neil Chamberlain, the Yale labor relations expert whose wisdom we have consulted on various occasions in previous chapters. His seminal contribution, *The Union Challenge to Management Control,* is as relevant today as it was when it appeared in 1948.

In that turbulent time, at the very beginning of the postwar glory days, Chamberlain wrote:

> It is difficult to reach any conclusion but that union officials . . . have generally adopted a flexible and evolutionary approach to the question [of management rights], with the consequence that into any statements acknowledging and accepting the existence of managerial prerogatives must be read the addendum "as of this moment."[1]

This idea that only "as of this moment" was labor willing to draw a clear line between management's rights and labor's demands is clearly in evidence in the thinking of chief executives during this period. Ira Mosher, president of the National Association of Manufacturers (NAM), related this story to the *New York Times* just a few months after the end of World War II:

> We drew up a list of some thirty-odd specific acts, such as the determination of prices, accounting procedures, and so forth, which it seemed clear to us must be reserved to management. Labor refused to accept a single one, and we were told officially by one of the labor delegates that the reason they had refused was that at some future time labor may want to bring any one of these functions into the realm of collective bargaining.[2]

In the years to come, labor would indeed intrude into a broader array of management functions.[3] As one union representative told Chamberlain, "There is no field over which the union will renounce jurisdiction if the welfare of its members is directly concerned."[4] Over the next forty years, more and more issues affecting workers' welfare would be brought to the bargaining table, and unions would successfully win the right to negotiate them. In the late 1940s, one prescient union leader predicted what has come to pass. "Collective bargaining," he said, "is only a transitional phase, leading into cooperation programs where the union will work out business matters with the company continuously, and not merely in fields specified in the contract, not merely as adjudications of rights established annually."[5] We predict that many in the leadership of labor and in management will see the desirability of taking this next step.

RIGHTS AND RESPONSIBILITIES IN THE ENTERPRISE

The traditional Workplace Contract has always been excruciatingly detailed on the question of the rights and responsibilities of labor and, in general terms, of management. The entire purpose of the standard contract—covering scores of issues in addition to the management-rights clause—is to make it as clear as possible what labor can expect from management and vice versa.

The Wagner Act of 1935 placed few restrictions on what unions could demand in the contract. Nevertheless, out of the practice of collective bargaining, the general lines of rights and responsibilities were set. Essentially management retained the right to chart the destiny of the organization, to set general policies, and to provide for short- and long-range planning. While most management-rights clauses are nowhere near as explicit, the one contained in the 1983 agreement between the climate control division of the Snyder General Corporation and Local 459 of the Sheet Metal Workers International Association provides a notion of what specific prerogatives are left to management. This traditional management-rights clause was deliberately titled by the parties "management responsibilities":

> The Union recognizes that it is the Company's right to *direct, plan* and *control* its operations and to supervise and direct its work force, including the right to establish new jobs, increase or decrease the number of jobs, change materials or equipment, schedule and assign work to be performed, hire, rehire, recall, transfer, promote or lay off employees according to production needs, subject to the express limitations and provisions of this agreement.
>
> Further the Union recognizes that for the Company to conduct its business efficiently, its management does hold unto itself exclusive

responsibilities to manage the business. Among these responsibilities, but not intended as a wholly inclusive listing, are the following: to decide the *products* to be manufactured, the *methods* of manufacture, the *materials and equipment* to be used; to discontinue any product, material or method of production; to introduce *new equipment*, machinery or processes as well as to change or eliminate existing equipment, machinery or processes; to terminate, discharge and discipline for just cause and to *establish rules and maintain order and efficiency in its operations.*[6] [Italics added.]

The management "responsibilities" clause essentially leaves productivity, quality, and innovation exclusively in the hands of corporate executives. The union has responsibilities under the traditional agreement, too, but these are primarily to its membership, not the enterprise. Hence management is responsible for producing a product or service that can be sold profitably, while labor is responsible for making sure the company's unionized workers get a "fair" share of the profits and just and equitable treatment from management.

In contrast to this traditional division of responsibilities is what Chamberlain termed "functional integration."[7] The key aspect of this managerial structure is that *both* sides are responsible to each other, to the firm, and to the public. Essentially, both management and labor have joint responsibility to all stakeholders in the enterprise—executives and stockholders, workers and consumers alike. In the modern setting, this would mean that management would have to pay relatively more attention than is the current practice to issues of employment security—one of the overriding issues traditionally placed in labor's domain. In return, unions would have to take on greater responsibility for the viability and profitability of the company, traditionally in management's domain. Together, corporate executives and union officials, according to Chamberlain's "functional integration," have a responsibility to the public to provide quality products and services at competitive prices while protecting the environment and the community.

In practice, functional integration would turn the customary union contract on its head. After decades of focusing on productivity, quality, and innovation as their responsibility, management would turn more of its attention to employment security. After decades of focusing on employment security as one of its primary objectives, labor would turn more of its attention to finding ways to aid the collective enterprise in "working smarter"; designing, engineering, and building quality; and innovating in the areas of new products, new processes, marketing, advertising, purchasing, and accounting. Functional integration is the workplace equivalent of "walking in the other person's shoes."

THREE FUNCTIONS OF MANAGEMENT

There are three functions that must be managed in any enterprise.[8] The first is the *directive* function. At the pinnacle of any organization, there must be those who provide the enterprise with direction, purpose, objectives, and goals. Traditionally, this function has been the sole domain of top management. It is what goes on at the level of the Chief Executive Officer (CEO) and the Board of Directors. The second is the *administrative* function. Normally the president (as distinct from the CEO) is the company's chief administrator, responsible not for choosing objectives or goals but for choosing among alternative ways to accomplish them.[9] The third function is *executive* in nature. Executives, as their name implies, are responsible for seeing that the alternative chosen to reach a particular objective is carried out. Large firms often have an executive vice president or executive director who oversees this responsibility. In fact, virtually all supervisors in the bureaucratic firm, from the executive vice president down through the ranks all the way to the line supervisor, are engaged in this function. The typical triangle-shaped hierarchical organizational chart reflects this division of responsibility. It is a form of Taylorism, this time for the upper echelon.

In the old-style, traditionally managed nonunion firm, all of these functions are the responsibility of management and management alone. In firms with standard (Track 1) union contracts, the union has limited executive functions in the sense that the rules and regulations in the contract restrict the types of executive decisions management may make. Collectively bargained limits on management's otherwise unilateral right to make decisions are "executive" in nature as are the negotiated wages, benefits, and other conditions of employment. In firms operating under the expanded contract containing Track 2 and Track 3 language, individual employees and union officials have limited responsibility for administrative functions. How a particular job will be accomplished may be decided by a team of workers or by a joint union-management committee.

What remains absent from most contracts, particularly in non-union settings, is any labor input into the "directive" function. What is to be produced and where, what investments will be made, and how a product or service will be marketed, advertised, and priced remain decisions not simply for management but for top management—the CEO, the Board of Directors, and only occasionally the president and executive director. Under functional integration in its most extensive form—and, indeed, in the Enterprise Compact to be described here—all three functions are shared throughout the organization.

THE ESSENTIAL STRUCTURE OF AN ENTERPRISE COMPACT

Virtually all the employee involvement programs in the United States today in the nonunion setting exist outside of any written contractual document between management and its employees. Employee involvement is established unilaterally by management, sometimes with consultation with workers but never through formal negotiations with them. In the union setting, Track 2 direct employee involvement and Track 3 representative involvement are written explicitly into a formal agreement.

An Enterprise Compact, as we define it, is a formal, legally binding, negotiated contract between unionized employees and management. It would include the standard Track 1, 2, and 3 provisions, and in addition would set out the enterprise objectives to be met jointly by the union and the company, delineate the rights and responsibilities of both parties to the compact, and provide explicitly for a sharing of the directive function over virtually all of the strategic decisions made currently by management alone. Its very essence is the elimination of the management-prerogatives clause in favor of joint responsibility for the well-being of the enterprise and its assorted stakeholders. The Enterprise Compact—in structure—is more like the agreement at Saturn than it is like the highly detailed traditional

Workplace Contract. It defines the employees' economic benefits and certain conditions of work but, in other respects, it is a living document that lays out goals and general organizational structures and leaves many details to be developed outside the contract itself. It is not a blueprint but a constitution.

The goals set forth in the Enterprise Compact should be of the following type:

- Both parties to the agreement strive to produce a globally competitive firm in terms of maximum feasible productivity growth, Six Sigma quality, and constant rejuvenation through innovation.
- Both parties agree to strive for reasonable levels of profitability to be shared in an equitable fashion among all stakeholders in the enterprise.
- Both parties agree to strive for the highest level of employment security for all employees of the firm and the highest possible level of compensation compatible with productivity growth and the competitive position of the enterprise.
- Both parties agree to strive to provide the highest level of benefit to the larger community compatible with profitable, competitive operations. This includes sincere concern for the environment and the safety of the firm's products or services, reasonable contributions to the tax base of the community, and the provision of a reasonable amount of direct contributions to the community in terms of training, volunteer, and philanthropic efforts.

It is impossible to *maximize* all four of these goals, given the constraints that each places on the remaining three. Instead of profit maximizing, the Enterprise Compact implicitly requires profit "satisficing." The parties to the compact must decide jointly about the trade-off between short-term profits, long-term market share, returns to stockholders and workers, and how much of the company's profit will be spent on community projects.

In reality, these choices are even more strictly limited by the nature of the competitive market and by Wall Street. Higher short-term profits through higher prices constrain long-term market share, while wage increases well above productivity growth lead to either noncompetitive prices or profits too low to maintain ready access to capital funds. Still, within these limits, labor and management must wrestle over the division of the economic pie between shareholder dividends and wage-earner pay—as they implicitly do within the bounds of the standard collective-bargaining regime. Under an Enterprise Compact, management and labor work *jointly* to maximize the size of the enterprise pie; across the bargaining table they negotiate the slices of the pie that are allocated to each of the stakeholder interests in the enterprise. It is in everyone's interest to boost productivity (within the principles governing a fair and reasonable work standard), to improve quality, and to promote innovation, as long as everyone has a role to play in distributing the benefits that come from improved competitiveness and profitability and increased market share.

THE SEVEN-POINT ENTERPRISE COMPACT

Putting the Enterprise Compact into practice requires an explicit agreement between management and labor over the fundamental issues of productivity, compensation, quality, innovation, and the functional integration of the directive, administrative, and executive functions of management. To make this matter concrete, we have summarized the basic issues in the Enterprise Compact in terms of seven critical provisions. These are in addition to, or in some cases substitutions for, traditional Track 1, 2, and 3 language in the expanded Workplace Contract. The following list describes what might be a typical three-year compact in a major manufacturing industry with relatively good productivity prospects:

A Sample Seven-Point Enterprise Compact for a Manufacturing Firm with Relatively Good Productivity Prospects

1. The union and management agree to target as a mutual goal 6 percent *productivity improvement* in each year of the compact.
2. Workers shall receive annual 3 percent *wage increases* (total compensation) plus cost-of-living protection in each year of the compact.
3. The company and the union agree to reduce the *prices* of its

products by 1 percent to 3 percent each year, after appropriately accounting for the difference between labor productivity growth and overall increases in total labor plus nonlabor costs.

4. *Quality* of the product will be a "strikable" issue. If the quality of the product at any time in the manufacturing process does not meet joint labor-management standards, the union has the right to close down the operation until quality standards are met.

5. The company agrees to abide by a *no-layoff* provision. Any necessary reductions in force must be accomplished through normal attrition and jointly negotiated incentives for early retirement.

6. The company agrees to establish with the union a bonus compensation system based on *profit sharing* and *gain sharing*.

7. The company and the union agree that all strategic enterprise decisions will be made through *joint action*. These decisions include, but are not restricted to, product pricing, the purchasing of inputs, marketing and advertising, methods of production, the introduction of new technology, investments in new capital and products, and the subcontracting of production. The existing management-rights clause in the traditional contract shall be deleted.

In this example, the jointly agreed-upon annual productivity target of 6 percent is well above the national average. This is because the hypothetical firm we have in mind has a recent history of 4 percent to 5 percent annual efficiency improvement, and we can anticipate that the parties might set a goal 20 percent to 25 percent above this average. The target would vary in other companies, of course, depending on their recent experience.

The 3 percent annual wage increase (that is, 3 percent increase in wages plus benefits) is based on the notion of setting wage increments relative to long-term national productivity growth—a principle that, within the context of the Enterprise Compact, we endorse. With a productivity growth target of 6 percent and total labor compensation rising by 3 percent, our hypothetical firm is in the position to reduce its prices *relative* to the national rate of inflation by somewhere between 1 percent and 3 percent. Firms that can expect to increase their productivity by a smaller percentage would be expected to meet the same wage increment, but would have to increase their relative prices or reduce their relative profits accordingly. Given profit and/or gain sharing as part of the Enterprise Compact, all the stakeholders in the firm have a strong incentive to boost productivity.

Let's explore each of the provisions of the Enterprise Compact in detail.

PROVISION 1: PRODUCTIVITY IMPROVEMENT

By controlling the "means and methods" of production, management has traditionally controlled the key factors that determine productivity. Under the Enterprise Compact, the tables are turned part way. Labor agrees to share responsibility for meeting productivity targets that are jointly developed. When one of us used the example in our seven-point list in a joint labor-management seminar at the Trenton, New Jersey, Fisher Guide division of General Motors—a plant that builds manual and power-assisted seat adjustment mechanisms and exterior trim for GM cars—our 6 percent productivity provision was met not with apprehension but with self-satisfied amusement. In its 1987 contract, Local 731 of the UAW and the management of the plant had placed at the very beginning of their contract "Document 1," which pledged management and the union to improve efficiency by *12* percent each year. The parties to the agreement noted that this increase could be achieved only through the "concept of continuous improvement"— part of the gospel spread by W. Edwards Deming. The Local 731 contract states:

> Continuous improvement is an ongoing customer driven process that enables all personnel to contribute to achieving our primary business goals of quality, cost, and delivery. We jointly recognize that all elements of the business—both the processes and personnel—can be improved. Through the concept of continuous improvement, we will strive for improvement relative to improved quality, improved methods and processes, reduced cost, improved efficiency, and the elimination of waste. This improvement concept must be instituted at all levels of the plant organization.[10]

At the time of the Trenton visit, the company and the union were in the third year of their agreement. They had met the 12 percent target in the first two years and were proudly on their way to meeting it in the third.

At other facilities where we advanced the provisions of the Enterprise Compact, in and outside the auto industry, the vision of a 6 percent productivity goal was met with skepticism. More than one worker wanted to know how to meet such a target without simple speedup. The answer we gave is that in virtually every shop and office, there are hundreds of small ways to improve productivity. When added together, they can result in the kind of efficiency gains witnessed at Trenton. In fact, one of the ways to improve productivity is not by working faster but by slowing down. A typical final auto assembly line runs at about sixty vehicles an hour. It is not unusual for six to eight of these sixty to be diverted to a repair bay to fix problems that were not caught during the course of the long trip down the assembly line. Chevrolets in the repair area are repaired in the same way Rolls-Royces are built—by hand and one at a time. This practice automatically reduces productivity. And the greater the amount of repair work, the greater the reduction in efficiency. At a slightly lower line speed, the number of "perfect" cars coming off the line is higher, and overall productivity can be enhanced.

Productivity can also be raised through the introduction of new technology and by changing work rules and production procedures. Under the full provisions of the Enterprise Compact with the no-layoff clause, labor has an unambiguously positive stake in higher productivity and therefore is less reticent to accept advanced techniques or to alter work rules—as long as it does not lead to unacceptable changes in the pace of work or increase the risk of accident or injury. A "productivity partnership" such as at Trenton is thus born, providing the possibility of increased competitiveness through stable or even reduced prices. At 6 percent a year, the efficiency of an establishment can be boosted by a compound rate of almost 20 percent over three years—sufficient to permit a firm to price its products aggressively against most import competition.

PROVISION 2: WAGE INCREASE + COLA

The second provision of the Enterprise Compact entails nothing new at all. It is merely an adaptation of the wage formula first laid out in the 1948 UAW-GM contract by Charles Wilson and Alfred Sloan (recall the discussion in chapter 2). With a 6 percent productivity increase each year in our hypothetical firm, the enterprise is in a good position to offer a 3 percent annual improvement factor (AIF) tied to national productivity growth. For reasons connected to the wage/price/profit/productivity nexus introduced in chapter 4, setting the wage package increase below the rate of productivity growth can provide the basis for an aggressive pricing strategy to rebuild market share.

Cost-of-living adjustments (COLA) should be maintained so that workers can feel secure that they are not putting their future real standard of living in jeopardy by buying into the compact. One revision in the COLA clause might be considered, however. When the clause was first introduced in the late 1940s, the United States was generally immune to price "shocks" emanating from external sources such as OPEC. By the 1970s, this was no longer true. In 1973 and again in 1979 when OPEC forced oil prices higher, workers with COLAs in their contracts were substantially protected against the price hikes. The problem was that the external price shock turned into a price-wage spiral that quickly led to double-digit inflation. Higher oil prices fed into a higher measured Consumer Price Index (CPI), which triggered COLA increases. These increases had to be covered by management, so it raised its product prices. These higher prices then fed back into the CPI, leading to round after round of "internally" generated inflation. The 1973 oil-initiated price-wage spiral was halted in 1975 only by a major recession. The 1979 OPEC-initiated spiral was finally tamed only through the Federal Reserve's triple whammy of skyrocketing interest rates—a very high price to pay for coaxing inflation back into the genie's bottle.

An alternative is for the government to design a formula for the CPI that treats external price shocks as a foreign-imposed tax rather than as a domestically generated price increase. The COLA clause could be rewritten so that such external shocks were excluded from the computation of the price adjustment factor, making it possible to avoid another round of externally initiated price-wage spirals. In Sweden with its national wage-setting policies, this was essentially done in 1973 and 1979, saving that country from the ravages of spiraling inflation experienced by the United States during the same period. Sweden and other countries took a single price "hit" without succumbing to an inflation spiral.

PROVISION 3: PRICE POLICY

Joint action over productivity improvement becomes a new responsibility for labor under Provision 1 of the Enterprise Compact. Giving it a voice in the pricing strategy of the enterprise endows it with a new right. Clearly, if productivity advances are simply taken in profits rather than attempts to secure long-term market share, labor has little to gain from exercising its responsibility to help boost efficiency. To counter this, workers must have the ability to influence pricing policy with an eye toward meeting global competition.

That labor should demand some voice in this area is scarcely a novel idea.[11] In 1947 and again in 1948, the UAW offered "to drop its wage demands in return for a substantial roll-back in prices."[12] A decade later, in the summer of 1957, Walter Reuther as president of the UAW dispatched a letter to the presidents of General Motors, Ford, and Chrysler specifically proposing that "each corporation reduce prices on 1958 models to levels averaging at least $100 below the prices for comparable 1957 models." If they did so, the UAW promised that it would "give full consideration to the effect of such reductions on each company's financial position in the drafting of our 1958 demands and in negotiations."[13] In the heady days of the first postwar generation, with no import competition on the horizon, the companies refused even to discuss the issue.

But taking the Wilson-Sloan AIF wage-setting principle to its logical conclusion suggests that it is also a good principle for setting prices. By relying on the wage/price/profit/productivity equation, increased productivity should permit firms to increase wages and profits without raising prices. If productivity can be boosted by *more* than wages during a contract cycle, then firms are in a position to lower prices without reducing profits. In the hypothetical example used here, with productivity rising by a healthy 6 percent (Provision 1) and wages rising by only 3 percent (Provision 2), there is ample room to reduce prices by an amount that reflects this reduction in unit labor costs.

A few caveats are in order, however. Since for any single firm, wages are only a fraction of total costs, prices cannot be reduced by the entire difference between the productivity growth rate and the wage increase—if other costs rise. This requires setting prices that are prorated between internal labor costs and other business expenses. Of course, if other costs of production decline—for example, the cost of energy or the price of purchased goods and services—pricing should take these lowered costs into consideration. Moreover, if somehow the entire economy adopted the provisions of the Enterprise Compact, it would be possible for every firm to cut prices because the costs of purchased inputs to *every* firm would fall as a result of lower unit labor costs throughout the economy. Lower prices would percolate from one industry to the next.[14]

Of course, even if total costs to the individual firm were to decline by 3 percent, it would take a deliberate act on the part of the firm to cut its prices by this amount. As noted in chapter 5, profit-maximizing firms might choose, regardless of their new lower costs, to maintain prices in an effort to boost short-term profits. In contrast, the union would likely have a strong interest in maximizing market share in order to boost employment security. Therefore, from the union's perspective, the entire cost savings should go toward reducing prices, while management might not want to see any of it used in this way. Under the Enterprise Compact, the union gains the right to play a role in this matter, with prices being negotiated along with the productivity target and the employee compensation package. What precise role labor should have in price setting, and how final decisions on these matters are made, are tricky questions, ones that we shall return to later in this chapter.

PROVISION 4: QUALITY AS A "STRIKABLE" ISSUE

As we noted in chapter 3, in many U.S. industries, products are simply priced out of the market. Imports may or may not be of equal or better quality than U.S. brands, but the import price is attractive to the price-conscious consumer. Apparel, textiles, and running shoes are good examples. In some of these cases, foreign costs are so much lower than those in the United States because of extraordinary differences in labor costs that it is virtually impossible to compete on price. In other cases (automobiles, photocopiers), price does make a difference. Eliminating "sticker shock" through lower prices could entice American consumers back to domestic brands. Provision 3 is aimed directly at these particular markets.

In most cases, however, price competition alone is hardly sufficient to win customers. While a competitive price may encourage consumers to take a second look at American goods, questionable quality often makes the difference between opting for the U.S.-made product or the competition's. Sony TVs sell at a premium in the United States precisely because they are judged to have better picture and sound quality and to be highly reliable.[15] As we noted in chapter 4, Six Sigma quality is still a goal that eludes virtually all American firms. It is precisely because quality is so important to competitiveness that labor must have a voice in setting quality standards and making certain that they are maintained. In the final analysis, workers should be able to overrule the supervisor who orders imperfect goods shipped in order to meet production targets. Stopping the assembly line—in essence, "striking" over quality—should be part and parcel of the Enterprise Compact.

As we noted in chapter 6, a large number of firms are already moving in this direction. At the GM-Toyota NUMMI plant, individual workers have the right to stop the line at any time to solve an assembly problem, without invoking disciplinary action. According to interviews conducted by Berkeley economists Claire Brown and Michael Reich, who have studied the plant, the line is stopped for an average of a half-hour per eight-hour shift.[16] Quality circles and quality networks are additional mechanisms used to pursue "perfect" production.

Yet quality begins well before assembly. For a product to be successful, quality must be designed and engineered into it. As Deming is fond of telling his audiences: "Routine 100 percent inspection to improve quality is equivalent to planning for defects, acknowledgment that the process has not the capability required for the specifications. Inspection to improve quality is too late, ineffective, costly."[17] Labor must be involved in more than simply "striking" over poor quality. It must play a critical role at every level of design and engineering so that once the product (or service) is ready for production, the "pieces fit right" and the whole works as it should. In this sense, quality as a strikable issue should mean that, properly implemented, it is seldom needed. With individual production employees responsible for "perfect" production in the plant through Track 2 mechanisms, and the union working on quality through Track 3 joint action committees at all levels of conception, design, and engineering, it should ultimately be possible to reach Six Sigma quality. By negotiating joint quality standards and boosting them over time, the union and corporate management not only set the benchmarks against which employees can decide whether "stopping the line" is in order, but they move the enterprise along the quality dimension from lower-level Sigma standards to higher ones. Negotiating the future involves, among many other things, negotiating quality.

PROVISION 5: EMPLOYMENT SECURITY

Up to this point, we have discussed the responsibilities for labor in the areas of enhanced productivity, quality, and, by inference, innovation in both product and process. In parallel fashion, management's compelling responsibility lies in the area of employment security. If workers are to help boost productivity, they must be assured that their efforts will not pay off in terms of making themselves redundant. Management must be willing to accept the equivalent of a "no-layoff" clause as its contribution to the Enterprise Compact.

The importance of job security was underlined by Ronald Henkoff, writing in *Fortune* magazine in early 1990:

> In each of the past three years, according to surveys by the American Management Association, roughly a third of American companies have cut their payrolls.
>
> Downsizing has become an opiate for many companies. Administered in repeated doses, it can hurt product quality, alienate customers, and actually cut productivity growth. It can foster an organization so preoccupied with bean counting, so anxious about where the ax will fall next, that employees become narrow-minded, self-absorbed, and risk-averse.
>
> More than half the 1,468 restructured companies surveyed by the Society for Human Resource Management reported that employee productivity either stayed the same or deteriorated after layoff.

Henkoff concludes that, "contrary to the Duchess of Windsor's famous dictum, you *can* be too thin."[18]

As we noted in chapter 6, a number of companies have based their employment policies on a no-layoff practice. Hallmark and Lincoln Electric, to name but two, profess that their employment security policies have been the centerpiece of their good employer-employee relations. As Robert Levering suggests in his book, *A Great Place to Work: What Makes Some Employers So Good (and Most So Bad),* a company's long-term commitment to its employees—making a company "just like a family"—is one of the few factors that contribute mightily to a strong reciprocal commitment of workers to their employers.[19]

When firms like Digital Equipment are finally forced by competitive pressures to reduce their work force, they have often attempted to do this by normal attrition and by monetary inducements to early retirement rather than outright layoffs. Under the Enterprise Compact as we envision it, these would constitute the main forms of work-force reduction, with the actual structure negotiated by the parties. For short-term or seasonal reductions, the parties might negotiate a program similar to the automobile industry's Supplemental Unemployment Benefit (SUB) system. The firm would agree to put aside on an ongoing basis a stipulated amount of money per employee hour of work that would fund a SUB program. Then, when business conditions warranted, workers would be paid out of the SUB fund while they are out of work. The actual size of the fund and the formula for disbursement would be negotiated by the parties.

The 1990 GM-UAW contract expands on the SUB formula substantially, by adding employment security to income security.[20] Under the contract, GM agreed that no worker would be subject to more than thirty-six weeks of "volume-related" layoff during the three-year contract. Thus, even if there is a downturn in market demand, when the thirty-six-week limit is exhausted, GM must recall the worker. If no job is available, the employee must be placed in the joint UAW-GM Job Opportunity Bank Security (JOBS) program, with full pay and benefits. Workers in the JOBS bank may be assigned to an array of nonproduction tasks at GM or loaned out to community groups for employment at GM's expense. GM has pledged in excess of $4 billion to support this program along with SUB.

Of course, there is always the latent possibility of catastrophic downturns in a firm's fortunes that lead to inevitable layoffs. An Enterprise Compact no-layoff provision should have an escape clause to handle such extreme cases. This can be done by negotiating in advance what constitutes a "catastrophic" circumstance and setting aside funds for special involuntary severance payments, job-placement services, and training and relocation allowances. Even the catastrophic circumstance, except so-called acts of God (for example, floods or hurricanes), should permit firms to provide affected employees with ample advance notice of impending layoff. All of this can be negotiated as part of the new pact between labor and management.

PROVISION 6: PROFIT AND GAIN SHARING

The Enterprise Compact need not incorporate any form of employee compensation beyond regular wages and benefits. As we noted in the last chapter, however, there is convincing evidence that profit-sharing and gain-sharing plans make good economic sense. Along this line, Levine and Tyson have identified four characteristics of a firm's industrial relations system that are likely to be associated with higher productivity: job security; measures to build group cohesiveness; guaranteed individual rights; and profit sharing and gain sharing.[21] They note that profit or gain sharing on the one hand and participation on the other are essentially symbiotic. Workers who share responsibility for improving productivity or profits naturally want to share in the rewards of their efforts. Workers who benefit directly from profit or gain sharing want to have a voice in strategic decisions that determine the level of profits or productivity gains.

In negotiating a profit-sharing and/or gain-sharing plan as part of the Enterprise Compact, the parties must address whether the bonus should be based on profits or productivity gains—or both. Should a bonus be paid to workers who help boost the efficiency of the firm, even if that improvement does not pay off in terms of higher profits because of external factors? Conversely, should workers be paid a bonus if profits increase despite no improvements in productivity or quality? Such philosophical issues have no set answers, and the empirical literature does not unambiguously suggest that one is better than the other for boosting productivity. The formula for bonuses is best left as a matter of negotiation between the parties to the compact.

PROVISION 7: JOINT ACTION

Joint action forms the very centerpiece of the Enterprise Compact, transforming the fundamental decision-making structure of the firm. If labor is to assume greater responsibility for productivity, quality, and innovation and receive guarantees of employment security, it is necessary for labor to play a much greater role in the strategic decision making of the enterprise.

Moving toward decision making at the highest level of the firm is part of the evolutionary process we have traced in previous chapters. The traditional Workplace Contract, operating primarily on Track 1, introduced joint decision making over such workplace issues as wages, benefits, and conditions of work. Management was forced through union pressure—and ultimately the strike weapon—to cede a portion of its authority to specific contract language granting certain rights to employees. Track 2 provided for direct employee input in workplace decisions, particularly over issues of work organization, quality, and the methods and processes of production or the provision of services. Finally, Track 3 expanded the issues over which the union held joint authority to such matters as the structure and administration of employee assistance programs, education and training, health and safety, and quality improvement. Joint action concerning strategic decision making goes beyond Tracks 1, 2, and 3 to cover virtually *all* decisions made by the enterprise at every level—on the plant floor, at the division level, and at the level of the company's Board of Directors.

An explicit union role in strategic matters is not totally without precedent. The 1941 collective-bargaining agreement between New York City apparel firms and the International Ladies' Garment Workers Union (ILGWU) provided for a collaborative role between the manufacturers and union leaders in improving the efficiency of the industry—even to the extent that the union did its own testing of firm-level productivity. The union demanded this provision in order to assist companies in improving their productivity so that the ILGWU could recoup for its members wages lost during the depression.[22] It even sent its own industrial engineers into a plant to explore various ways to improve productivity.

A modern reincarnation of the ILGWU joint action provision can be found in the Textile/Clothing Technology Corp., known as $(TC)^2$.[23] As in the 1941 instance, the impetus for $(TC)^2$ in 1980 did not come from the apparel or textile industry, but from the union—in this case from Murray H. Finley, then president of the Amalgamated Clothing and Textile Workers Union (ACTWU). Searching for a way to improve productivity in the apparel industry so as to stem the import tide, Finley teamed up with three men's suit manufacturers with which his union had contracts—Hartmarx (formerly Hart, Shaffner and Marx), Palm Beach, and Greif—as well as with the menswear division of the textile giant, Burlington Industries. Former U.S. Secretary of Labor John Dunlop acted as adviser. Finley reasoned that only by automating the apparel shops could his union members remain globally competitive. Automation would no doubt reduce the need for workers in plants that adopted new technologies, but the long-term loss in employment could be even more drastic if automation were not implemented.

Finley found it difficult to convince additional apparel firms to join (TC)², for they always had the opportunity to move offshore to obtain a lower-wage work force. But this was not true for the large domestic textile firms that provided the raw material for the clothiers. They were susceptible to Finley's automation argument, and a number of them— including the predominantly nonunion producers J. P Stevens, Du Pont, and the Russell Corp.—joined Burlington Industries in this endeavor.[24] In one meeting in 1983 with Finley and the CEOs of these firms in attendance, (TC)² raised $5 million for technology research. Draper Labs at MIT and the Singer Co. were selected to receive contracts to develop automated sewing systems and automatic cloth-transfer machines. By 1986, the joint union-management–sponsored technology corporation had established the National Apparel Technology Center in Raleigh, North Carolina, and was receiving matching grant funding from the federal government for research and training. While (TC)² is not written into any ACTWU contract, the continuing presence of the union on its board assures that many of the new technologies in the apparel and textile industries will be the product of joint union-management action.

On a much smaller scale, innovative production systems are being designed and implemented through collaborative union-management efforts. In 1987, for example, the UAW local at the Trenton, New Jersey, GM seat mechanism and trim facility—the local that set 12 percent productivity targets in its collective-bargaining agreement— won in its local contract the right to establish "joint forward planning" meetings with top management to work out any and all matters related to pursuing the goal of "continuous improvement." The joint forward planning meetings between management and labor developed the "synchronous," or "just-in-time" manufacturing system now being used in the plant, implemented team concept throughout the facility, and jointly instituted a statistical quality-control process toward a zero-defect goal.[25]

While these are all rightly characterized as falling within Track 3, the parties have left open the possibility of dealing with virtually any issue related to productivity and quality. This could cover relations with suppliers, marketing the division's products to other GM divisions and other companies, making innovations in current products, and even generating new ones. In fact, at the Oklahoma City GM assembly plant, the local union is already involved in reviewing vendor quality and price information, and it plays a meaningful role in selecting which vendors obtain contracts.[26] Finally, at the Fisher Guide Coldwater Road Plant in Michigan, the UAW local union won the right to have five "hourly advisers" work at the business-unit level of the company (the top rung of in-plant management). These advisers work on a one-to-one basis with the plant's business managers and are privy to all R&D and product-design conferences held at the divisional level. The Work in America Institute calls this the "elevation of the process of jointness to the higher levels of plant management."[27]

Under the Enterprise Compact, joint strategic planning goes beyond the plant or even the division level. It reaches all the way to the level of the CEO and covers the full range of issues that any chief executive must address. As the following list makes clear, these issues cover not only strategic decisions directly concerning employment and compensation but financial matters, pricing policies, and relations with suppliers, trade associations, the government, and consumers. From labor's perspective, all of these are critical to employment security, and from management's perspective, full cooperation and input from labor are the surest route to meeting productivity, quality, and innovation targets consistent with profitable operation.

Strategic Joint Action Functions in the Enterprise Compact

I. Finance: Control over Money
   1. Raising of necessary capital
   2. Dividend policy
   3. Retained earnings policy
   4. Accounting practices
   5. Budgeting

II. Personnel: Control over Workers
   1. Type of personnel
   2. Size of work force
   3. Hiring, dismissal, allocation, promotion, and discipline of work force
   4. Wages, hours, and benefits
   5. Health, safety, and social conditions

III. Procurement: Control over Materials
1. Purchase of raw material
2. Organization of suppliers and subcontractors

IV. Production of products or services
1. Design and engineering
2. Types of machinery and equipment utilized
3. Job content
4. Methods of operation
5. Rates of operation
6. Standards of quality
7. Maintenance operations

V. Distribution of products or services
1. Quantities of production
2. Sales policies
3. Distribution organization
4. Marketing
5. Advertising
6. Inventory policy
7. Credit policies

VI. Enterprise Coordination or "Cabinet" Activities
1. Determination of product line
2. Internal company organization
3. Selection of key administrative and executive personnel
4. Research and development policy
5. Expansion or contraction of capacity decisions
6. Plant location
7. Prices of products
8. Trade, industry, and government relations
9. Public relations
10. Consumer relations

Source: Adapted from Neil Chamberlain, *The Union Challenge to Management Control* (New York: Harper and Brothers, 1948), pp. 46–47.

IMPLEMENTING THE ENTERPRISE COMPACT

How the Enterprise Compact can be put into practice remains an open question. The experiences at Saturn, at NUMMI, with (TC)², and the plant-level joint action projects between the UAW and General Motors point in one direction: joint committees operating at the plant, division, and enterprise levels. At the plant level, it is possible to expand the activities of Track 3 joint committees to cover nearly all of the decisions made by plant managers and their close associates. This covers such matters as plant layout, introduction of new technology, and relations with suppliers, other company divisions, and the local community. At the division level, the union and the company can create joint committees to make strategic decisions about product design, product engineering, marketing, accounting, advertising, and distribution. And, finally, at the corporate level, union representatives can join the Board of Directors in an American-style form of "co-determination"—with the union playing a role in making key decisions over what products or services will be produced, what prices will be charged, what investments will be made, where subcontracting will be used, whether expansion or contraction in capacity is warranted, and ultimately whether to merge, acquire, or even go out of business.

Such extensive empowerment of labor almost always sets off alarms. For those who do not automatically dismiss the idea, two questions invariably arise. One concerns the degree of worker and union expertise necessary to deal with such complex issues as pricing policy, finance, or the introduction of new technology. Workers and union representatives raise this issue themselves. More often, of course, management does. The second question has to do with the nature of the decision-making process envisioned in the compact. Just how democratic should the process be? In the case where consensus cannot be reached on a particular matter between management and labor, who is empowered to make the final decision? While both of these issues— expertise and empowerment—contain thorny problems that will have to be worked out in practice, there are some guidelines that may be of help.

On worker and union expertise, one should take note of the fact that workers and union representatives possess a great deal of knowledge about production methods, quality improvement, and needed innovation at the plant level. The hundreds of firms with successful employee involvement and joint action programs have demonstrated this to the satisfaction of both managers and union representatives. The nearly universal absence of any meaningful participation in strategic policy does pose a problem, however. To overcome this deficit, companies and unions might create joint training programs for selected groups of workers and union representatives. "Retooling" union officials, for example, to be "multicrafted" in both the grievance process *and* the fundamentals of double-entry accounting could be done by sending them to a local community college. Some might even pursue an MBA.

Similarly, workers and union officials can learn the basics of pricing policy, investment strategy, and technology innovation. Of course, in any one enterprise only a few workers and representatives need be trained in these sophisticated skills, so the overall expense in terms of dollars and time is limited. In addition, many of these skills need not be mastered by workers or union representatives themselves. The union can hire consultants to represent their interests, as many do today for the purpose of negotiating collective-bargaining agreements or as specialists in finance, actuary science, occupational safety and health, time study, or law. In a relatively brief period of time, the combination of internal training, outside classroom experience, and the hiring of consultants could bring a union up to speed in many of the intricacies of strategic decision making.[28] Moreover, in many cases managers themselves have no more expertise than workers or union representatives. They, too, rely on internal or external consultants to provide them with alternatives and cost-benefit analyses so that they can choose among various policies based on their own beliefs about where the enterprise should be headed. Bringing union representatives into the loop does not markedly change the need for expertise.

Empowerment is by far the more challenging problem. Negotiating the details of democratic decision making within the firm is at best a delicate matter. In this case, we can provide only a few guidelines. First, experience along the more limited Tracks 2 and 3 suggests that most decisions at the plant, division, and perhaps even enterprise levels can be made by consensus. In the introduction of a major new technology at a particular plant, for example, one could envision either a temporary or a permanent joint committee comprising the plant manager, a number of engineers from the parent company, and a small number of union representatives who would consider the technology alternatives available to them. The committee would be responsible for identifying the best and worst attributes of each technology and the costs associated with implementing the various alternatives. From such a study, consensus might arise with little trouble—particularly given employment security and gain sharing.

But what happens when, after full deliberation, there is no consensus? One possibility is that the final decision still rests with management. Labor has had full consultation, but defers to management when a disagreement cannot be resolved—not unlike the president of the U.S. Senate (the vice president of the United States) casting the deciding vote when there is a tie vote in the chamber. An alternative is for both sides to submit their positions to a jointly selected mediator who attempts to forge a consensus. Still a third possibility is interest arbitration, whereby management and union representatives to the joint committee agree to submit the case to a neutral arbitrator or arbitration panel which is empowered to make a binding decision. Setting strict time limits on each step in the process, once consensus cannot be reached, can expedite the mediation or arbitration process enormously.[29]

At the highest level of the firm—the corporate Board of Directors—labor will have representation. How many seats on the board is open to negotiation. Recall that, at Chrysler, the union had just one member; at Weirton Steel, the number was three out of fourteen. At Western Airlines, before its merger into Delta, each of the four unions representing employees at the company was allotted one seat on the Board.[30] An "outsider" with both extensive experience in the international labor movement and membership on other corporate boards was selected as the Teamsters' representative. The airline pilots union chose a rank-and-file member with hands-on knowledge of airline operations. The remaining two unions, the Air Transport Employees (ATE) and the Association of Flight Attendants (AFA), appointed their own presidents to round out labor's participation on the Western Airlines Board. In a crisis, the union board members made a number of important contributions to the operation of the firm. But in the end, minority membership on the Board could not prevent the company from being merged into Delta, resulting in the termination of many of the EI innovations put in place by the expanded Board as well as of three of the four bargaining units.[31] Co-determination in this instance, as well as others, is no panacea. Whether introducing joint participation before Western Airlines had reached a critical juncture would have saved the company is anyone's guess.

EXPANDING THE ENTERPRISE COMPACT THROUGHOUT THE ECONOMY

We do not want to give the impression, by our examples, that the Enterprise Compact is or should be restricted to the private sector or just manufacturing. Expanding it to the private, nonmanufacturing sector requires little alteration in the basic formulation of the seven-point program. Hotels and restaurants, hospitals, banks, and construction sites can all adapt the compact to their own circumstances, adjusting the productivity, wage, pricing, and quality targets to their own particular settings.

The compact is applicable in the public sector as well—witness the UHPA in Hawaii—although in this case there is the further complication of legislative control over the "enterprise." Usually there are laws stipulating the nature of public services (such as welfare or mental health services) that place constraints on what management and labor are permitted to do in "directing" an agency or public office. In this case, labor simply suffers under the same constraints as traditional public management. The difference under the Enterprise Compact, as opposed to the traditional Workplace Contract, is that labor has a direct voice in writing the specific regulations that govern how policies are put into practice. This is true in social work and in schools, in prisons and in highway projects. In primary and secondary schools, for example, the union might play a direct role along with the school board in establishing new educational innovations. In Kentucky, where many of the teachers are represented by the National Education Association (NEA), a sweeping school reform instituted in 1990 "involves a dramatic shift of power to teachers," according to *Business Week*.[32] The new Kentucky law requires every school to form a teacher-dominated governing council that can override a wide range of state rules and even union-established practices. The councils have the right to alter class size, to rearrange or extend the school day, and to decide what new staff to hire. In a case of dramatic role reversal, the Kentucky plan relegates school boards and principals, who are outnumbered on the councils, to advisory standing.[33] Whether the Kentucky experiment will work to improve the schools, to boost grades and attendance, and to reduce dropout rates is not yet known, but it should provide an interesting case of worker empowerment in the public sector for years to come.

THE FUTURE OF THE ENTERPRISE COMPACT

While the seven-point Enterprise Compact described here will no doubt appear radical and even ominous to those who have no experience beyond the traditional work organization, we believe that over time its precepts will become commonplace. In the same way that management was once appalled at the thought of labor demanding the right to bargain collectively over wages and working conditions, management today is often dubious of our prescription for a productivity/ quality/employment security compact based on full joint participation and functional integration at all levels of the firm. Still, in the same way that management came to abide—and, in some cases, even to support—collective bargaining under the requirements of the law, we believe management will come to see the Enterprise Compact as an instrument for producing mutual gains for stockholders and workers alike. Similarly, unions that may be loath to take on more responsibility will learn from experience the essential importance of their involvement in the policy-making aspects of managing the enterprise as the path to serve the interests of their members more effectively.

The provisions of the compact are by no means set in stone. Through experimentation in many settings, we expect them to be honed and improved. As MIT's Thomas Kochan puts it: "It is clear there is no single best way to achieve participation in strategic decisions. . . . What we need is a period of experimentation and learning."[34] One hopes that in the process, managers, workers, and union representatives will increasingly embrace the concept of joint action at all levels of the enterprise; that they will separate personalities from problems; that they will focus on their basic mutual interests, not entrenched positions; that they will generate a variety of possible outcomes before making final decisions; and that they will insist on objective standards as the basis of what is to be accomplished.[35] More or less—and for better, not worse—parties to traditional collective bargaining are learning these lessons and are in a position to apply them to decision making at the strategic level of the firm. Given the exigencies of global competition and the need for America to improve dramatically its productivity, quality, and innovation performance, the Enterprise Compact may prove to be precisely the social instrument for meeting these challenges.

CHAPTER 10

Creating a Benign Climate for the New Labor-Management Accord

I am not an advocate for frequent changes in laws and institutions. But laws and institutions must go hand in hand with the progress of the human mind. As that becomes more developed, more enlightened, as new discoveries are made, new truths discovered and manners and opinions changed with the change of circumstances, institutions must advance also to keep pace with the times.

—Thomas Jefferson

We began this book by nostalgically recounting the "glory days"—the postwar era marked by American economic hegemony, profitable enterprise, and a steadily rising standard of living, built in part on the traditional Workplace Contract. It has now been nearly twenty years since the beginning of the "silent depression."[1] Since 1973, average wages have declined and family income has stagnated as American industry and its work force struggle to maintain their competitiveness in global markets.

To end the silent depression, we have argued that U.S. industry must boost its productivity, improve the quality of its products and services, and find ways to become more innovative in both the goods we produce and the manner in which we produce them. None of this will come about by a quick technological fix. We are convinced that only a fundamental restructuring of the nature of labor-management relations will do the trick. We must unleash the full potential of the work force to concentrate on producing in the most efficient manner possible nothing less than the highest quality, most innovative goods and services on earth. Throughout much of the economy, current employee-employer relations provide few incentives and even fewer avenues for this to take place.

We have suggested in the preceding chapters that there is potentially great promise in the employee involvement experiments that have proliferated during the past two decades. The very best of them have led to increased productivity and quality while boosting job satisfaction and security. None of them, however—not even the grand experiment in Spring Hill, Tennessee—has crossed the threshold to the full Enterprise Compact that we believe holds at least one important answer to ending the silent depression. Transforming labor relations from the adversarial system of the Workplace Contract to the cooperative system of the Enterprise Compact may be just the metamorphosis that the American production system needs.

Yet fostering the development of a labor-management compact capable of producing an American economic renaissance requires a benign socioeconomic climate—something we have not seen for at least a decade. Such a climate requires encouragement from both labor and management in the private sector and nurturance from government.

UNION VERSUS MANAGEMENT: BURYING THE HATCHET

The first step toward an Enterprise Compact demands a profound change in attitude on the part of both union leadership and corporate executives toward one another—and toward the work force. In some industries this has already begun, but in too many others tempers have flared on both sides of the fence. Management has traditionally viewed the union as something to be tolerated at best, more often to be repelled. Union leaders, in turn, have often viewed management as the enemy. For both it amounts to: "What's good for them must be bad for us."

Corporate attitudes have hardened in recent years, in part, because executives under the threat of global competition and deregulation realize the need for flexibility and continual adjustments to survive. They view the traditional Workplace Contract as overly rigid and, in the words of the Harvard law professor Paul Weiler, "containing provisions that are as outmoded as the production techniques in use when the terms were first negotiated."[2] They view unions as inflexible, concerned only with protecting their members' short-term interests even at the expense of the viability of the firm.

Part of this *is* a legitimate concern, but most of it reflects a stereotype of union behavior that, if ever true, is certainly at variance with most union behavior today. Still, this misconception has often led management to use anti-union tactics that flagrantly flaunt the law. Weiler points out that in the 1950s, when union organizing was still in full flower, the National Labor Relations Board (NLRB) annually secured a right of reinstatement for nearly one thousand workers whom it found had been illegally fired for supporting a union and its activities. In the 1980s, with much less organizing under way and a less sympathetic labor board, the rate hit ten thousand cases a year. Weiler goes on to note that

> though American business grudgingly tolerated unions for a quarter century after World War II, a large majority of American firms now make it a basic aim of corporate strategy to remain union-free in their domestic, if not foreign, operations. This strategy influences their patterns of investment, their location decisions, the design of their employment package, even the types of employees that they interview and hire.[3]

Hard times reinforce anti-management as well as anti-union animus. In the face of deindustrialization and the displacement of millions of jobs, union leaders have naturally moved to protect their members' rights under existing contracts. A change in the language of labor agreements that seems to add to management's flexibility with respect to its disposition of labor seems often to be a concession that cannot be politically tolerated. Thus, a vicious cycle—partly real, partly perceptual—is set in motion: management will not tolerate unions; unions dig in their heels against any further erosion in their membership in firms that are already organized.

Unions also have a perceptual problem with the workers they are trying to organize. American unions are often portrayed as large, bureaucratic organizations that may be necessary for "oppressed" workers tied to assembly lines or the machine, but are irrelevant or even counterproductive for the growing ranks of professional and "knowledge" workers. Americans want to retain their individuality, their creativity, and flexibility on the job. The perceived rigidity of contract language suggests to some workers that to gain the employment securities built into the typical labor agreement, they must sacrifice a degree of flexibility on the job that they are unwilling to concede. Most workers do not particularly like the paternalism of the "boss" who cannot be easily avoided; they are wary of the possible paternalistic attitude of the union, which can be.

This challenge has by no means gone unnoticed. In August 1982, the AFL-CIO Executive Council established the Committee on the Evolution of Work. Its charge was "to review and evaluate changes that are taking place in America in the labor force, occupations, industries and technology." In the course of its study, the committee found that three-quarters of the unorganized work force agree that unions in general improve wages and working conditions. An even larger number—80 percent—agree that "unions are needed so that the legitimate complaints of workers can be heard." Among nonunion employees, however, a majority expressed reservations that "unions stifle individual initiative" and "fight change." The conclusion the committee drew from these facts is candidly stated:

> It is apparent . . . that the labor movement must demonstrate that union representation is the best available means for working people to express their individuality on the job and their desire to control their own working lives, and that unions are democratic institutions controlled by their members and that we have not been sufficiently successful on either score.

A series of recommendations was issued, targeted toward organizing the unorganized and establishing collective bargaining for them. The committee suggested, based on a broad survey of the work force, that

> collective bargaining is not, and should not be, confined by any rigid and narrow formula; the bargaining process is shaped by the times, the circumstances and the interplay between particular employers and employees. It is the special responsibility of the individual unions

that make up the labor movement to make creative use of the collective bargaining concept and to adapt bargaining to these times and to the present circumstances.[4]

Frankly, unions must establish to the satisfaction not only of the already organized but particularly of the unorganized that the labor movement is deeply conscious of the needs and desires of working people that go beyond wages, benefits, and working conditions—basic as they continue to be. Workers want to exercise more freedom in the workplace, they want a greater measure of control over their work lives, and they expect to be treated with dignity at work. The growth in recent years in the membership of service-sector and public-sector unions, and unions of college and university employees, may well reflect an affirmative response of those unions to the needs and desires of the workers described in the AFL-CIO committee study.

Inasmuch as unions move away from the rigid structure of the traditional Workplace Contract toward acceptance of both the rights and the responsibilities embodied in the Enterprise Compact, it will be up to management to respond accordingly. It can accept the union movement's commitment to work toward improvements in productivity, quality, and innovation in return for a partnership in strategic decision-making power within the firm, or it can continue to press for a union-free environment. In our opinion, if labor does not move toward the ideas embodied in the Enterprise Compact, or if management refuses to join labor in this undertaking, the American economy will suffer for it.

LABOR LAW REFORM

Government can help. First, it must desist from playing a destructive role in labor-management relations, and, second, it should boost its affirmative one. In the 1930s, Franklin Roosevelt endorsed unionism by supporting the Wagner Act and encouraging the spread of industrial unionism. In the 1980s, Ronald Reagan, despite having once been president of the Screen Actor's Guild, did much to encourage management to reject unions and their role in the economy. Firing the nation's air traffic controllers when they went on strike in 1981 signaled to

management that acting tough toward unions would be not only tolerated but countenanced. Selecting conservative, pro-management
members to the National Labor Relations Board had the same effect.
In labor-management circles, "Reaganism" meant a resurrection of
management prerogatives and a stricter circumscription of union
rights. Reagan moved the nation away from the essential elements of
the Enterprise Compact, compromising rather than enhancing America's competitiveness in the global marketplace.

This was most obvious in the decisions made by the "new" NLRB,
often described as the most conservative in the entire fifty years of its
existence.[5] The elevation of management rights is revealed in a number
of key rulings by the board, particularly in the area of the relocation of
work. In *Otis Elevator*, the pre-Reagan board ruled that United Technologies Corporation (Otis's parent company) had violated its collective-bargaining agreement by refusing to bargain with its union over
the transfer of unionized workers from one of its facilities in New Jersey
to another in Connecticut.[6] In subsequent rulings by the U.S. Supreme
Court, as well as the NLRB, the union's right to bargain over such
matters as plant shutdowns and relocations was severely limited. In
1981, for example, in *First National Maintenance Corp.*, the court ruled
that companies had no obligation to bargain over, or even to provide
advance notice of, the closure of a plant: "the harm likely to be done
to an employer's need to operate freely in deciding whether to shut
down part of his business for purely economic reasons outweighs the
incremental benefit that might be gained through the union's participation in making the decision."[7]

In commenting on this case, Gordon Clark, formerly of Carnegie
Mellon University, notes that in following the court's logic, the crucial
issue for the NLRB has become "the right of management to conduct
its business without undue interference from labor over decisions to
restructure operations, close and open plants, introduce labor saving
technology, and the like."[8] Indeed, in reviewing the original Otis Elevator case in 1984, the NLRB reversed its earlier position and denied the
union's claim that moving jobs from one facility to another violated the
collective-bargaining agreement.[9] The board made a similar ruling in
Milwaukee Spring II, once again reversing a pro-union, pro-employee
ruling involving relocation of work from a unionized to a nonunionized
facility during the term of a collective-bargaining contract.[10]

According to former Secretary of Labor John Dunlop, such decisions are symptomatic of a much deeper problem with current labor law. Dunlop has argued that the Wagner Act itself, along with its amendments, is no longer adequate in a global economy.[11] Even with a more liberal NLRB, the act is at best ambiguous about the role of labor in strategic decisions incorporated in the Enterprise Compact. The now-famous *Yeshiva* decision of the U.S. Supreme Court in 1980 is suggestive of the legal problems that could undercut movement toward the type of joint labor-management action envisioned in our compact.[12] In that decision, the nation's highest court ruled that the faculty at a private university is not eligible under the Wagner Act for officially sanctioned union representation because it performs "managerial" functions related to hiring and other "administrative" policies. According to Charles Heckscher: "What that decision says, strictly speaking, is that any employee who has the discretion to *think* on the job, to use judgment in interpreting commands—anyone, that is, whose job has not been reduced to mindless routine—is excluded from the framework of representation.[13]

While this case has not, at least so far, interfered with the type of employee involvement program in place at Saturn, it obviously prevents certain employees from having union representation and has a potentially chilling effect on pushing participation beyond this transitional stage. At a minimum, *Yeshiva* suggests that the government is neutral toward the Enterprise Compact; if enforced rigorously, it could be antagonistic to it.

For this reason, while it is not absolutely necessary to amend the Wagner Act to promote employee involvement, rewriting it so as to give participatory management a government imprimatur would have the salutary effect of encouraging management and labor to consider adopting the spirit, and perhaps the provisions, of the Enterprise Compact. Putting the nation's basic labor relations law on the side of economic competitiveness through employee participation would be one good way to advance a benign labor-management relations climate in the United States. Government action should be directed not toward accentuating division and controversy but, rather, toward assisting workers and managers to reach the higher ground of joint action in problem solving.

ENHANCING THE ROLE OF THE U.S. DEPARTMENT
OF LABOR

Beyond legislation pertinent to constructing a better legal environment for the success of participatory labor-management relations is the role the federal government can play in assisting companies and unions willing to promote joint cooperation. In this regard, the U.S. Department of Labor's Bureau of Labor-Management Relations and Cooperative Programs (BLMR) is to be applauded for its active, positive role in promoting joint efforts. Established in 1978, the BLMR was "created to promote cooperative labor-management relations efforts and enhance the quality of working life, while improving the productivity and competitiveness of American industry."[14] It regularly sponsors conferences and symposia, and publishes and disseminates a newsletter, *Labor Relations Today*, a series of Labor-Management Cooperation *Briefs*, and case study reports on employee involvement programs throughout the country.

It also sponsors a research program responsible for engaging scholars and practitioners in the evaluation of EI experiments and participatory management, as well as acting as an information clearinghouse to facilitate the exchange of information among employers, unions, and others interested in joint labor-management programs and innovative workplace practices. Moreover, the BLMR's Industrial Adjustment Service helps state and local governments, unions, and employers develop joint labor-management programs to ease the impact of, or avoid worker dislocations resulting from, plant closings or layoffs. The staff conducts state and regional workshops for officials interested in such efforts and provides follow-up technical assistance in designing and implementing these programs. Many of these workshops are conducted in cooperation with the Federal Mediation and Conciliation Service.[15]

Consistent with the schizophrenic nature of the U.S. government, the BLMR works hard to inspire labor-management cooperation while the top leadership in Washington—including the White House, the NLRB, and often the Supreme Court—does little to discourage a continued adversarial, if not openly hostile, relationship between labor and management. Reversing this attitude, and providing the BLMR with more resources and a clearer mandate to advocate joint participation, if not the specific provisions in the Enterprise Compact, would add needed strength to the employee involvement movement. Regrettably, in 1992 the Bush administration did just the opposite, sharply cutting back the activities of the BLMR, drastically reducing its staff, and curtailing budgetary support.

LABOR-MANAGEMENT COUNCILS

At the state and local levels, the recent period has witnessed the development of areawide labor-management councils. These have helped to sponsor new experiments in employee involvement and serve as a forum for discussing their merits and demerits. In some cases their formation was initiated and financially supported by local or state government. In others, they are strictly the creatures of the private sector, financed by private contributions from both management and labor.

The remarkable turnaround in the fortunes of the community of Jamestown, New York, resulted in part from the development of an active labor-management council in that city. Stanley Lundine, at the time mayor of Jamestown, later a congressman and currently lieutenant governor of New York, brought together representatives of the business community and the labor movement in the area. They joined forces to stem the tide of businesses leaving the area and were successful in inducing new enterprises to locate there. The economic base of Jamestown was stabilized, in large measure as a result of a communitarian spirit embraced by government, management, and labor.

The apparent success of Jamestown stimulated other communities to create their own area labor-management councils, and various states set aside funds to assist them. In Ohio, Centers of Labor-Management Cooperation were created under state statute and given funding from the Ohio Department of Economic Development. Companies and unions can join together under the aegis of a university, as in Toledo, or under a separately established association, as is the case with the Northwest Ohio Center. Such centers schedule conferences so that labor and management representatives can come together not only to learn about current developments in cooperative activities but to receive educational information and training about the creation and administration of inside-the-plant joint action practices.

Similarly, in Pennsylvania funding is made available to such organizations as the Northwestern Pennsylvania Area Labor-Management Council. The state government also provides financing for projects through its MILRITE (Making Industry and Labor Right in Today's Economy) Council. Here, too, assistance to promote joint programs between management and labor is made available through in-plant third-party assistance, workshops and seminars, and informational training programs. The council, typical of many like it throughout the country, lists as its goals and objectives:

A. To aid in the improvement of labor-management communication and relationships in Northwestern Pennsylvania.
B. To improve the ability of labor and management to work together.
C. To improve the quality of work life in area industry.
D. To help revive the region's economic climate.
E. To create job stability and to attract new industry to the area.[16]

New York State has established an Industrial Cooperation Council through Executive Order No. 55 signed by Governor Mario Cuomo. The council brings together leaders from New York's business and labor communities to discuss mutual problems that go far beyond workplace issues. Its specific responsibilities include:

Examining the issues of industrial productivity, competitiveness, and adaptation to new technology.
Developing new approaches to financing industrial innovation and expansion, including prudent use of pension funds and institutional investments.
Providing information, training and technical assistance for groups regarding industrial restructuring and new forms of management and financing, including employee ownership.
Proposing programs to assist individuals and communities adversely affected by plant closings, major layoffs, and other changes in the economy.
Recommending policies concerning federal activities which affect the future of New York's economy.[17]

Beyond these government-sponsored activities are a multitude of privately established and privately funded area labor-management councils around the country. Their activities generally focus on joint efforts between the labor movement and participating companies in the area to improve the business climate in their respective communities, to create jobs, and to keep jobs from moving away from the area. The Indiana Labor and Management Council (ILMC), for example, was "formed to promote productivity, competitiveness and the Quality of Working Life."[18] Other area labor-management committees of note have been established in southwestern Illinois, in Muskegon and Kalamazoo, Michigan, in the tricounty Lansing, Michigan, area, and in Oakland County, Michigan. Obviously, we believe that such labor-management councils should be encouraged throughout the nation.

In addition, community colleges and universities should assume a more significant, active role in advancing the concept of employee involvement practices. Core programs in schools of business administration might well give the same attention to this subject as they do to courses devoted to finance, marketing, and investment. While schools of business administration now appear to be more prone than in the past to offer such courses, the emphasis on human resources still seems to be of secondary significance within the curriculum. One notable exception is Northern Michigan University, which carries out regular training sessions throughout the upper peninsula of Michigan and has produced an extraordinarily useful orientation and training manual for work-site labor-management cooperation.[19]

ORGANIZING THE UNORGANIZED

It is impossible for workers to maintain a legally sanctioned, independent voice apart from management unless they belong to a union recognized by the NLRB (or state government). Thus the Enterprise Compact, as we have described it, cannot exist outside the union setting. The problem, of course, is that at the present time nearly 85 percent of the labor force is not covered by a legally binding collective-bargaining agreement. So no matter how felicitous it might be to entertain the idea of spreading the compact nationwide, until a greater proportion of the work force is organized, the Enterprise Compact can be instituted in only a very limited arena.

Since the turn of the century, America has witnessed two great waves of unionization. The first was among the construction trades. With massive immigration to the United States in the first decade of this century, millions of bricklayers, carpenters, plumbers, electricians, and laborers were needed to meet the enormous building boom in major cities throughout the country. The specialized skills of many of these tradesmen made it possible for them to successfully demand union recognition through the American Federation of Labor. While there were millions of unskilled workers who might cross a picket line to take a job, few had the required skills that contractors demanded.

The second wave of unionization occurred in the mass-production manufacturing industries during the 1930s. The captains of industry had assembled thousands of workers in individual factories, producing conditions ripe for union organizing. Through the Wagner Act, industrial unions—assembled into the Congress of Industrial Organizations (CIO)—were provided the legal means to confront management efforts to keep unions out of their plants. Within a matter of a few short years, millions of blue-collar workers in private industry joined unions, swelling the ranks of the United Auto Workers, the United Steelworkers, the International Union of Electrical Workers, and dozens of labor organizations in other industries.

Following President Kennedy's executive order in 1961 recognizing the rights of public employees to join unions, the nation witnessed a third wave of union organization. As part of that wave came such unions as the American Federation of Government Employees (AFGE), the American Federation of State, County, and Municipal Employees (AFSCME), and the teachers' unions.

Who might be part of a fourth wave that is needed today? While we can only speculate, one group would comprise professional workers who might very likely be attracted to the provisions of the Enterprise Compact. There is already a rise in independent professional workers in the National Writers Union (NWU), formed to represent authors and journalists in dealing with book, magazine, and newspaper publishers. Architects, engineers, scientists, accountants, auditors, lawyers, and professional medical personnel (in addition to nurses, who are already well organized in some cities) represent other groups of "knowledge workers" who could benefit from joining unions, particularly those committed to the concepts we have been outlining.

There is also the possibility of new organizing at the other end of the labor market—among the lesser-skilled work force. With the polarization of earnings in America has come a proliferation of low-wage employment.[20] Many of the new low-wage jobs have gone to women, minority workers, and recent immigrants. One possibility, largely untapped, would be expanding the civil rights movement into a labor-organizing movement, perhaps working with existing unions or forming new ones. As just one example, the United Farm Workers union had strong ties to both civil rights and Latino organizations. The women's labor organization, 9 to 5, has been successful in encouraging union activity in enterprises employing large numbers of women.

The federal government could remove some of the barriers to such new labor organizing by updating NLRA legislation, which no longer provides a level playing field for union-organizing drives. The Wagner Act, as interpreted by the courts, permits employers to hire "permanent replacements" if their workers go out on strike. The act makes it illegal for employers to fire workers because of strike activity, yet if a company hires "permanent replacements," it is not required to give the striking employees their old jobs back when the strike is over. In 1983, for example, when 1,700 Phelps Dodge copper miners went on strike, the company hired permanent replacements. When the union called off the strike, Phelps Dodge refused to allow any of the strikers to come back to work. To this day, not a single striker has regained his job. The same is true of the 5,600 workers at Greyhound. In other cases—at Hormel Meatpacking in Minnesota and International Paper in Jay, Maine—only a small fraction of the original strikers ever reclaimed their jobs.[21] As Paul Weiler told Business Week: "If a company discriminated against blacks or women and said: 'We didn't fire them, we just permanently replaced them,' it would get laughed out of court."[22]

In permitting the hiring of permanent replacements, the law creates two serious problems. The first is that it has a tremendous "chilling" effect on unions trying to organize new workers. All management has to do is hint that if organizing were ever to lead to a strike, workers may lose their jobs despite their apparent protection under the original Wagner Act. This gives pause to any worker when deciding whether or not to join a union. Moreover, as was true in the International Paper case, hiring permanent replacements can shred the social fabric of a community, pitting brother against brother and father against son. International Paper's action so soured labor and community relations in Maine that the Republican governor of that state, along with the president of the state's largest manufacturing employer, Bath Iron Works, joined forces to author legislation that would have prohibited the hiring of replacement workers ("strikebreakers") by any Maine employer for the first ninety days of a strike. The law passed both Houses of the state legislature, but ultimately was ruled unconstitutional by the Maine Supreme Court when it was challenged by a number of Maine employers. As of this writing, the U.S. House of Representatives has passed a bill that would ban the hiring of permanent replacements nationwide. President Bush has vowed to veto it if the Senate goes along with the House. Clearly this would once again send the wrong signal to management and labor. The right signal is to encourage unions to organize and to play a constructive role in rebuilding U.S. competitiveness. To do this, unions should not be marginalized, let alone explicitly or implicitly ostracized.

Indeed, the federal government could take some positive steps toward providing a level playing field in union recognition campaigns. According to Weiler, "sharply restricting the length of [union certification] election campaigns would reduce the time and temptation for employers to use illegitimate tactics to intimidate their employees."[23] In order to bring fairness to play in those situations in which management flagrantly and crudely violates employees' rights in union-organizing drives, Weiler also proposes that injured employees be given the right to sue for general damages in a jury trial rather than allow the National Labor Relations Board to assess fines—bearing in mind that such NLRB awards average only about $2,000 a case.

Permitting interim injunctions in claims of unfair labor practices would also help, since delays in the final adjudication of claims before the NLRB commonly take several years.[24] Our continuing political battles over these and many other labor relations issues puts the United States far behind most other industrialized nations in promoting harmony in the world of industrial relations.

TAKING UP THE CHALLENGE

Moving away from the view of labor as simply a cost item to be minimized and of unions as organizations to be avoided is the first step toward the Enterprise Compact. In the union setting, this will require putting aside old grudges and moving ahead to a new labor-management relationship. In the nonunion setting, it means considering the positive roles that a union can play within the context of the Enterprise Compact and being willing to give up some prerogatives in order to gain a partner.

Labor, particularly organized labor, must do precisely the same. It must also be willing to take on responsibilities it has often shunned in the past, and to develop new expertise to fulfill a new role. As John Hoerr has urged:

> If unions are to make a serious contribution in any of these new areas, perhaps the biggest challenge of all will be an internal one: developing their own human resources. As the global economy becomes more complex and the efforts of companies to respond to it more diverse, unions are going to have to learn new skills and develop new kinds of expertise. The union leader of the future will, most likely, have to combine the political instincts of the traditional organizer with the business savvy of the best global manager.[25]

The Enterprise Compact calls for a vision of the future that extends well beyond current thinking and current practice. Its roots lie deep within the democratic heritage of our people and our nation. At its heart is an appeal to management to lay aside its overemphasis on the adversarial resistance to unionism and its characterization of workplace democratization as hopelessly utopian and inefficient.

In like fashion, its appeal to labor is to exercise the responsibilities attendant to managing the affairs not just of the workplace but of the entire enterprise. That means careful and persistent attention to issues of productivity, quality, and innovation. Many labor-management issues will continue to be controversial, but clearly labor and management have more in common than in conflict. Together, embracing a common vision of the future, they can join in a compact that benefits all stakeholders in the nation.

Notes

Chapter 1: A New Vision for American Enterprise

1. A case in point is John F. Welch, Jr., chairman of General Electric. According to John Holusha of the *New York Times,* Welch, "who earned the nickname Neutron Jack on his reputation for eliminating people while leaving buildings standing, has gone through a conversion and is now preaching corporate pacifism." Using GE's 1991 annual report as his pulpit, Welch intoned, "We cannot afford management styles that suppress and intimidate." He urged his own company to "have the self-confidence to empower others and behave in a boundaryless fashion." "Trust and respect between workers and managers is essential," he wrote. For greater detail on Jack Welch's "conversion," see John Holusha, "A Call for Kinder Managers at G.E.," *New York Times,* March 4, 1991, p. D1.

2. The 30 percent statistic is based on a sample of 12,449 manufacturing plants employing more than 100 employees as of December 31, 1969. See David Birch, *The Job Generation Process* (Cambridge, Mass.: MIT Program on Neighborhood and Regional Change, 1979), app. D. For additional statistics on plant closings and their employment effect, see Barry Bluestone and Bennett Harrison, *The Deindustrialization of America: Plant Closings,*

Community Abandonment, and the Dismantling of Basic Industry (New York: Basic Books, 1982).

3. William J. Abernathy, Kim B. Clark, and Alan M. Kantrow, *Industrial Renaissance* (New York: Basic Books, 1983), p. 9.

4. See Bennett Harrison and Barry Bluestone, *The Great U-Turn: Corporate Restructuring and the Polarizing of America* (New York: Basic Books, 1988).

5. Lester Thurow, *The Zero-Sum Society* (New York: Basic Books, 1985), p. 47.

6. Michael J. Mandel and Aaron Bernstein, "Dispelling the Myths that Are Holding Us Back," *Business Week*, December 17, 1990, special report, *Can You Compete?* pp. 66–70.

7. See, for example, Edward F. Denison, *Trends in American Economic Growth, 1929–1982* (Washington, D.C.: Brookings Institution, 1985).

8. During 1979–85, the annual growth in multifactor productivity averaged 2.1 percent in the manufacturing sector. In the nonfarm nonmanufacturing sector, the annual growth rate was −0.4 percent. Finance and insurance productivity dropped by 2.0 percent per year; the overall efficiency of the real estate industry fell by 3.2 percent; and construction declined by 2.0 percent. See Martin Neil Baily and Alok K. Chakrabarti, *Innovation and the Productivity Crisis* (Washington, D.C.: Brookings Institution, 1988), table 1.3, p. 6.

9. The Barry Associates results are cited in Sherwood Kerker, "Why Productivity Is Down," *St. Louis Post Dispatch*, September 21, 1980.

10. Aaron Bernstein, *Grounded: Frank Lorenzo and the Destruction of Eastern Airlines* (New York: Simon and Schuster, 1990), p. 7.

11. Eric Weiner, "Lorenzo to Leave Airline Industry in Deal Selling Continental Stock," *New York Times*, August 10, 1990, p. 1; and Floyd Norris, "A Good Deal? Yes, for Lorenzo," *New York Times*, August 10, 1990, p. D8. In an ironic footnote to this story, the parent company, Continental, which had been run by Lorenzo, declared bankruptcy five months later. See Mark Ivey and Michael Oneal, "The Lorenzo Legacy Haunts Continental," *Business Week*, December 17, 1990, p. 28.

12. On the Greyhound case, see Thomas C. Hayes, "Greyhound Takes the Road to Bankruptcy," *New York Times*, June 10, 1990, p. E3; David Moberg, "Greyhound Strikers Bid for the Wheel," *In These Times*, June 20–July 3, 1990, p. 7; and Wendy Zellner, "Labor May Still Have Greyhound Collared," *Business Week*, November 26, 1990, p. 60.

13. Robert Levering, Milton Moskowitz, and Michael Katz, *The 100 Best Companies to Work for in America* (New York: Signet Books, 1984), p. xvi.

14. Ibid., p. 98.

15. Ibid., p. 183.

16. Nancy Marx Better, "A Hidden Upside in All the Downsizing," *New York Times,* October 27, 1991, p. 25.

17. Thomas J. Peters and Robert H. Waterman, *In Search of Excellence: Lessons from America's Best-Run Companies* (New York: Harper and Row, 1982), p. 238.

18. Paraphrased from John Maynard Keynes, *The General Theory of Employment, Interest and Money* (London: Macmillan, 1973).

19. Henry Ford, with Samuel Growther, *Today and Tomorrow* (New York: Doubleday, 1926), p. 160.

20. See Alan Farnham, "The Trust Gap," *Fortune,* December 4, 1989.

21. Ibid., pp. 56–57.

22. Ibid., p. 56.

23. Between 1986 and the end of 1991, IBM downsized its worldwide payroll from 407,000 to 350,000. All of this was done through normal attrition and generous voluntary early retirement programs. In late 1991, as part of its continuing restructuring program, it hinted at trimming another 20,000 staff during the coming year. As the *Wall Street Journal* reports, IBM's voluntary packages have been getting less generous, and therefore the company may have to resort to "more stick and less carrot as it makes its next round of cuts" (Paul B. Carroll, "IBM Is Likely in 1992 to Trim 20,000 Positions," *Wall Street Journal,* November 20, 1991, p. A3).

24. Bart Ziegler, "IBM Chairman Outlines Revamp to Skeptical Analysts," *Boston Globe,* December 10, 1991, p. 45.

25. Peters and Waterman, *In Search of Excellence,* p. 239.

26. Levering, Moskowitz, and Katz, *The 100 Best Companies,* p. 102.

27. Interview with Maryann Komejan, corporate secretary and manager of communication and public relations, Donnelly Corporation, March 17, 1992.

28. L. William Seidman and Steven L. Skanche, *Productivity: The American Advantage* (New York: Simon and Schuster, 1989).

29. Ibid.

30. *Proceedings of the Special Collective Bargaining Convention* (Detroit, Mich.: UAW, 1967), p. 118.

31. Roger E. Smith, the chairman of General Motors Corporation, at the groundbreaking ceremony for the UAW-GM Human Resource Center, Auburn Hills, Michigan, May 9, 1985.

32. See Jolie Solomon, "Taking a Stand: If You Think the Pressure to Be Politically Correct Is Tough on Campus, Try It in the Corner Office,"

Boston Globe, July 21, 1991, p. 45. Solomon does not focus specifically on labor-management issues. But she notes a number of examples where CEOs who took positions counter to major business lobbying groups or conservative "research centers" have been slammed in the conservative press and publicly ridiculed. Control Data Corporation's CEO, Lawrence Pearlman, had to defend himself against corporate lobbyists and the National Association of Manufacturers when he testified in favor of federal legislation that would have mandated "family leave" for employees. *CEO* magazine denounced the chief executive of the H. J. Heinz Co. as "capitulating" to "enviroterrorists" just because he announced that the company's Star Kist tuna division would begin harvesting in a way that protects dolphins. Most corporate executives—with the exception of such media stars as Chrysler's Lee Iacocca—prefer to keep their names out of public view and therefore are loath to take stands that are considered "controversial."

33. John T. Dunlop, "Conflict or Co-operation: Which Way Is Industrial Relations Heading?" (Larry Sefton Memorial Lecture, Woodworth College, University of Toronto, March 12, 1985), p. 8.

34. Robert M. Kaus, "The Trouble with Unions," *Harper's* June 1983, as reprinted in *The Transformation of Industrial Organization,* ed. Frank Hearn (Belmont, Calif.: Wadsworth, 1988), pp. 140, 141.

35. After five weeks, the school-bus drivers' strike ended with no wage increase, but some concessions on job security. To his credit, Lynn Williams, the president of the United Steel Workers union to which the local school bus drivers were affiliated, intervened to end the strike on terms that would not further break the budget for Boston schools. See Diego Ribadeneira, "Bus Drivers OK Contract to End Strike," *Boston Sunday Globe,* October 27, 1991, p. 1.

36. CBS Television, "60 Minutes," November 24, 1991.

37. These statistics are from Roper polls, as reported in the *UAW Washington Report* 31 (September 26, 1990): 1.

38. See Richard B. Freeman and James L. Medoff, *What Do Unions Do?* (New York: Basic Books, 1984). Studies showing similar results are discussed in chapter 7 herein.

39. Quoted in Diane Ravitch, ed., *The American Reader* (New York: HarperCollins, 1990), p. 3.

40. See "Agreement Between Harvard Industries and Its ESNA Division and the International Union, United Automobile, Aerospace and Agricultural Implement Workers of America and Its Local 726," October 14, 1991.

41. Peter F. Drucker, *The New Society: The Anatomy of Industrial Order* (New York: Harper and Row, 1949; New York: Harper Torchbook, 1962), p. 106.

42. Abernathy, Clark, and Kantrow, *Industrial Renaissance,* p. 93.

43. See John Hoerr, "The Strange Bedfellows Backing Workplace Reform," *Business Week,* April 30, 1990, p. 57.

44. See William L. Weiss (co-chair of the Collective Bargaining Forum), Ameritech Distinguished Speaker Series Lecture, November 29, 1989 (East Lansing, Mich.: Ameritech Publishing and the School of Labor and Industrial Relations, Michigan State University, 1990). The original Collective Bargaining Forum report that discusses the workable compact is found in U.S. Department of Labor, Bureau of Labor-Management Relations, *New Directions for Labor and Management* (April 1988).

45. Remarks by UAW Local 1853 President Michael Bennett, Automotive News World Conference (Detroit, Mich., January 15, 1991), p. 10.

Chapter 2: The Glory Days and the Traditional Workplace Contract

1. Council of Economic Advisers, *Economic Report of the President, 1989* (Washington, D.C.: Government Printing Office), table B-32, p. 344.

2. For an extraordinary account of wartime shipbuilding, see Mark S. Foster, *Henry J. Kaiser: Builder in the Modern American West* (Austin, Tex.: University of Texas Press, 1989), chap. 5.

3. By the end of the war, nearly 300,000 airplanes had been produced, 86,000 tanks, and 55,000,000 tons of shipping. The navy procured some 71,000 new ships, from landing craft to aircraft carriers. The nation's steel production nearly doubled, aluminum output grew by sixfold, and an entire new industry produced over 700,000 tons of synthetic rubber annually. Records were broken every year in the production of wheat, corn, livestock, cotton, and other staples. See Foster Rhea Dulles, *The United States since 1985* (Ann Arbor, Mich.: University of Michigan Press, 1959), pp. 448–49.

4. Average weekly hours of production for workers in durable manufacturing reached 44.0 in 1945, up from 39.2 in 1940. See U.S. Department of Labor, Bureau of Labor Statistics, *Handbook of Labor Statistics,* Bulletin 2217 (Washington, D.C.: Government Printing Office, June 1985), table 70, p. 186.

5. *Economic Report of the President, 1989,* table B-32, p. 344.

6. See Leo M. Cherne, *The Rest of Your Life* (New York: Doubleday, 1944).

7. See Foster, *Henry J. Kaiser,* p. 129.

8. U.S. Bureau of the Census, *Statistical Abstract of the United States, 1986* (Washington, D.C.: Government Printing Office, December 1985), table 1311, p. 731.

9. Ibid., table 930, p. 545; table 1041, p. 598. According to *Fortune* magazine, more than half of all American families now own two or more cars, and fewer than one in ten has no car at all. See Sylvia Nasar, "Do We Live As Well As We Used To?" *Fortune,* September 14, 1987, p. 40.

10. The War Production Board (WPB) closed down passenger car assembly lines and banned the manufacture of radios for civilians. It drastically curbed, in the words of one historian, "the production of hundreds of other articles from lawnmowers to girdles, from typewriters to zippers, [and] restricted the use of cloth by decrees limiting the length of women's skirts and eliminating the cuffs on men's trousers" See Dulles, *United States Since 1865,* p. 448.

11. It is estimated that during the war, disposable personal income exceeded the production value of civilian goods by more than $20 billion. Without rationing, this excess of consumption demand would have led to even a steeper inflation than the 30 percent experienced between December 1941 and December 1945. See Dulles, *United States Since 1865,* p. 451; and *Economic Report of the President, 1989,* table B–62, p. 378.

12. The 1980s were famous for seemingly unrestrained consumerism, but unlike the immediate postwar spending spree, the consumption "boom" in the 1980s was spurred by debt finance rather than out of household savings. This permitted families in the late 1940s and throughout most of the next two decades to improve their standards of living without accumulating massive amounts of debt. On consumer debt during the Reagan years, see A. Gary Shilling, *The World Has Definitely Changed* (New York: Lakeview Press, 1986), p. 15.

13. By 1950 real annual personal consumption was more than 45 percent greater than before the war. Between 1946 and 1950, Americans spent more than $320 billion on fixed residential investment (in 1982 dollars). This was equivalent to 5.7 percent of the real GNP generated during that period. For the sake of comparison, during the Vietnam-induced "boom" (1965–1969), residential investment as a percentage of GNP was 4.8 percent, and during the most recent "boom" period, 1983 through 1987, it was 4.9 percent. Computed from *Economic Report of the President, 1989,* table B-2, p. 310.

14. Ibid.

15. *Handbook of Labor Statistics,* table 63, p. 174.

16. With the growth in consumption and investment, production expanded rapidly. Even in *slow-growth* sectors like textiles, mining, and iron and

steel, total U.S. output was 26 percent, 25 percent, and 7 percent higher in 1959 than from 1947 to 1949. In the leading growth industries, the overall production levels doubled and tripled in the span of a single decade. Using the Federal Reserve Board Industry Groupings Production Index, Vatter reports the following index values for 1960 (1947 to 1949 = 100):

Industry	Production Index
Aircraft	368
Electric utilities	289
Chemicals	255
Natural gas	228
Electric machinery	222
Rubber and plastic products	200

17. See Paul Krugman, *The Age of Diminished Expectations* (Cambridge, Mass.: MIT Press, 1990), fig. 6, p. 12. The 3 percent record productivity growth during the 1950s exceeded even that during 1940s, including the war years, when the entire economy was geared at a feverish pitch.

18. From a high of $89.4 billion in 1944, demobilization saw federal purchases of goods and services fall to as little as $13.6 billion in 1947. See *Economic Report of the President, 1989,* table B-1, p. 309.

19. These figures are in nominal terms. In terms of 1944 purchasing power, the real-dollar equivalents for these three years are as follows: 1944—$96 billion; 1947—$12 billion; and 1953—$39 billion. Calculated from ibid., table B-79, p. 401, and table B-2, p. 311.

20. Executive Office of the President, Office of Management and Budget, *Historical Tables: Budget of the United States, Fiscal Year 1990* (Washington, D.C.: Government Printing Office, 1989), table 3.1, "Outlays by Superfunction and Function: 1940-1994," pp. 39-40.

21. For a well-documented account of the G.I. Bill and its economic impact, see Congressional Research Service, "Veterans' Education Assistance Programs," Report 86-32 EPW (Washington, D.C.: Library of Congress, January 31, 1986).

22. Louis Galambos and Joseph Pratt, *The Rise of the Corporate Commonwealth* (New York: Basic Books, 1988), p. 140.

23. The data on federal government spending in the postwar era are taken from *Historical Tables,* table 3.1, pp. 39-45. All figures are in nominal terms.

24. The figures for highways and education were computed from *Economic Report of the President, 1989,* table B-83, p. 405.

25. For an enlightened discussion of this era, see Robert Kuttner, *The End of Laissez Faire: Economics and National Purpose After the Cold War* (New York: Simon and Schuster, 1990).

26. Ibid., p. 59.

27. In today's dollars, it would be equivalent to a staggering $110 billion. See "Reckoning the Price of Providing Aid to the Soviets," *Boston Globe*, July 8, 1990, p. 10. By contrast, federal outlays for international development and humanitarian assistance in 1990 amounted to a mere $4.8 billion. See *Historical Tables*, table 3.3, p. 57.

28. Calculated from data in *Economic Report of the President, 1989*, table B-2, pp. 310–11.

29. In 1929, the value of total imports into the United States was equivalent to 5.7 percent of GNP. In 1949, it was a mere 3.8 percent and even in 1959, only 4.7 percent. It was only in 1969 that the import share of GNP regained its pre-depression level. Calculated from Council of Economic Advisers, *Economic Report of the President, 1986* (Washington, D.C.: Government Printing Office, 1986).

30. The source of these statistics is the U.S. Bureau of the Census, *Census of Manufacturers, 1972* (Washington, D.C.: Government Printing Office, 1975), table 5, pp. SR2-6 through SR2-49.

31. The basic concept underlying Davis-Bacon is that contractors on government projects should not be able to undercut the wages paid construction workers by establishing wages lower than those generally prevailing in the area where the project is located.

32. See C. Arthur Williams, John G. Turnbull, and Earl F. Cheit, *Economic and Social Security*, 5th ed. (New York: Wiley, 1982), p. 588.

33. The "rule of 72" is a mathematical rule of thumb permitting one to calculate quickly the number of years it takes for something growing at a given annual rate to double in value. Simply dividing the annual growth rate into the number 72 yields the approximate number of years needed to double the quantity in question. In this particular case, 72 divided by 3.7 yields 19.5 years. Real GNP (in 1982 dollars) was $1,109 billion in 1948. Nineteen years later, in 1967, it was $2,271 billion. If GNP had grown by only 2 percent a year during the postwar period, it would have taken nearly twice as long (thirty-six years) for it to double. The point is that small differences in growth rates over suitably long periods of time yield extremely different overall levels of output.

34. *Economic Report of the President, 1989*, table B-95, p. 417.

35. Ibid., table B-88, p. 410.

36. The Dow-Jones Industrial Average for 1949 averaged 179.48. By 1952 it was up to 270.76. Only two years later, it had reached 442.72. By the end of the decade, it was 632.12. See ibid., table B-94, p. 416.

37. Dulles, *United States Since 1865,* p. 472.

38. Major strikes, according to the BLS definition, are those that continue for one full day or shift or longer and that involve 1,000 workers or more. See *Handbook of Labor Statistics,* "Technical Notes," p. 408, and table 123, p. 409. Other data suggest that the number of all work stoppages (including those in smaller firms) reached a peak of 4,600 in 1946 and averaged over 2,500 per year in the decade following the war. See Michael Goldfield, *The Decline of Organized Labor in the United States* (Chicago: University of Chicago Press, 1987), fig. 6, p. 41.

39. U.S. Department of Commerce, *Historical Statistics of the United States: Colonial Times to 1970* (Washington, D.C.: Government Printing Office, 1975), pt. 1, pp. 176–78. Of the 17 million, 10.6 million workers belonged to the American Federation of Labor (AFL), 4.6 million belonged to the Congress of Industrial Organizations (CIO), and another 1.8 million were in unions not affiliated with either—notably, members of the Teamsters.

40. The general relationship between productivity and wages had actually been raised by the UAW in earlier negotiations. In the course of the 113-day strike against General Motors in 1945–46, Walter Reuther, then vice president of the UAW and director of its General Motors department, flagged the argument in support of the union's wage demands: "The grim fact is that if free enterprise in America is to survive . . . it must master the technique for providing full employment at a high standard of living, rising year by year to keep pace with the annual increase in technological efficiency." At a later date he described the strike in these terms: "It [the strike] was about the right of a worker to share . . . in the fruits of advancing technology. The other issue was why should workers be victimized by inflationary forces over which they have no control, which erode their real wage position?" (cited in Frank Cormier and William J. Eaton, *Reuther* [New York: Prentice-Hall, 1970], p. 292).

41. Based on government statistics that demonstrated long-run average increases in labor productivity of approximately 2 percent a year, GM offered, and the union ultimately accepted, a 3-cent-per-hour wage increase effective the first day of the contract and another at the beginning of the second year. To protect workers from the "ravages of inflation," the company offered another automatic wage boost: a cost-of-living adjustment calculated on the basis of the U.S. Bureau of Labor Statistics' Consumer Price Index (CPI). Under the GM plan, also accepted by the union, a cost-of-living allowance was implemented on the day the contract was signed. This meant an immediate 8-cent-an-hour wage boost plus a quarterly COLA adjustment equal to 1 cent per hour for each future 1.14-point increase in the government's price index. Coming on

top of the 18.5-cent-per-hour general increase negotiated in March 1946 and an 11.5-cent-per-hour boost negotiated in a special "reopener" agreement just thirteen months later, the average UAW member at GM enjoyed an overall wage gain of 41 cents per hour between March 1946 and April 1948. For the typical worker this amounted to a hefty 30 percent increase in base pay, close to what Reuther and the UAW had demanded. By 1948 the base wage (including AIF and COLA) for the typical GM assembly-line worker was $1.44 per hour. Fringe benefits paid by the company (including the employer's share of Social Security, holiday, and vacation costs) cost GM the equivalent of another 18 cents per hour. The economic highlights of UAW–General Motors contracts from 1937 through 1990 are found in a booklet published by the UAW Research Department, "Collective Bargaining Gains by Date of Settlement" (Detroit, Mich.: UAW Solidarity House, February 27, 1988). For more detail, see Harry C. Katz, *Shifting Gears: Changing Labor Relations in the U.S. Automobile Industry* (Cambridge, Mass.: MIT Press, 1985), table 2.2, p. 23. The value of fringe benefits is based on calculations found in Robert M. MacDonald, *Collective Bargaining in the Automobile Industry* (New Haven, Conn.: Yale University Press, 1963), p. 40.

42. This does not mean that the same percentage wage increase was applied to all workers each year. In some instances, skilled trades classifications received a larger "cents-per-hour" increase in order to reverse the narrowing of the percentage wage gap with production classifications caused by flat COLA adjustments.

43. The formula governing the quarterly adjustments in the cost-of-living allowance was based on the relationship between the average wage rate at GM and the CPI at a specific point in time. Thus, in March 1948 the average wage rate was $1.48 per hour. The CPI stood at 130. The result of the average wage rate divided by the CPI is 1.14. From time to time, as the CPI base was changed by the Bureau of Labor Statistics, the negotiating parties altered the COLA formula to reflect these changes. Thus, in 1990 the COLA formula stood at a one-cent rise in the COLA for each .26 rise in the CPI (1967 = 100).

44. These figures refer to contracts covering 1,000 workers or more. The high-water mark for COLA clauses was 1977. Particularly in the wake of double-digit inflation during the early 1980s, many companies forced their unions to agree to abandon the price escalator clauses in their contracts. By 1986, the proportion of major contracts with a COLA clause had declined from 61 percent to 50 percent. See Stuart E. Weiner, "Union COLAs on Decline," in *Collective Bargaining Negotiations and Contracts*, ed. Bureau of National Affairs, (Washington, D.C.: Bureau of National Affairs, October 23, 1986), sec. 16, p. 2.

45. Despite periodic changes in the COLA formula in line with the increase in the CPI, UAW members were not completely protected against inflation. Under very rapid increases in the CPI, as in the period from 1979 through 1981, the formula did not quite keep up with inflation. Nevertheless, COLA protection allowed UAW members to minimize the potential harm from inflation and make real economic gains in each contract.

46. These statistics prepared by the UAW Research Department were presented by Walter Reuther to the Twelfth Constitutional Convention of the UAW in Milwaukee, Wisconsin, on July 10, 1949. The entire speech can be found in Henry M. Christman, ed., *Walter P. Reuther: Selected Papers* (New York: Pyramid Press, 1964), pp. 30–37.

47. *Economic Report of the President, 1989,* table B-87, p. 409. Corporate profits reported here refer to corporate profits with inventory valuation and capital consumption adjustments.

48. The spotlight on negotiated benefits and improvements in existing benefits was so powerful in some industries that it led negotiators from time to time to reallocate future COLA adjustments toward defraying their cost. Thus, increases in COLA might be converted to help finance a benefit improvement rather than be applied directly to wage rates.

49. Later, in the era of deep and widespread layoffs in major manufacturing industries, companywide seniority actually led to the formation of a whole class of employees now known at General Motors as the "GM Gypsies." Under contract language first negotiated in 1955, "Paragraph 96" employees and, in later contracts, "Document 28" employees have the right to follow their jobs when production is shifted from one facility to another. They do not have the right to "bump" existing employees at the new facility, but they have the right to be hired in before new workers are offered jobs. At GM, the transfer of production has been so extensive that it is not unusual to find workers who have worked in three or four different plants in different states and regions of the country during the 1980s. While not an official record, one worker at the GM Fort Wayne, Indiana, truck plant has worked in eight shops in various states. In this case, workers have the unappetizing choice of repeatedly pulling up stakes and moving to where the work is or permanently losing their GM paychecks. For a fascinating account of the GM Gypsies, see Russell Eckel (Ph.D. diss., Boston College, forthcoming).

50. Under the 1947 Taft-Hartley amendments to the National Labor Relations Act (NLRA), paragraph 14b permits states to outlaw the union shop. Twenty states, mostly in the South and the agricultural Midwest have such "right-to-work" laws. In these states, unions have often insisted on "agency shop" protection where workers are not required to

join the union but must pay an "agency fee" to cover their fair share of union costs associated with negotiating contracts and representing workers in grievances. The courts have ruled that agency shop clauses are legal, since under the NLRA, union representatives must defend all workers in an organized bargaining unit, whether paying dues or not.

51. This composite management-rights clause was derived from a number of provisions that appear in a variety of contracts, including those negotiated between the UAW and General Motors, Ford, and Chrysler; the UAW and International Harvester; and the United Steel Workers and the USX Corporation.

52. See Edwin F. Beal and James P. Begin, *The Practice of Collective Bargaining*, 4th ed. (Homewood, Ill.: Irwin, 1972), pp. 310–22.

53. As quoted in Neil Chamberlain, *The Union Challenge to Management Control* (New York: Harper and Brothers, 1948), p. 3.

54. Quoted in William Serrin, *The Company and the Union* (New York: Knopf, 1973), p. 165.

55. The union security clause in the 1950 contract did not provide for a full union shop. It did not require then-current employees who were not already members of the union to sign membership cards and pay union dues as a condition of employment. Union members, however, were required to maintain their union membership and pay dues. The 1955 UAW-GM contract and each successive contract have contained the full union shop clause applicable to all bargaining unit employees.

56. Quoted in Serrin, *Company and the Union*, p. 170.

57. Reprinted in *United Automobile Worker*, June 1950, p. 3.

58. "Sympathetic pressure" refers to the pressure on wages and benefits felt in one industry, often not unionized, from the rise in wages in another. "Pattern bargaining" refers to cases where the provisions of a negotiated union contract in one firm are adopted by other firms in the same industry or transferred to other sectors of the economy represented by other unions. Both sympathetic pressure and pattern bargaining were extremely common during much of the early postwar period. See Otto Eckstein and Thomas A. Wilson, "The Determinants of Money Wages in American Industry," *Quarterly Journal of Economics* 76 (August 1966): 379–414.

59. As it turned out, the unanticipated inflation caused by the Korean War led the UAW to demand a wage reopener well before the termination of the five-year agreement. In opposition to the stance initially taken by the corporation, the UAW argued that its contracts were "living documents" that had to be altered before their expiration date in the event of extraor-

dinary and unforeseen changes in economic conditions. The existing COLA formula failed to fully protect workers against the rising tide of prices because its inflation protection was not retroactive and it was not based on a straight percentage adjustment in the Consumer Price Index. After a string of local strikes, GM reluctantly agreed to reopen the contract. The result was an agreement that boosted the AIF from 4 cents to 5 cents per hour each year, added another 10 cents for skilled workers, and readjusted the COLA formula. Pension benefits were improved as well, with an increase from $1.50 to $1.75 per month per year of service. Similar contracts were penned almost immediately with Ford and Chrysler. Despite the brief interruption in "labor peace," the AIF/COLA formula was sustained. Ironically, the auto industry itself turned to the "living document" interpretation of the contract when it requested labor cost relief during the 1981–82 recession. With layoffs mounting, the UAW agreed to reopen the three-year 1979 contract five months early. It consented to aid the industry by granting a deferral of contractual cost-of-living benefits and the cancellation of certain holiday and bonus provisions.

60. These estimates are found in U.S. Department of Labor, Bureau of Labor Statistics, *Handbook of Labor Statistics,* Bulletin 2070 (Washington, D.C.: Government Printing Office, 1980), as reported in Michael Goldfield, *The Decline of Organized Labor in the United States* (Chicago: University of Chicago Press, 1987), table 1, p. 10.

61. Eckstein and Wilson, "Determinants of Money Wages."

62. See Richard Edwards and Michael Podgursky, "The Unraveling Accord: American Unions in Crisis," in *Unions in Crisis and Beyond,* ed. Richard Edwards, Paolo Garonna, and Fraz Todtling (Dover, Mass.: Auburn House, 1986), p. 23.

63. The data for these comparisons and those to follow are calculated from *Handbook of Labor Statistics,* Bulletin 2217, table 80, pp. 202–3.

64. See Sumner Slichter, James J. Healy, and E. Robert Livernash, *The Impact of Collective Bargaining on Management* (Washington, D.C.: Brookings Institution, 1960); and Thomas A. Kochan, Harry C. Katz, and Robert B. McKersie, *The Transformation of American Industrial Relations* (New York: Basic Books, 1986), esp. pp. 55–59.

65. See *Handbook of Labor Statistics,* Bulletin 2217, table 81, pp. 204–6.

66. Information supplied to authors by John Dunlop, National Education Association staff, March 18, 1992.

67. For recent data on unionization rates by industry and occupation, see U.S. Bureau of Labor Statistics, Department of Labor, *Employment and*

Earnings (Washington, D.C.: Government Printing Office, January 1991), table 58, p. 229.

A keener sense of the growth in the public sector can be gleaned from data comparing membership in 1955 and 1989 for the key AFL-CIO unions operating primarily in the public sector:

	Membership	
Union	1955	1989
American Federation of State, County & Municipal Employees	99,000	1,090,000
American Federation of Teachers	40,000	544,000
National Association of Letter Carriers	100,000	201,000
American Federation of Government Employees	47,000	156,000

(*Source:* Bureau of National Affairs, "American Federation of Labor and Congress of Industrial Organizations Paid Membership," *Daily Labor Report* [December 8, 1989]: E-1)

68. The UAW, for instance, as an industrial union, represents nonfaculty employees in Michigan at Wayne State University in Detroit, Oakland and Eastern Michigan universities, Wayne County Community College, Northern Michigan University, and Michigan Technical University; in Iowa at Black Hawk College; in New York at Columbia University, Cornell University, and Barnard College; in Massachusetts at Boston University, the University of Massachusetts at Amherst, and the Berkeley School of Music; and at the University of California at Berkeley.

69. For details on the trend in the union/nonunion wage differential, see George Johnson, "Changes over Time in the Union/Non-Union Wage Differential" (University of Michigan, February 1981, Mimeographed), table 2, as reported in Richard B. Freeman and James L. Medoff, *What Do Unions Do?* (New York: Basic Books, 1984), p. 53.

70. See Bennett Harrison and Barry Bluestone, *The Great U-Turn: Corporate Restructuring and the Polarizing of America* (New York: Basic Books, 1988), fig. 5.2, p. 119.

71. The standard measure of income equality used by the U.S. Census Bureau is the "Gini Index." In 1947, the index stood at .376. By 1968 it had fallen to .348, the lowest point in modern U.S. history. See U.S. Department of Commerce, Bureau of the Census, *Money Income of Households, Families, and Persons in the United States: 1984* (Washington, D.C.: Government Printing Office, 1986). For a detailed discussion of the Gini Index and the trend in inequality, see Harrison and Bluestone, *The Great U-Turn*, esp. pp. 128–31.

72. *Economic Report of the President, 1989*, table B-30, p. 342.

73. The actual wording of Article II, Section 2, states that "representatives and direct taxes shall be apportioned among the several States which may be included within this Union, according to their respective numbers, which shall be determined by adding to the whole number of free persons, including those bound to service for a term of years, and excluding Indians not taxed, three fifths of all other persons." This provision, known as the "three-fifths" compromise, along with one permitting the continued importation of slaves, was the price extracted by the southern states as a condition for them joining the Union. For a brief discussion of these issues, see Michael Kraus, *The United States to 1865* (Ann Arbor: University of Michigan Press, 1959), pp. 257–60.

Chapter 3: Goodbye to the Glory Days

1. The average price index (1982 to 1984 = 100) for motor fuels nationwide increased from 28.4 in 1972 to 42.2 in 1974. See Council of Economic Advisers, *Economic Report of the President, 1989* (Washington, D.C.: Government Printing Office, January 1989), table B-59, p. 375. The year-end spot price of Arabian light crude rose from under $2.00 per barrel in 1972 to about $4.00 a barrel in 1973 to $10.00 at the end of 1974. See *Petroleum Intelligence Weekly*, as reported in Jane Fitz Simon, "Military Budget Cuts Now Being Considered," *Boston Globe*, August 7, 1990, p. 30.
2. *Economic Report of the President, 1989*, table B-62, p. 378.
3. Ibid., table B-45, p. 359.
4. See James B. Sumrall, Jr., "Diffusion of the Basic Oxygen Furnace in the U.S. Steel Industry: A Vintage Capital Model" (Ph.D. diss., 1977, Boston College,), p. 14.
5. These data are from *Annual Statistical Reports* of the American Iron and Steel Institute and reported in Bertrand Bellon and Jorge Niosi, *The Decline of the American Economy* (Montreal: Black Rose Books, 1988), table 2.4, p. 51.
6. See Stephen Wheelright, "What Do All These Products Have in Common?" as reported in A. Blanton Godfrey and Peter J. Kolesar, "Role of Quality in Achieving World Class Competitiveness," in *Global Competitiveness*, ed. Martin K. Starr (New York: Norton, 1988), p. 21.
7. See Bennett Harrison and Barry Bluestone, *The Great U-Turn: Corporate Restructuring and the Polarizing of America* (New York: Basic Books, 1988), table 1.1, p. 9.
8. U.S. Department of Commerce, International Trade Administration, *United States Trade: Performance in 1987* (Washington, D.C.: Government

Printing Office, 1988), p. 6, as reported in Michael L. Dertouzos, Richard K. Lester, and Robert M. Solow, *Made in America* (Cambridge, Mass.: MIT Press, 1989), p. 32.

9. See Barry Bluestone, "Is Deindustrialization a Myth? Capital Mobility versus Absorptive Capacity in the U.S. Economy," *Annals of the American Academy of Political and Social Science* 475 (September 1984): 39–51.

10. These statistics are reported in Samuel Bowles, David Gordon, and Thomas Weisskopf, "Power and Profits: The Social Structure of Accumulation and the Profitability of the Postwar U.S. Economy," *Review of Radical Political Economics* 18 (Spring–Summer 1986). Comparable profit statistics can be found in reports of the U.S. Bureau of Economic Analysis of the Department of Commerce, as reported in Louis Uchitelle, "Corporate Profitability Rising, Reversing Fifteen-Year Downturn," *New York Times*, November 30, 1987, p. 1; T. P. Hill, *Profits and Rates of Return* (Paris: Organization for Economic Cooperation and Development, 1979), table 6.4, p. 125; and Daniel M. Holland and Stewart C. Myers, "Profitability and Capital Costs for Manufacturing Corporations," *American Economic Review* 70 (May 1980), 321.

11. See Barry Bluestone and Bennett Harrison, *The Deindustrialization of America* (New York: Basic Books, 1982), table 6.1, p. 148.

12. Ibid., esp. pp. 25–48.

13. Candee S. Harris, "The Magnitude of Job Loss from Plant Closings and the Generation of Replacement Jobs: Some Recent Evidence," *Annals of the American Academy of Political and Social Science* 475 (September 1984): 15, 19. These numbers exclude business enterprises with fewer than 100 employees.

14. See *Economic Report of the President, 1989,* table B-43, p. 356.

15. See *UAW Research Bulletin* (November 1989): 1.

16. See Bellon and Niosi, *The Decline of the American Economy,* table 2.1, p. 46.

17. For a review of a sample of these, see Bluestone and Harrison, *The Deindustrialization of America,* esp. pp. 49–81.

18. A number of industry studies using data through 1980 suggest that unions in the one-time oligopolistic sector were able to retain their wage and benefit gains at the expense of profit margins, but only in the very early years of import competition. See Thomas Karier, "Unions and Monopoly Profits," *Review of Economics and Statistics,* (February 1985): 34–42; Thomas Karier, "New Evidence on the Effect of Unions and Imports on Monopoly Power," *Journal of Post-Keynesian Economics* 10 (Spring 1988): 414–27; Paula Voos and Larry Mishel, "The Union Impact on Profits: Evidence from Industry Price-Cost Margin Data,"

Journal of Labor Economics (January 1986): 105–33; and Richard B. Freeman, "Unionism, Price-Cost Margins, and the Return to Capital," National Bureau of Economic Research Working Paper no. 1164 (Cambridge, Mass.: NBER, 1983). Freeman and Medoff sum up the essence of this research by suggesting, "What unions do is to reduce the exceedingly high levels of profitability in highly concentrated industries toward normal competitive levels" (Richard B. Freeman and James L. Medoff, *What Do Unions Do?* [New York: Basic Books, 1984], p. 186).

19. James E. Anderson, David W. Brady, Charles S. Bullock III, and Joseph Stewart, Jr., *Public Policy and Politics in America,* 2d ed. (Monterey, Calif.: Brooks/Cole, 1984), pp. 296–97.

20. A brief list of these books includes Thomas J. Peters and Robert J. Waterman, *In Search of Excellence* (New York: Harper and Row, 1983); Tom Peters, *Thriving on Chaos—Handbook for a Management Revolution* (New York: Knopf, 1987); Rosabeth Moss Kanter, *The Change Masters: Innovation and Entrepreneurship in the American Corporation* (New York: Simon and Schuster, 1983); W. Edwards Deming, *Out of Crisis* (Cambridge, Mass.: Massachusetts Institute of Technology, 1982); Peter F. Drucker, *Managing in Turbulent Times* (London: Pan Books, 1980).

21. Maryann Keller, *Rude Awakening* (New York: Morrow, 1989), p. 21.

22. Harrison and Bluestone, *Great U-Turn,* p. 23.

23. Roughly speaking, if all firms are treated as a single unit, capital inputs amount to no more than 30 percent of the economy's total costs. Labor accounts for the rest. See Alan Blinder, ed., *Paying for Productivity* (Washington, D.C.: Brookings Institution, 1990), p. 2.

24. "A Survey of Mexican Plant Owners," *Automotive News,* May 2, 1988.

25. *UAW Research Bulletin* (February 1991): 8.

26. See Philip Mirowski and Susan Helper, "Maquiladoras: Mexico's Tiger by the Tail?" *Challenge,* May–June 1989, pp. 25–26.

27. Akio Morita, as quoted in Norman Jonas, "The Hollow Corporation," *Business Week,* March 3, 1986, p. 57.

28. The source for these statistics is the U.S. Bureau of Labor Statistics, *Handbook of Labor Statistics* (Washington, D.C.: Government Printing Office, 1989), as reported in Thomas Karier, "Trade Deficits and Labor Unions: Myths and Realities," in *Unions and Economic Competitiveness,* ed. Lawrence Mishel and Paula Voos (Armonk, N.Y.: Sharpe, 1992), table 1, p. 19.

29. See Thomas A. Kochan, Harry C. Katz, and Robert B. McKersie, *The Transformation of American Industrial Relations* (New York: Basic Books, 1986), pp. 68–69.

30. See table 3.3 in Kochan, Katz, and McKersie, *American Industrial Relations*, p. 71.

31. For a graphic story about the steel industry using this metaphor, see John P. Hoerr, *And the Wolf Finally Came* (Pittsburgh, Pa.: University of Pittsburgh Press, 1988).

32. See Daniel J. B. Mitchell, "Recent Union Contract Concessions," *Brookings Papers on Economic Activity* 1 (1982): 171–72. For the record, wages at Chrysler were restored to auto industry levels in subsequent years as the corporation regained profitability.

33. Ibid., pp. 170–71.

34. Daniel J. B. Mitchell, "Shifting Norms in Wage Determination," *Brookings Papers on Economic Activity* 2 (1985): 585 (table 5). Mitchell's tabulation is based on the results of biweekly surveys conducted by the Bureau of National Affairs, Inc., covering union settlements involving fifty or more employees.

35. Ibid., p. 593.

36. Two-tier contracts have proven less attractive to management in recent years because of the antagonism they implicitly engender between senior and junior employees. Labor unions have fought them successfully in many industries. Only 4 percent of contracts signed in 1990 contained such a provision. See Bureau of National Affairs, Inc., *Daily Labor Report*, no. 37 (February 27, 1991): 2.

37. Mike Davis, *Prisoners of the American Dream* (London: Verso–New Left Books, 1986), p. 152.

38. Robert J. Flanagan, "Wage Concessions and Long-Term Union Wage Flexibility," *Brookings Papers on Economic Activity* 1 (1984):186 (table 1), 192 (table 3).

39. For one of the most elaborate discussions of the shift to flexible specialization, see Michael J. Piore and Charles F. Sabel, *The Second Industrial Divide* (New York: Basic Books, 1984). Some firms agreed to provide extra "pay-for-knowledge" to workers who learned multiple skills.

40. For further discussion of the impact of flexible manufacturing on unions and the traditional Workplace Contract, see John Hoerr, "What Should Unions Do?" *Harvard Business Review* 69 (May–June 1991): 30–45.

41. See Michael Goldfield, *The Decline of Organized Labor in the United States* (Chicago: University of Chicago Press, 1987), p. 51.

42. Ibid., p. 226.

43. See Charles R. Hulten and James W. Robertson, "Corporate Tax Policy and Economic Growth: An Analysis of the 1981 and 1982 Tax Acts: Changing Domestic Priorities" (Washington, D.C.: Urban Institute, December 1982, discussion paper).

44. For a discussion of deregulation under the Reagan administration, see

Michael D. Reagan, *The Politics of Policy* (Boston: Little, Brown, 1987); "Deregulating America," *Business Week*, November 28, 1983, pp. 80–96; and Harrison and Bluestone, *Great U-Turn*, pp. 99–102.

45. For a more detailed discussion of changes in the legal philosophy of the National Labor Relations Board, see Gordon L. Clark, "Prospects for Labor Law Reform" (Pittsburgh, Pa.: Center for Labor Studies, School of Urban and Public Affairs, Carnegie Mellon University, October 24, 1986, working paper), p. 8.

46. These numbers refer to corporate profits throughout the entire economy, adjusted for inventory valuation and capital consumption allowances. The source for these data is *Economic Report of the President, 1989*, table B-87, p. 409.

47. GM's profit recovery, unlike that of Ford or Chrysler, was not primarily due to its domestic auto operations. Rather, its foreign auto plants, its financing unit—the GM Acceptance Corporation (GMAC)—and its recently acquired Hughes Division were responsible for the bulk of its increased profitability. Throughout the 1980s, GM continued to lose domestic market share not only to the Japanese and other foreign competitors, but to Ford and Chrysler as well.

48. *UAW Research Bulletin* (April 1987): 27–29.

49. These statistics refer to corporate profits with inventory valuation adjustment, but without capital consumption adjustments. See *Economic Report of the President, 1989*, table B-89, p. 411.

50. See Samuel Bowles, David Gordon, and Thomas Weisskopf, "Power and Profits: The Social Structure of Accumulation and the Profitability of the Postwar U.S. Economy," *Review of Radical Political Economics* 18 (Spring/Summer 1986): 132–67, as revised and reported to the authors by Weisskopf in December 1987 to reflect new government capital stock series.

51. The data on personal consumption expenditures and installment credit are from Council of Economic Advisers, *Economic Indicators* (Washington, D.C.: Government Printing Office, October 1990), pp. 1, 29.

52. *Economic Report of the President, 1987*, table B-45, p. 359; and *Economic Indicators*, p. 15.

53. See Barry Bluestone, "The Great U-Turn Revisited: Economic Restructuring, Jobs, and the Redistribution of Earnings" in *Jobs, Earnings, and Employment Growth Policies in the United States*, ed. John D. Kasarda (Boston: Kluwer, 1990).

54. To remain in the middle class in the face of declining *weekly* earnings, families worked harder and longer in the 1980s. According to the U.S. Bureau of Labor Statistics, the number of workers "moonlighting" (i.e., holding more than one job simultaneously) rose from 4.7 percent in 1975

to 6.2 percent in 1989. This was particularly true among women, where the percentage moonlighting increased from 2.9 percent to 5.9 percent. In addition, more and more workers were putting in long hours. The proportion of the work force working 49 hours or more per week increased from 18 percent in 1970 to nearly 24 percent in 1989. According to Louis Harris and Associates, the median number of leisure hours taken each week by adults eighteen and over declined by a startling 10 hours, from 26.2 in 1973 to 16.6 hours in 1987. See Peter T. Kilborn, "Tales from the Digital Treadmill," *New York Times,* June 3, 1990, sec. 4, p. 1.

55. *Economic Report of the President, 1989* table B-30, p. 342. In 1980 the federal government counted 13.0 percent of all persons in poverty; by 1987— before the slowdown in the economy at the end of the decade—the poverty rate was up to 13.5 percent.

56. Katherine L. Bradbury, "The Shrinking Middle Class," *New England Economic Review* (September–October 1986): 52.

Chapter 4: What Went Wrong?

1. For a ranking of U.S. manufacturing industries by their trade balance status, see National Academy of Engineering, "The Technological Dimensions of International Competition" (Washington, D.C.: NAE, 1988), p. 18. Boeing Aircraft has been the number-one U.S. exporting firm for years. In 1990, the company had export sales of over $16 billion. These sales represented more than 58 percent of its total sales. Among America's fifty biggest exporters, there were ten in addition to Boeing whose exports were 20 percent or more of its total sales. These were McDonnell-Douglas (aerospace products), Caterpillar (heavy machinery, engines, turbines), Hewlett-Packard (computers, electronics), Motorola (communications equipment, semiconductors), Unisys (computers), Intel (microcomputer components), Compaq Computer (computers), Sun Microsystems (computers), FMC (armored military vehicles, chemicals), and Ethyl Corporation (specialty and petroleum chemicals). Note that of these top ten, six are related to computer manufacturing. See James Beeler, "Exports: Shim 'Em Out," *Fortune,* Spring/Summer 1991, p. 59. See also Jonathan Kapstein, Patrick Oster, Kevin Kelly, and Paul Magnusson, "Why Europe Is in Dollar Shock," *Business Week,* March 4, 1991, pp. 36–37; Christopher Farrell, Michael J. Mandel, Keith Hammonds, Doris Jones Yang, and Paul Magnusson, "At Last, Good News: The Stunning Turnaround in Trade Is No Fluke," *Business Week,* June 3, 1991, pp. 24–25; and Sylvia Nasar, "Boom in Manufac-

tured Exports Provides Hope for U.S. Economy," *New York Times*, April 21, 1991, p. 1.

2. See Alan M. Kantrow in the introduction to Alan M. Kantrow, ed., *Survival Strategies for American Industry* (New York: Wiley, 1983), p. 2.

3. As the economist William Baumol writes: "There has undoubtedly been a protracted fall off [in productivity growth] from the early postwar peak, and it certainly was pronounced. But it is that peak which looks like the aberration, and the decline from it may well prove to be a return to historical growth rates." As such, the glory days, according to Baumol, were idiosyncratic, in large measure due to the postwar exploitation of accumulated innovative ideas left dormant during the Great Depression and the extraordinary amount of investible savings hoarded during the war. In historical terms, the argument goes, we are not doing badly at all. See William J. Baumol, "Productivity Growth, Convergence, and Welfare: What the Long-Run Data Show," *American Economic Review* 76 (December 1986): 1081–82. For a review of Baumol's research, see Alicia H. Munnell, "The Growth Puzzle," *American Prospect*, no. 3 (Fall 1990): 120–22.

4. See Paul Krugman, *The Age of Diminished Expectations* (Cambridge, Mass.: MIT Press, 1990), p. 12.

5. The six industries that have *not* experienced a decline in productivity are food, textiles, apparel, furniture, nonelectrical machinery, and electrical machinery—including computers. That at least several of these productivity "performers"—textiles, apparel, and nonelectrical machinery—are still subject to intense international price competition suggests that productivity growth alone is not sufficient to generate a trade balance or surplus. The fourteen manufacturing industries suffering declines in productivity are tobacco products, lumber, paper, printing and publishing, chemicals, petroleum refining, rubber, leather, primary metals, transportation equipment, instruments, miscellaneous manufactures, and stone, clay, and glass. See American Productivity Center, *Multiple Input Productivity Indexes* 6 (December 1986), table 3a, as reported in Martin Neil Baily and Alok K. Chakrabarti, *Innovation and the Productivity Crisis* (Washington, D.C.: Brookings Institution, 1988), table 1-3, p. 6.

6. See Edward F. Denison, *Estimates of Productivity Change by Industry* (Washington, D.C.: Brookings Institution, 1989), table 3-1, p. 40.

7. U.S. Department of Labor, Bureau of Labor Statistics, *Productivity and the Economy: A Chartbook*, Bulletin 2298 (Washington, D.C.: Government Printing Office, March 1988), chart 5, p. 11.

8. As theory would predict, the "boomlet" in manufacturing productivity helped to stabilize U.S. prices and led to expanded exports. Between

1973 and 1983, when productivity growth was dismal, U.S. merchandise exports (in nominal dollars) increased by a factor of 2.83, while merchandise imports soared by a factor of 3.81. Between 1983 and 1989, partly as a result of productivity-enhanced stable prices, the expansion in U.S. exports kept pace with the expansion of foreign merchandise imports. Both rose by approximately 80 percent. These statistics are computed from data contained in Council of Economic Advisers, *Economic Report of the President, 1989* (Washington, D.C.: Government Printing Office, 1989), table B-102, p. 424; and Council of Economic Advisers, *Economic Indicators* (Washington, D.C.: Government Printing Office, October 1990), p. 35.

9.   The merchandise trade deficit peaked in 1987 at $160 billion. In the following three years, it fell to $127 billion, $116 billion, and $108 billion, respectively. Partly as a result of the 1990–91 recession, the trade balance fell further to an annualized rate of less than $74 billion by the end of 1991. See *Economic Indicators,* March 1992 p. 36.

10.   The MIT Commission on Industrial Productivity estimates that between 1979 and 1986, 36 percent of the improvement in labor productivity was due simply to industry jettisoning employees. See Michael L. Dertouzos, Richard K. Lester, and Robert M. Solow, *Made in America* (Cambridge, Mass.: MIT Press, 1989), p. 31.

11.   Baily and Chakrabarti, *Innovation and the Productivity Crisis,* pp. 5–7; and Lawrence Mishel, "Manufacturing Numbers: How Inaccurate Statistics Conceal U.S. Industrial Decline," *EPI Study Series* (Washington, D.C.: Economic Policy Institute, 1989).

12.   Gene Koretz, "The Surge in Factory Productivity Looks Like History Now . . ." *Business Week,* October 8, 1990, p. 24.

13.   Computed from data in Council of Economic Advisers, *Economic Indicators* (Washington, D.C.: Government Printing Office, August 1991).

14.   Denison, *Estimates of Productivity Change,* table 3-1, p. 40.

15.   "Productivity Rise First in Six Quarters," *New York Times,* August 7, 1990, p. D4.

16.   See Edward F. Denison, *Trends in American Economic Growth, 1929–1982* (Washington, D.C.: Brookings Institution, 1985).

17.   See Edward F. Denison, *Accounting for Slower Economic Growth: The United States in the 1970s* (Washington, D.C.: Brookings Institution, 1979).

18.   Quoted in Baily and Chakrabarti, *Innovation and the Productivity Crisis,* p. 33.

19.   See Dertouzos, Lester, and Solow, *Made in America.*

20.   See Alicia H. Munnell, "Why Has Productivity Growth Declined? Productivity and Public Investment," *New England Economic Review* (January/February 1990): 4.

21. Ibid., pp. 9–10.
22. As quoted in *Wall Street Journal,* January 6, 1981, p. 1.
23. The calculations that provide this estimate are figured in the following manner:

How much more investment in capital would have been necessary during the period 1980 to 1987 in order to meet the 3.8 percent GNP growth rate of 1948 to 1969, given the slow growth in multifactor productivity (.4 %) from 1979 to 1987?

1. The relationship between output growth, multifactor productivity growth, labor force growth, and investment (capital growth) is the following:

$$\% \; Q \text{ growth} = \% \text{ MFP growth} +$$
$$(s_k \times \% \text{ K growth}) + (s_l \times \% \text{ L growth})$$

where Q_t = real output
MFP_t = index of multifactor productivity
K_t = real capital input
L_t = real labor input
s_k = capital share
s_l = labor share

2. For 1960 to 1969, the relevant data are:

$$4.5\% = 1.8\% + (.359 \times 4.1\%) + (.641 \times 1.9\%)$$

3. For 1979 to 1987, the relevant data are:

$$2.7\% = .4\% + (.348 \times 4.0\%) + (.652 \times 1.4\%)$$

4. Simulating a 3.8% growth rate for 1979 to 1987 (the actual average real GNP growth rate for the early post–World War II era), given the .4% growth in multifactor productivity, assuming the actual capital and labor shares, and given the actual labor force growth rate, yields a capital growth rate of 7.1%:

$$3.8\% = .4\% + (.348 \times X) + (.652 \times 1.4\%)$$

Solving for X yields 7.1%.

5. Between 1980 and 1987, real gross domestic investment grew from $509.3 billion to $674.8 billion, or 4.1% per year.

6. To fulfill a growth rate of 7.1% a year, real gross domestic investment would have had to grow to $823 billion by 1987. Over the eight-year period, the total *additional* investment would have amounted to over a half trillion dollars—$535 billion. If all of this were to have come from added savings, consumption between 1980 and 1987 would have

been cut by a little more than 3 percent ($535 billion ÷ $15.8 trillion = 3.3%).

(*Sources:* Growth equation and data for calculating capital investment are from Munnell, "Why Has Productivity Growth Declined?" pp. 5, 9. Consumption and investment data are from Council of Economic Advisers, *Economic Report of the President, 1989,* table B-2, p. 310.)

24. William A. Ruch and James C. Hershauer, *Factors Affecting Worker Productivity,* (Tempe, Ariz.: Bureau of Business and Economic Research, Arizona State University, 1974), pp. 36–37.

25. James P. Womack, Daniel T. Jones, and Daniel Roos, *The Machine That Changed the World* (New York: Rawson, 1990), p. 99.

26. Quoted in Robert H. Hayes, "Why Japanese Factories Work," in *Survival Strategies for American Industry,* ed. Alan M. Kantrow (New York: Wiley, 1983), p. 239.

27. See Andrew Pollack, "The Computer Age: Still a Work in Progress," *New York Times,* August 11, 1991, sec. 4, p. 1.

28. The statistics on R&D spending are from an October 1986 article by Martin Baily appearing in *Science,* as reported in Laura D'Andrea Tyson, "Competitiveness: An Analysis of the Problem and a Perspective on Future Policy," in *Global Competitiveness,* ed. Martin K. Starr (New York: Norton, 1988), p. 99.

29. Thomas A. Stewart, "The New American Century: Where We Stand," *Fortune,* Spring/Summer 1991, p. 18. As late as 1980, of the top six U.S. patent winners, five were U.S. corporations. General Electric led the race, with RCA, the U.S. Navy, AT&T, and IBM among this list. In 1990, only GE and IBM made the top ten.

30. See Tyson, "Competitiveness: An Analysis," p. 99.

31. William J. Broad, "In the Realm of Technology, Japan Looms Ever Larger," *New York Times,* May 28, 1991, p. C1.

32. See Baily and Chakrabarti, *Innovation and the Productivity Crisis,* p. 59.

33. See Dertouzos, Lester, and Solow, *Made in America.*

34. Ibid., p. 13.

35. See Doron P. Levin, "Toyota Tercel Priced to Swell Buyer Base," *New York Times,* September 25, 1990, p. D5.

36. See Jim Mateja, "Domestic Car Prices Rise 3% as Japanese Hold Line," *Boston Globe,* October 22, 1990, p. 48.

37. Even when American firms had the opportunity to challenge the Japanese and other foreign competitors after the devaluation of the dollar in the mid-1980s, U.S. firms generally failed to do so. When devaluation forced foreign firms to increase their prices, American firms could have held the line on theirs, thereby capturing greater market share. Instead,

many opted for short-term higher profits. In the auto industry, as well as others, this proved devastating. In 1986, each lost point in auto market share cost U.S. manufacturers nearly 115,000 lost sales. The market share calculations are found in Kim B. Clark, W. Bruce Chew, and Takhiro Fujimoto, "Product Development in the World Auto Industry," *Brookings Papers on Economic Activity* 3 (1987): 731.

38. W. Edwards Deming, *Quality, Productivity, and Competitive Position* (Cambridge, Mass.: Center for Advanced Engineering Study, MIT, 1982), pp. 14–15.

39. These examples are reported in Don C. Jackson, "Technology Hemorrhage in an Open Society," *Business in the Contemporary World* (Autumn 1989): 105.

40. George Gilder, "The Revitalization of Everything: The Law of the Microcosm," *Harvard Business Review* 66 (March–April 1988): 53, as reported in Jackson, "Technology Hemorrhage," pp. 104–5.

41. As quoted in Howard Gleckman, "The Darman Diet for Bloated Businesses," *Business Week,* March 13, 1989, p. 102.

42. See Robert Reich, *The Next American Frontier* (New York: Times Books, 1983).

43. Thomas A. Stewart, "Lessons from U.S. Business Blunders," *Fortune,* April 23, 1990, p. 141.

44. These data were culled from *Mergers and Acquisitions* 21 (May/June 1987): 57, as reported in Frank R. Lichtenberg and Donald Siegel, "Productivity and Changes in Ownership of Manufacturing Plants," *Brookings Papers on Economic Activity* 3 (1987): 644 (table 1).

45. See Carla Rapoport, "Japan's Capital Spending Spree," *Fortune,* April 9, 1990, p. 92.

46. See Andrei Shleifer and Lawrence H. Summers, "Hostile Takeovers as Breaches of Trust," Department of Economics, Harvard University, unpublished paper (1987), as referenced in Lichtenberg and Siegel, "Productivity and Changes in ownership," p. 645.

47. Gregory L. Miles, " 'If We Knew Everything We Know Now . . .' " *Business Week,* January 15, 1990, p. 54.

48. For an excellent summary of this argument, see Dale Belman, "Unions, the Quality of Labor Relations, and Firm Performance," in *Unions and Economic Competitiveness,* ed. Lawrence Mishel and Paula Voos (Armonk, N.Y.: Sharpe 1991).

49. Besides Belman's work in this area, see the seminal study by Richard B. Freeman and James L. Medoff, *What Do Unions Do?* (New York: Basic Books, 1984).

50. The actual differential varies significantly from industry to industry and from occupation to occupation. In the heyday of unions in the 1960s,

according to Stanford economist and chairman of President Bush's Council of Economic Advisers, Michael Boskin, unionized unskilled laborers earned as much as 25 percent more than those who were unorganized. On the other hand, the union/nonunion wage differential for sales workers was an almost insignificant 2.3 percent. See Michael J. Boskin, "Unions and Relative Real Wages," *American Economic Review* 62 (June 1979): 469.

51. Charles Brown and James Medoff, "Trade Unions in the Production Process," *Journal of Political Economy* (June 1978): 355–78.

52. For productivity estimates in the cement industry, see Kim B. Clark, "The Impact of Unionization on Productivity: A Case Study," *Industrial and Labor Relations Review* 33 (July 1980): 451–69; in the construction industry, see Steven G. Allen, "Unionized Construction Workers Are More Productive," *Quarterly Journal of Economics* 99 (May 1984): 251–96; for hospitals, see Charles A. Register, "Wages, Productivity, and Costs in Union and Nonunion Hospitals," *Journal of Labor Research* (Fall 1988); in the mining industry, see M. Connerton, R. B. Freeman, and J. L. Medoff, "Industrial Relations and Productivity: A Study of the U.S. Bituminous Coal Industry" (Cambridge, Mass.: Harvard University, 1983, Mimeographed).

53. For example, a positive 25 percent union productivity premium in bituminous coal during the 1960s was found to have turned to *negative* 25 percent in the mid-1970s as a result of the stormy industrial relations climate that developed in the industry as unionized mines tried to extract major concessions from their workers. See Connerton, Freeman, and Medoff, "Industrial Relations and Productivity." Similarly, Graddy and Hall find some evidence that conflictual labor relations reduce productivity in the banking industry by up to 25 percent. See Duane B. Graddy and Gary Hall, "Unionization and Productivity in Commercial Banking," *Journal of Labor Research* (Summer 1985): 6.

54. In cross-sectional studies, Mansfield, Link, Hirsch and Link, and Turleckyi have suggested that highly organized industries suffer an annual productivity growth rate deficit of at most 5 percent to 6 percent. Sveikaskaus and Sveikaskaus, Freeman and Medoff, and Allen in other research have concluded that there is no evidence to support any claim of a productivity growth effect. See Edward Mansfield, "Basic Research and Productivity Increase in Manufacturing," *American Economic Review* 70 (December 1980): 863–71; Albert N. Link, "Productivity Growth, Environmental Regulations, and the Composition of R&D," *Bell Journal of Economics* 13 (Autumn 1982); 548–54; Barry T. Hirsch and Albert N.

Link, "Unions, Productivity, and Productivity Growth," *Journal of Labor Research* 5 (Winter 1984); Nestor Turleckyj, "What Do R&D Numbers Tell Us About Technological Change?" *American Economic Review* 70 (May 1980): 55–61 C. D. Sveikaskaus and L. Sveikaskaus, "Industry Characteristics and Productivity Growth," *Southern Economic Journal* 48 (January 1982): 769–74; Freeman and Medoff, *What Do Unions Do?* and Steven G. Allen, "Declining Unionization in Construction: The Facts and the Reasons," *Industrial and Labor Relations Review* 41 (April 1988): 343–59.

55. Freeman and Medoff, *What Do Unions Do?*
56. In the construction industry, Steven Allen found that 10 percent of the union productivity advantage was due to the reduced need for supervision. See Steven G. Allen, "Unionization and Productivity in Office Building and School Construction" (Raleigh, N.C.: North Carolina State University, January 1983, Mimeographed), pp. 27–30.
57. Freeman and Medoff, *What Do Unions Do?* p. 183.
58. John Hoerr, *And the Wolf Finally Came: The Decline of the American Steel Industry* (Pittsburgh, Pa.: University of Pittsburgh Press, 1988), as reprinted in *Work in America* 13, (September 1988): 2.
59. On manufacturing wage growth, see Lawrence Mishel and David M. Frankel, *The State of Working America* (Armonk, N.Y.: Sharpe, 1991), p. 259.
60. Niccolò Machiavelli, *The Prince* (Baltimore: Penguin Books, 1961), p. 51.
61. "Modern operating agreements" are by no means a child of the 1980s or 1990s. John L. Lewis, for instance, as president of the United Mine Workers Union during the 1930s insisted that the mine owners invest in modern technology in order to increase productivity. On the West Coast in the 1960s, the International Longshoremen's and Warehousemen's Union, under the legendary Harry Bridges, reached accord with the dock owners on mechanization and modernization, making wholesale changes in work rules in return for a no-layoff policy and earnings guarantees. The outline of this "epochal" agreement appears in the union's newspaper, *The Dispatcher*, October 31, 1960.
62. See Ramond A. Katzell and Daniel Yankelovich, *Work, Productivity, and Job Satisfaction* (New York: Psychological Corporation, 1975), pp. 103, 115, 117.
63. See Dertouzos, Lester, and Solow, *Made in America*, p. 268.
64. Auto industry losses nearly put Chrysler out of business and threatened Ford's existence. Total employment in the domestic motor vehicle industry plummeted from over a million in 1978 to less than 700,000 in four

years. During the same period, the construction industry jettisoned over 350,000 workers, while basic steel lost over 160,000. For employment data by major industry category, see U.S. Department of Labor, Bureau of Labor Statistics, *Handbook of Labor Statistics*, Bulletin 2217 (Washington, D.C.: Government Printing Office, 1985), tables 64 and 65, pp. 176–77.

65. Calculated from *Economic Report of the President, 1989*, table B-108, p. 431.

66. Tyson, "Competitiveness: An Analysis," p. 101.

67. See David Aschauer, "Is Public Expenditure Productive?" *Journal of Monetary Economics* 23 (March 1989). From 1950 to 1970, public infrastructure investment expanded at 4.3 percent annually, and total factor productivity grew at a healthy 1.75 percent per year, consistent with annual labor productivity growth of about 3 percent. In the subsequent period between 1970 and 1985, investment in airports, highways, sewer systems, and other public works declined to an average annual rate of only 1.5 percent. What happened to private-sector productivity when infrastructure investment slowed? It declined to less than 1 percent per year.

68. See Alan S. Blinder, "Are Crumbling Highways Giving Productivity a Flat?" *Business Week*, August 29, 1988, p. 16.

69. Alicia H. Munnell, "Why Has Productivity Growth Declined? Productivity and Public Investment," *New England Economic Review* (January/February 1990): 18.

70. Dertouzos, Lester, and Solow, *Made in America*, p. 112.

71. See William Celis III, "Scholastic Tests Show Decline in Verbal Skills," *New York Times*, August 28, 1990, p. B5. The average math SAT scores for 1967, 1981, and 1990 were 492, 466, and 476, respectively.

Certainly, not all of the education deficit can be laid on the doorstep of too little government spending on primary and secondary schools. Still, our nation, which prides itself on its public schools, has fallen behind in its funding of education. Larry Mishel and Edith Rasell of the Washington-based Economic Policy Institute were surprised when they compared America's spending on schools with that of our leading economic competitors. They found that the United States was no longer leading and was in fact far behind in the pack. If government spending on *all* levels of education, including colleges and universities, is the object of interest, the United States does pretty well. In terms of school expenditure per dollar of gross domestic product (GDP), America is tied for second place with the Netherlands. Only Sweden spends more.

When the analysis is restricted to kindergarten through grade twelve, however, the story changes dramatically. The United States is not first or second in school spending; it is fourteenth. Ahead of it are Sweden, Austria, Switzerland, Norway, Belgium, Denmark, Japan, Canada,

West Germany, France, the Netherlands, Great Britain, and Italy. Of the richest developed countries, only Australia and Ireland spend a smaller share of their GDP on primary and secondary schooling. In terms of another measure, expenditure per pupil, the United States in 1988 ranked ninth among the top sixteen developed countries. The United States was behind Switzerland, Sweden, Norway, Japan, Denmark, Austria, West Germany, and Canada. See M. Edith Rasell and Lawrence Mishel, "Shortchanging Education: How U.S. Spending on Grades K–12 Lags Behind Other Industrial Nations," *EPI Study Series,* (Washington D.C.: *Economic Policy Institute,* 1989).

Private business has attempted to make up for the shortcomings in the formal education system. One estimate suggests that firms are spending collectively about $30 billion a year on improving the skills of their employees. The snag is that only 8 percent of this money is being spent on verbal and math skills, most training is narrowly targeted, and a disproportionate share goes to employees who are college graduates or executives in postgraduate programs. Nowhere near enough trickles down to the workers at the plant level to boost their productivity growth to global standards. See Robert Reich, "Blackboard Jingle," *American Prospect* (Fall 1990): 8–12.

72. John Bishop, "Is the Test Score Decline Responsible for the Productivity Growth Decline?" *American Economic Review* 79 (March 1989): 192.

73. Translated into readily meaningful terms, the test score drop meant GNP in 1980 was nearly 1 percent less than it would have been if test scores had remained at their 1966 level. By 1987, the United States was forfeiting 1.9 percent of its GNP because of this failing. By the year 2010, according to Bishop, the nation's GNP will have suffered a 4.4 percent deficit as a result of the declining scholarship produced in U.S. schools.

While a number of equally well trained economists doubt Bishop's precise estimates, few deny the link between test scores, scholastic ability, and the nation's output or ability to compete. One of these is the Brookings Institution's Henry J. Aaron, who argues that "the drop in test scores came too late and applied to too small a proportion of the work force to explain the productivity slowdown" ("Politics and Professors Revisited," *Papers and Proceedings of the American Economic Association* 79 [May 1989]: 8–9). Nonetheless, he believes that longer school days, weeks, and years can improve academic performance and help accelerate economic growth.

74. See Dertouzos, Lester, and Solow, *Made in America,* p. 21.

75. Robert Reich, as reported in Curtis J. Lang, "The Hole in America's Stocking," *Village Voice,* December 25, 1990, p. 40.

76. Dertouzos, Lester, and Solow, *Made in America,* p. 21.

77. One of the best books on this subject is Robert Kuttner, *The End of Laissez Faire* (New York: Knopf, 1991).

78. The original theory of free trade traces its routes to the nineteenth-century writings of David Ricardo. A "new view" of trade is developing among standard theorists that departs somewhat from the original laissez-faire doctrine. Given economies of scale and externality or spill-over effects, the new view suggests that nations can, under specific conditions, improve their overall welfare through a strategic set of market barriers. Leading researchers in this branch of neoclassical theory include Paul Krugman, Avinash Dixit, James Brander, and Barbara Spencer. For an introduction to the new view, see Paul Krugman, *Rethinking International Trade* (Cambridge, Mass.: MIT Press, 1990).

79. Canada substituted at the beginning of 1991 a value-added tax for its old manufacturers' excise tax. Under the new levy system, Canadian exporters receive a rebate equal to the amount of the tax they have paid on purchases related to their foreign sales. Under the old tax they did not. As a consequence, Canadian manufacturers will become more competitive. They are expected to boost their exports by at least $1.25 billion a year—on top of the better than $8 billion annual surplus they already enjoy with the United States. See Clyde H. Farnsworth, "New Tax to Aid Canada on Trade," *New York Times*, January 21, 1991, p. D1.

80. This and the following examples of industrial policy in practice are drawn from Dertouzos, Lester, and Solow, *Made in America*.

81. See Steven Greenhouse, "There's No Stopping Europe's Airbus Now," *New York Times*, June 23, 1991, p. F1.

Chapter 5: Management Rights and Union Demands

1. Milton Friedman, "The Social Responsibility of Business Is to Increase Its Profits," *New York Times Magazine*, September 13, 1970, pp. 32–33, 122–26.

2. Peter F. Drucker, *Management: Tasks, Responsibilities, Practices* (New York: Harper Colophon, 1985), p. 40.

3. Quoted in John Daintith, Hazel Egerton, Rosalind Fergusson, Anne Stibbs, and Edmund Wright, eds., *The Macmillan Dictionary of Quotations* (New York: Macmillan, 1987), p. 92.

4. Walter Reuther, "How to Raise Wages Without Increasing Prices" (Detroit: UAW, n.d.), p. 20, transcript of speech, quoted in Neil Chamberlain, *The Union Challenge to Management Control* (New York: Harper and Row, 1948), p. 97.

5. The original theoretical work on profit "satisficing" was done in the late

1950s by William Baumol, a Princeton University economist. See William Baumol, *Economic Theory and Operations Analysis* (Englewood Cliffs, N.J.: Prentice-Hall, 1971). The Harvard economist John Kenneth Galbraith popularized the idea in his book *The New Industrial State* (Boston: Houghton Mifflin, 1967).

6. Even the most modest comparison reveals important similarities between the guilds of medieval Europe and the craft unionism of the late nineteenth and twentieth centuries in Europe and the United States. In both cases, those with specific skills organized to protect jurisdiction over entry to their craft and exercised control over the regulations that governed it. The major differences are that the master guildsman was, in his own right, the equivalent of an entrepreneur, and the guild was as much an association of employers as it was a union of artisans. Operating within a restricted economic and geographic area, the guild association and its members had the equivalent of monopoly power and controlled what are generally characterized today as management rights. In contrast, the contemporary craftsperson has largely lost his or her ironclad control of the marketplace and normally works as an employee under the direction of a contractor. Nonetheless, modern craft unions have been constituted for precisely the same purpose as the earlier guilds: to maintain for their members a satisfactory standard of living by protecting the jurisdiction of their skills and by enhancing the dignity of their craft—a benign combination of "bread and roses."

7. John Cameron Simonds and John T. McEnnis, *The Story of Manual Labor* (New York: Peale, 1886).

8. William Lazonick, *Competitive Advantage on the Shop Floor: Organization and Technology in Capitalist Development*, Occasional Paper no. 10 (New York: Center for Labor-Management Policy Studies, Graduate School and University Center, City University of New York, July 1990), p. 4.

9. Ibid., p. 5.

10. See George Lodge, *The New American Ideology* (New York: Knopf, 1975), pp. 9–11, as summarized in Michael Beer, Bert Spector, Paul R. Lawrence, D. Quinn Mills, and Richard E. Walton, *Managing Human Assets: The Groundbreaking Harvard Business School Program* (New York: Free Press, 1984), p. 42.

It is interesting to note that the moral basis for opposition to the spread of industrial unionism during the 1930s was similarly based on the alleged sacred nature of property rights. Consider the position of S. M. DuBrul, the director of the labor economics section of General Motors, in a speech delivered before the Institute of Public Affairs at the University of Virginia on July 14, 1934:

To sum up, society has determined certain rights called "property rights." In a corporation, the stockholders have delegated some of those rights to the Management and holds the Management accountable for the preservation and development of their best long-term interests. The Management of a business, therefore, is accountable primarily to the owners from whom it receives its authority. . . .

The very act of accepting authority constitutes an agreement to exercise it in accordance with the aims and interests of the person from whom it is obtained, and the use of this authority in a contrary manner is a violation of the terms of its acceptance. . . .

The Management, in its delegation of authority, is bound to make certain to the best of its ability that the authority will be used only in accordance with the interests of the business. This precludes it from delegating authority to anyone whose interests may be in conflict with those of the owners of the business. These are the principles that are involved in so many of the labor controversies of the moment. (Quoted in Chamberlain, *The Union Challenge*, p. 133. For the record, note the capitalization of the word *management* throughout the speech!)

11. "Helpful Hints and Advice to Employees" (Detroit, Mich.: Ford Motor Co., 1915, brochure), p. 3.

12. Richard Edwards, *Contested Terrain: The Transformation of the Workplace in the Twentieth Century* (New York: Basic Books, 1979), p. 18.

13. Dan Clawson, *Bureaucracy and the Labor Process* (New York: Monthly Review Press, 1980), p. 130.

14. Frank Hern, ed., *The Transformation of Industrial Organization* (Belmont, Calif.: Wadsworth, 1988), p. 9.

15. Edwards, *Contested Terrain*, p. 53.

16. Speech of Charles M. Schwab before the American Society of Mechanical Engineers, December 1927, as reported in David Brody, *Workers in Industrial America* (New York: Oxford University Press, 1980), p. 48.

17. Owen D. Young, as quoted in *Nation's Business*, no. 17, April 1929, and as reported in Brody, *Workers in Industrial America*, p. 50.

18. Quoted in Brody, *Workers in Industrial America*, p. 57.

19. According to Edwards, International Harvester was a leader of the welfare capitalism strategem. By 1920, I-H had branched out into new areas: a plant safety program; a medical plan providing free physical examinations for new employees; dental examinations; hospital facilities; a visiting nurse program; home instruction in hygiene; a supplementary profit-sharing plan; social clubs; and library facilities for workers. Some of the benefits, including a pension system, were reserved for workers who refused to join a union and avoided taking part in strikes. See Edwards, *Contested Terrain*, p. 92.

20. Robert Levering, Milton Moskowitz, and Michael Katz, *The 100 Best Companies to Work for in America* (New York: Signet Books, 1987), p. 21.

21. According to the labor historian David Brody, by 1927, 800,000 employees had invested over a billion dollars in stock ownership plans in 315 different companies. Companies offered their own employees group insurance for accident, illness, and death. Close to six million workers were covered by such plans by 1928. Pensions were offered by at least 350 major firms before the early 1930s. See Brody, *Workers in Industrial America*, p. 54.

22. Walter Lippman, *Interpretations, 1933–1935* (New York: Macmillan, 1936), as cited in Charles C. Heckscher, *The New Unionism* (New York: Basic Books, 1988), p. 90. According to one 1926 survey cited by Edwards, 80 percent of fifteen hundred of the largest U.S. companies had some form of welfare program, and about half had "comprehensive" schemes. See Edwards, *Contested Terrain*, p. 95.

23. See Stuart Brandes, *American Welfare Capitalism, 1880–1940* (Chicago: University of Chicago Press, 1976), p. 28.

24. Frederick Winslow Taylor, *The Principles of Scientific Management* (New York: Norton, 1967).

25. As cited in Daintith et. al., *Macmillan Dictionary of Quotations*, p. 280.

26. The following discussion of Gilbreth's and Henry Gantt's contributions to scientific management is loosely based on an account in Peter F. Drucker, *Management*, pp. 200–202.

27. Ibid., p. 202.

28. Adam Smith, *The Wealth of Nations* (New York: Random House, 1937).

29. Taylor, *Scientific Management*, p. 59.

30. Edwards reports, based on the historical research of Milton Nadworny, that the experience with Taylorism at the American Locomotive Company was not atypical of firms that tried to implement the system:

> One of Taylor's early converts, David Van Alstyne, began introducing elements of the efficiency system. But higher management, which saw the program as experimental, was not ready to undertake the scale of changes required for full implementation. Under pressure to obtain results, Van Alstyne began taking shortcuts, and the full system was never installed. This experience repeated the past—at Bethlehem [Steel], Taylor himself had been fired before he was able to complete the job. (*Contested Terrain*, p. 101)

> For more detail, see Milton Nadworny, *Scientific Management and the Unions, 1900–1932* (Cambridge, Mass.: Harvard University Press, 1955), pp. 27–28.

31. Barbara Garson, *The Electronic Sweatshop: How Computers Are Transforming the Office of the Future into the Factory of the Past* (New York: Simon and Schuster, 1988), p. 37.

32. See Carl Botan and Maureen McCreadie, "Separating Minds from Hands: Information Technology and Policy in the Workplace" (Paper presented to the Annual Conference of the American Society for Information Service, Washington D.C., November 1989), pp. 7–9.

33. Ibid., pp. 12–13.

34. The GE experience is related in Edwards, *Contested Terrain*, pp. 105–10.

35. Peter F. Drucker, *The New Society: The Anatomy of Industrial Order* (New York: Harper and Row, 1949; New York: Harper Torchbook, 1962), p. 308.

36. H. L. Arnold and L. F. Faurote, *Ford Methods and the Ford Shops* (New York: Engineering Magazine Co., 1915), as quoted in Richard C. Edwards, "The Social Relations of Production at the Point of Production," in *Essays on the Social Relations of Work and Labor,* ed. Olivia Clark, Jerry Lembcke, and Bob Marotto, Jr. (special issue of *Insurgent Sociologist* 8 [Fall 1978]: 117).

37. Calculated from Lance Davis, *American Economic Growth: An Economist's History of the United States* (New York: Harper and Row, 1972), as reported in Edwards, *Contested Terrain*, p. 135. Harry Braverman reports that the number of administrative workers in the U.S. economy relative to the number of production workers increased from 1 in 8 in 1909 to more than 1 in 5 in 1947. See Braverman, *Labor and Monopoly Capital* (New York: Monthly Review Press, 1974), p. 240.

38. The roots of managerialism actually go back to the late 1940s. Peter Drucker argued for the creation of "autonomous self-governing plant communities" where management would not simply consult with its workers but would have them make decisions for themselves. Only in this way, Drucker thought, would "it be possible for workers and middle management to see the enterprise from the angle of vision of top management, and for top management to see the enterprise from the angle of vision of the worker and middle management" (*The New Society,* p. 302).

39. Heckscher, *New Unionism,* p. 85.

40. Douglas McGregor, *The Human Side of Enterprise* (New York: McGraw-Hill, 1960).

41. Heckscher, *New Unionism,* p. 102.

42. According to surveys conducted by the business-backed Conference Board, executives at 31 percent of large, "double-breasted" firms (i.e., multiplant companies with both union and nonunion establishments) reported in 1977 that it was as important to keep as much of the company nonunion as it was to achieve the most favorable bargain possible. By 1983, the percentage of managers responding in this way had jumped to 45 percent. See Audrey Freedman, *Managing Labor Rela-*

tions (New York: Conference Board, 1979), and Audrey Freedman, *The New Look in Wage Bargaining* (New York: Conference Board, 1985).

43. For an interesting review of the techniques offered by management consultants for avoiding unions, see Phillis Payne, "The Consultants Who Coach the Violators," *AFL-CIO American Federationist,* September 1977, pp. 22–29.

44. Phillip S. Foner, *History of the Labor Movement in the United States* (New York: International, 1947), p. 65.

45. Howard Wachtel, *Labor and the Economy* (Orlando, Fla.: Academic Press, 1984), p. 454.

46. National Commission on Unemployment Compensation, *Unemployment Compensation: Final Report* (Washington, D.C.: Government Printing Office, 1980), p. 8.

47. Gordon F. Bloom and Herbert R. Northrup, *Economics of Labor Relations* (Homewood, Ill.: Irwin, 1981), p. 601.

48. Associated Industries of Massachusetts, *Industry,* December 29, 1923, as reported in Barry Bluestone and Bennett Harrison, *The Deindustrialization of America* (New York: Basic Books, 1982), pp. 240–41.

49. Wachtel, *Labor and the Economy,* p. 492.

50. In 1984 there were nearly half a million beneficiaries of the Black Lung Benefit Program—nearly 150,000 miners and more than 325,000 widows and dependents. Total payments from federal general tax revenues and mine operators exceeded $1.5 billion. See U.S. Department of Commerce, *Statistical Abstract of the United States, 1986* (Washington, D.C.: Government Printing Office, 1985), table 636, p. 374.

51. Wachtel, *Labor and the Economy,* p. 448.

52. Foner, *History of the Labor Movement,* pp. 78–81.

53. Wachtel, *Labor and the Economy,* p. 415.

54. See James E. Anderson, David W. Brady, Charles S. Bullock III, and Joseph Steward, Jr., *Public Policy and Politics in America* (Monterey, Calif.: Brooks/Cole, 1984), p. 314.

55. This particular case involved the Miners' National Association of Clearfield County, Pennsylvania, in a struggle against a reduction in wages. See Foner, *History of the Labor Movement,* pp. 457–58.

56. Anderson et al., *Public Policy,* p. 314.

57. In the 1920s, the U.S. Supreme Court interpreted the Clayton Act in a series of decisions that, among other things, effectively removed picketing from the protection of Section 20 (*American Steel Foundaries v. Tri-City Central Trades Council,* 1921) and invalidated certain collective bargaining agreements (*United States v. Brims,* 1926).

58. Herbert R. Northrup and Gordon F. Bloom, *Government and Labor* (Homewood, Ill.: Irwin, 1963), p. 22.

59. Cited in UAW Education Department, *Quotations of Significance to Union Leaders* (Detroit: UAW, May 1968), p. 4.

60. See Howard Dickman, *Industrial Democracy in America* (LaSalle, Ill.: Open Court, 1987), pp. 262–70.

61. Introduction by Walter P. Reuther to Edward Levinson, *Labor on the March* (New York: University Books, 1938).

62. Between 1935 and 1938, national union membership rose from 3.6 million to 8 million. The percentage of the nonagricultural labor force belonging to unions swelled from 13.2 percent to 27.5 percent during this three-year period. See Michael Goldfield, *The Decline in Organized Labor in the United States* (Chicago: University of Chicago Press, 1987), table 1, p. 10.

63. See Robert M. Kaus, "The Trouble with Unions," *Harper's*, June 1983, as reprinted in *The Transformation of Industrial Organization*, ed. Frank Hearn (Belmont, Calif.: Wadsworth, 1988), p. 143.

64. Beer et al., *Managing Human Assets*, pp. 48–49. For a more general statement of the countervailing power theory, see John Kenneth Galbraith, *American Capitalism* (Boston: Houghton-Mifflin, 1952).

65. See Sanford Cohen, *Labor Law* (Columbus, Ohio: Merrill, 1964), p. 169, as discussed in Wachtel, *Labor and the Economy*, op. 423.

66. See U.S. Department of Labor, Bureau of Labor Statistics, *Handbook of Labor Statistics, 1978*, Bulletin 2000 (Washington, D.C.: Government Printing Office, 1979), table 151, p. 508; and *Handbook of Labor Statistics, 1980*, Bulletin 2070 (1981), table 167, p. 415.

67. *Secondary boycotts* are those where union workers picket a job site to protest not the actions of their employer but the activities of another party such as a subcontractor or nonunion supplier. *Jurisdictional strikes* occur when a union brings a job action in an attempt to get workers to switch allegiance from another union to it. A *union shop* is one in which a worker must join the appropriate union bargaining unit within a stipulated number of days after being hired by a unionized employer. Currently, twenty-one states, mostly in the South, have taken advantage of paragraph 14b and prohibited the union shop. These are commonly designated by the union contested term, "right-to-work" states.

68. U.S. Department of Commerce, *Historical Statistics of the United States: Colonial Times to 1970* (Washington, D.C.: Government Printing Office, 1975), pt. 1, pp. 176–78.

69. Drucker, *New Society*, p. 107.

70. Neil W. Chamberlain, *The Union Challenge to Management Control* (New York: Harper and Brothers, 1948), p. 49.

71. Excerpt from a speech by Sidney Hillman as the invited guest speaker at a luncheon of a manufacturers' club in Montreal, Canada, held in

January, 1918. See Matthew Josephson, *Sidney Hillman: Statesman of American Labor* (New York: Doubleday, 1952), p. 190.

Chapter 6: Employee Involvement in Action

1. Thomas J. Peters and Robert H. Waterman, Jr., *In Search of Excellence* (New York: Harper and Row, 1982).
2. Listing the "best" of anything is always a dangerous practice, as Peters and Waterman learned. A number of their "best-run companies" began to fail soon after the publication of their book. Changes in the nature of the computer market badly damaged the profits of the minicomputer makers Digital Equipment and Wang, the latter close to bankruptcy by the end of the 1980s. Atari, a division of Warner Brothers, has, for all practical purposes, been supplanted by the Japanese-designed Nintendo system. General Motors has continued to lose market share not only to the Japanese but to its domestic rival, Ford. NCR has been the successful target of a hostile takeover by AT&T. So it goes.
3. Peters and Waterman, *In Search of Excellence,* p. xxii.
4. Ibid., p. xxv.
5. As reported in John Hoerr, "The Payoff from Teamwork," *Business Week,* July 10, 1989, p. 56.
6. As reported in Edward Cohen-Rosenthal and Cynthia E. Burton, *Mutual Gains: A Guide to Union-Management Cooperation* (New York: Praeger, 1987), p. 47.
7. See Cohen-Rosenthal and Burton, *Mutual Gains,* p. 60. According to Robert Cole, one of the leading authorities on the Japanese system of workplace cooperation:

> The number of [Japanese] firms with formal joint consultation systems has continued to grow. [A] 1980 survey of 434 firms sampled in the private sector reports that 98.6 percent of the firms had *company level* joint consultation systems (with little variance by firm size). Sixty-four percent had *plant level* joint consultation systems, ranging from 37 percent of those firms with under 300 employees to 94.3 percent of those firms with 10,000 or more employees. Finally, 16.6 percent had *workshop level* joint consultation machinery. ("Participation and Control in Japanese Industry" [Paper presented at the Conference on Productivity, Ownership, and Participation, May 24–25, 1983], p. 8)

8. Bill Saporito, "Cutting Costs Without Cutting People," *Fortune,* May 25, 1987, p. 27.
9. Ibid.

10. Irvine O. Hockaday, Jr. (CEO of Hallmark Co.), in an interview with Bill Saporito, *Fortune*, May 25, 1987, p. 31.

11. Robert Levering, Milton Moskowitz, and Michael Katz, *The 100 Best Companies to Work for in America* (New York: New American Library, 1984), p. 472.

12. According to the National Association of Suggestion Systems (indeed, there is such an organization!), in 1988 American workers dropped over one million ideas into their firms' suggestion boxes. Management adopted almost 300,000 of these, roughly 29 percent, and thereby saved $2.2 billion. This is a fine record, says the association, but it does not come close to the standard set in Japan. The Japanese Human Relations Association reports that Japanese companies with worker-suggestion programs average more than 2,000 ideas per 100 workers, compared to 13 per 100 in the United States. Close to 80 percent of the Japanese suggestions are adopted. See "Topics of the Times," *New York Times*, January 23, 1990, p. A22.

13. Charles C. Heckscher, *The New Unionism: Employee Involvement in a Changing Environment* (New York: Basic Books, 1988), p. 16. See also Severyn T. Bruyn, *A Future for the American Economy* (Stanford, Calif.: Stanford University Press, 1991), pp. 91–92.

14. Heckscher, *New Unionism*, p. 103.

15. Harold E. Edmundson and Steven C. Wheelright, "Outstanding Manufacturing in the Coming Decade," *California Management Review* 31 (Summer 1989): 82 (exhibit 3).

16. "Chicago Bank Eliminates 'Paperwork Assembly Line,'" *World of Work Report* 11 (November 1986): 1.

17. Ibid., p. 2.

18. Peter F. Drucker, *The New Society: The Anatomy of Industrial Order* (New York: Harper and Row, 1949; New York: Harper Torchbook, 1962), pp. 103–4.

19. Paul Weiler, "Who Will Represent Labor Now?" *American Prospect*, no. 2 (Summer 1990): 82–83.

20. The largest joint union-management education venture in virtually the entire world is sponsored by the UAW-GM Human Resource Center (HRC) housed in Auburn Hills, Michigan. The HRC has recently expanded its Paid Education Leave (PEL) program to target every UAW member working in a GM facility, together with local union and plant-level management officials. Every worker will be paid to go through a special one-week "global awareness" program taught by college and university instructors from the communities where plants are located. The curriculum is jointly developed by the company and the union with the aim of helping every member of the GM "community" understand

how changing global conditions affect the industry and the union. This program is underwritten by a special fund set aside in the collective bargaining agreement.

21. To cite just one example, a joint alcoholism rehabilitation program was initiated at GM in 1972. It later developed into a broad employee assistance program with a national joint committee comprised of both corporate and international union representatives. Similar joint committees were then established in virtually all of the company's plants nationwide. By the end of 1990, the total number of "clients" referred to the joint Employee Assistance Program at GM exceeded 145,000. Recovery rates, as reported by the corporation and the union, are more than twice the national average and are attributable to active follow-up, continuous concern, and ongoing case management.

22. Along this line, joint programs have been initiated covering a variety of strategies and mechanisms in the attempt to slow rising costs. Among them are effective utilization review, offering health maintenance organization or preferred provider coverage as well as managed care services, and educating employees about benefit plan design and health insurance purchasing. Obtaining data from hospitals and health care insurers and jointly reviewing the information help the parties to make decisions that may reduce costs. A study of so-called community medical practice, for instance, may provide information pointing to abuse of medical procedures (e.g., unusually high utilization of surgical procedures such as caesarean births) and open the opportunity to put pressure on the medical profession to be more attentive to practices that may unnecessarily increase costs.

23. For example, in a May 3, 1989, letter to the president of the United Steelworkers Union, Lynn Williams, Bethlehem Steel Corporation agreed to establish a "National Policy for Steel Committee" comprising top management and union officials. Among the stated purposes of the committee is "consideration of and possible development of an appropriate national health policy."

24. In a comprehensive declaration on the subject, the AFL-CIO Executive Council asserts that "by virtue of their ownership interest, all workers are entitled to equal participation with employers in the administration and investment of pension fund assets to ensure that the funds are being managed in their interest" (cited in "Labor and Investments" [Washington, D.C.: Industrial Union Department, AFL-CIO, 2d quarter pamphlet 1990,], p. 4.

25. To be sure, unions such as the Amalgamated Clothing and Textile Workers (ACTWU) and the International Ladies' Garment Workers (ILGWU) have for many years managed the pension funds established

under their contracts with employers in the clothing industry. In fact, their member retirees receive their monthly pension checks directly from the international union headquarters.

26. One can now add to these the joint committees that are responsible for overseeing the effective implementation of negotiated prepaid legal services programs and the tuition assistance programs, which enable employees to advance their skills and education, including college and university studies and technical or vocational training.

27. See William N. Cooke, *Labor Management Cooperation* (Kalamazoo, Mich.: Upjohn Institute, 1990), table 3.1, p. 62.

28. See Thomas A. Kochan, Robert B. McKersie, and John Chalykoff, "The Effects of Corporate Strategy and Workplace Innovations on Union Representation," *Industrial and Labor Relations Review* 39 (July 1986). In addition, a 1983–84 survey of approximately 350 unionized firms in Wisconsin shows that roughly 60 percent have established either shop-floor teams or joint committees. See Paula Voos, "Managerial Perceptions of the Economic Impact of Labor Relations Programs," *Industrial and Labor Relations Review* (January 1987): 195–208.

Chapter 7: Does Participation Work?

1. See William N. Cooke, *Labor-Management Cooperation* (Kalamazoo, Mich.: Upjohn Institute, 1990), esp. pp. 6–16.

2. A 1983 New York Stock Exchange survey of large companies reveals that cost cutting is the number-one reason firms initiate "quality of work life" (QWL) programs. Three out of five respondents (58 percent) mentioned this factor. Combating low morale within the work force was mentioned by 46 percent. Thirty-eight percent hoped that QWL would improve productivity; 24 percent were counting on it to improve quality. See New York Stock Exchange, "People and Productivity: A Challenge to Corporate America" (New York: NYSE, 1983).

3. Michael Beer and his colleagues at the Harvard Business School note that there may be something of a self-fulfilling prophecy here:

Managers' assumptions about the capacity of employees to participate in decisions are likely to be pessimistic because their assumptions are shaped, in part at least, by their experiences in organizations that do not afford employees opportunities to participate and influence. Thus, a self-fulfilling prophesy develops in which employees are not offered an opportunity to influence because of pessimistic management assumptions, and those assumptions are formed by past practices which have left employees dependent and unskilled in the participative process. (Michael Beer, Bert Spector, Paul R. Lawrence, D. Quinn Mills, and

Richard E. Walton, *Managing Human Assets: The Groundbreaking Harvard Business School Program* [New York: Free Press, 1984], p. 61)

4. *U.E. Guide to Wage Payments Plans, Time Study and Job Evaluation,* United Electrical, Radio and Machine Workers, 1943, p. 8, as quoted in Neil Chamberlain, *The Union Challenge to Management Control* (New York: Harper and Brothers, 1948), p. 4.

5. Preamble to the United Automobile Workers of America (UAW) Constitution, UAW-CIO, 1935, p. 7.

6. Preamble to the "Constitution of the International Union, United Automobile, Aerospace and Agricultural Implement Workers of America (UAW)," 1980, p. 3.

7. On this point, see Beer et al., *Managing Human Assets,* p. 58.

8. Victor Reuther, "Foreword" to Mike Parker and Jane Slaughter, *Choosing Sides: Unions and the Team Concept* (Boston: South End Press, 1988), p. v.

9. See Charles Heckscher, *The New Unionism* (New York: Basic Books, 1988), p. 130. According to Heckscher's own analysis of the 1977 Quality of Employment Survey conducted by the U.S. Department of Labor, unions won only 8 percent of their organizing campaigns in manufacturing industries using QWL programs, as opposed to a 36 percent success rate in these industries overall. It may be noted that union opposition to the concept of joint action has no influence on a management that is unorganized. The argument proposed by union leaders who support the EI concept is that more innovative organizing strategies are required. They pointed out, that, in such instances, management has full authoritarian control of the process with the attendant possibility of abuse, but that union representation provides the employees with co-equal status in defining and implementing the process and making certain that its benefits accrue to the employees and are not determined solely by management.

10. The concept of "management-by-stress" is detailed in Mike Parker and Jane Slaughter, *Choosing Sides: Unions and the Team Concept* (Boston, Mass.: South End Press, 1988).

11. See Mike Parker, *Inside the Circle: A Union Guide to QWL* (Boston, Mass.: South End Press, 1985). See also Andy Banks and Jack Metzgar, "Participating in Management: Union Organizing on a New Terrain," *Labor Research Review* 13 (Fall 1989): 1–55.

12. The MIT Commission on Industrial Productivity came to very much the same conclusion: "Sustained labor-management cooperation has been limited by the deep-seated antiunion attitudes of many American managers and a corresponding distrust on the part of many American union

leaders of new forms of employee participation and work organization" (Michael L. Dertouzos, Richard K. Lester, and Robert M. Solow, *Made in America* [Cambridge, Mass.: MIT Press, 1989], p. 94).

13. For more detail on this survey, see "Dramatic Gains in Attitudes toward Work and Quality," *World of Work Report* 7 (December 1982): 89–91.

14. Ibid., p. 90.

15. The Boeing survey results are reported in Thomas A. Kochan and Joel Cutcher-Gershenfeld, *Institutionalizing and Diffusing Innovations in Industrial Relations*, BLMR 128 (Washington, D.C.: U.S. Department of Labor, Bureau of Labor-Management Relations and Cooperative Programs, 1988), p. 7. It should be noted that the union representing the workers at Boeing, the International Association of Machinists (IAM) opposes the joint action concept and cautions its local unions about getting involved in such programs.

16. See U.S. General Accounting Office, *Survey of Corporate Employee Involvement Efforts* (Washington, D.C.: Author, 1987, Mimeographed).

17. A Canadian survey carried out in the early 1980s involving nearly 1,000 participants in twenty carefully selected large firms concluded that chief executives, middle managers, and blue- and white-collar workers in "democratically" structured firms reported marginally less intergroup conflict than those working in "hierarchical" companies. Problem-solving modes of operation are used more and workers' input is ignored less in the democratically structured firms. The author concludes that "perhaps the emphasis on friendly relations among employees in the democratic workplaces puts pressure on superiors to smooth over differences of opinion" (Donald V. Nightingale, *Workplace Democracy: An Inquiry into Employee Participation in Canadian Work Organizations* [Toronto: University of Toronto Press, 1982], esp. chap. 5).

18. William N. Cooke, *Labor-Management Cooperation* (Kalamazoo, Mich.: Upjohn Institute, 1990).

19. The three collected annual data from 1979 through 1986 for fifty-three plants of a major American automobile manufacturer; see Harry C. Katz, Thomas A. Kochan, and Jeffrey H. Keefe, "Industrial Relations and Productivity in the U.S. Automobile Industry," *Brookings Papers on Economic Activity*, 3 (1987): 685–715. While they surveyed chief industrial relations managers in each of these facilities, they also gathered data from corporate records on the number of written grievances, employee absentee rates, product quality audits, and the ratio of supervisors to production workers in each plant. In addition, they developed a productivity measure in a subset of final vehicle assembly plants, in this case, the number of "standardized" production worker hours required to assemble a vehicle. The labor efficiency data were "standardized" for the

complexity of the automobile. Cars with more options, for example, take more time to assemble than "stripped" vehicles. The labor standards used in this study were based on the company's own industrial engineering reports on product complexity. See Katz, Kochan, and Keefe, "Industrial Relations and Productivity."

20. Ibid., p. 702.

21. One auto plant that Katz, Kochan, and Keefe did not study was the GM-Toyota joint venture, NUMMI, in Fremont, California. This plant uses the team concept and apparently, at least during the early 1980s, was almost as productive as Japanese plants operating in Japan. This suggests that teamwork can boost productivity and quality, but it by no means is an automatic process. See John F. Krafcik, "High Performance Manufacturing: An International Study of Auto Assembly Practice" (Cambridge, Mass.: International Motor Vehicle Program, MIT, January 1988, working paper).

22. Maryellen R. Kelley and Bennett Harrison, "Unions, Technology, and Labor-Management Cooperation," in *Unions and Economic Competitiveness,* ed. Lawrence Mishel and Paula B. Voos (Armonk, N.Y.: Sharpe, 1992).

23. The original survey was directed by Maryellen R. Kelley and Harvey Brooks and is described in Kelley and Brooks, *The State of Computerized Automation in U.S. Manufacturing* (Cambridge, Mass.: Center for Business and Government, John F. Kennedy School of Government, Harvard University, 1988).

   The actual survey was carried out by the Center for Survey Research at the University of Massachusetts at Boston between October 1986 and March 1987. The industries in the survey covered nonferrous foundries; cutlery, hand tools, and hardware; heating equipment and plumbing fixtures; screw machine products; metal forgings and stampings; ordnance and accessories; miscellaneous fabricated metal products; engines and turbines; farm and garden machinery and equipment; construction and related machinery; metalworking machinery and equipment; special industrial machinery; general industrial machinery and equipment; miscellaneous machinery, excluding electrical; electrical industrial apparatus; motor vehicles and equipment; aircraft and parts; guided missiles and space vehicles; engineering and scientific instruments; measuring and controlling instruments; and jewelry, silverware, and plateware. All told, in 1986, 25 percent of all U.S. manufacturing workers were employed in these industries.

   How do Kelley and Harrison explain what they themselves call "the 'perverse' effects of employee participation" they have found? One possibility that cannot be completely dismissed is that the correlation between EI and their measure of productivity performance is spurious. It is possible, perhaps even likely, that the firms that chose to introduce LMCs did so precisely because they were grasping for a solution to an already existing productivity crisis. Thus, the firms *with LMCs* would appear in the Kelley and Harrison survey as having poorer efficiency performance—even if the LMC did in fact improve productivity.

Another possibility is that many of these EI programs are in the infancy of their organizational development and therefore have not yet learned to walk, let alone run. Most analysts and practitioners alike readily admit that there are start-up costs associated with beginning EI and that productivity usually dips before it improves. Still, a third possibility offered by Kelley and Harrison is that companies that have introduced employee participation have not fundamentally changed their bureaucratic structures or implemented many of the other changes needed to boost productivity. EI alone may do little to improve efficiency and may actually disturb it.

More likely, we believe, is that this research—despite the care with which it was undertaken—fails to capture two critically important dimensions of the EI-productivity link. The first has to do with the measurement of "output." Kelley and Harrison had access to data only on the *level* of productivity at a given point in time. But what needs to be measured is the *change* in productivity over time as a result of implementing an EI system. It is the dynamics of the employee participation process, not the static conditions, that must be tallied. It is altogether possible that those firms that have introduced EI have done it precisely because they are plagued by low productivity. In this case, it is possible that *all* of them may have improved their productivity, even markedly, by resort to EI programs, but still remain below the efficiency levels in the non-EI/nonunion firms. This result would be fully consistent with the data presented by Kelley and Harrison.

The second factor has to do with "inputs." Counting the mere existence of a formal EI program captures virtually nothing about its extent and intensity. According to the Kelly and Harrison survey, over 42 percent of the single-plant facilities and almost 71 percent of the branch plants are coded as having formal labor-management problem-solving committees. No review of EI programs suggests anywhere near so much apparent attention to EI efforts, and it is likely that many of the reported programs are quite limited in scope. Hence, it is unclear what the negative finding really means, since the "input" is so imperfectly measured. It is hard to imagine that a well-functioning, powerful EI program in a nonunion setting would be tolerated by management if it reduced efficiency by 30 to 35 percent. It is equally difficult to imagine a weak program having much of an effect one way or the other.

24. U.S. Department of Labor, Bureau of Labor-Management Relations and Cooperative Programs, "Labor-Management Cooperation: 1989 State-of-the-Art Symposium," *BLMR Reports* 124 (1989): 17–20.

25. David I. Levine and Laura D'Andrea Tyson, "Participation, Productivity, and the Firm's Environment," in *Paying for Productivity*, ed. Alan S. Blinder (Washington, D.C.: Brookings Institution, 1990), table 1, pp. 192–95.

26. Keith H. Hammonds, "Corning's Class Act," *Business Week*, May 13, 1991.

27. The Work in America Institute has followed the development of the EI process at Ford Sharonville and, from time to time, has published brief reports concerning the operation in its publication, *World of Work Report* (see vol. 7, no. 12, December 1982, and vol. 9, no. 7, July 1984). Additional information on Sharonville was obtained from interviews conducted by the authors.

28. John Lippert, "Romeo: A Love Story," *Detroit Free Press*, May 20, 1991.

29. Ibid.

30. Thomas A. Stewart, "The New American Century," *Fortune* (special issue), Spring/Summer 1991, p. 22.

31. Terry Hammond-Smith, "Northern Telecom Employees Say Team Style Aids Plant, Workers," *Daily Labor Report* (Bureau of National Affairs, Inc.), June 1, 1990, p. C-1.

32. John Hoerr, "The Cultural Revolution at A. O. Smith," *Business Week*, May 29, 1989.

33. The New York Sanitation Department's Bureau of Motor Equipment has been the subject of many reports. Of these, the following are particularly useful. Ronald Contino, "Attached Report on Productivity Gains through Labor/Management Programs at the Bureau of Motor Equipment," Report to the Commissioner of the Department of Sanitation, New York City, April 19, 1982 (mimeograph); Ronald Contino, "Employee Participation: The Blue Collar Edge," *Public Works* (June 1987): 81–109; and "N.Y. Sanitation Shops Rival Private-Firm Performance," *Work in America* 12 (May 1987): 1.

34. Contino, "Employee Participation."

35. Cooke, *Labor-Management Cooperation*, p. 97.

36. See R. Drago, "Quality Circle Survival: An Exploratory Analysis," Department of Economics Working Paper, University of Wisconsin at Milwaukee, 1987, as reported in Thomas A. Kochan, "Adaptability of the U.S. Industrial Relations System," *Science*, April 15, 1988, p. 289.

37. Kochan, "Industrial Relations System," p. 289. See also Thomas A. Kochan, Harry C. Katz, and Nancy R. Mower, *Worker Participation and American Unions* (Kalamazoo, Mich.: Upjohn Institute, 1984).

38. Charles C. Heckscher, *The New Unionism: Employee Involvement in the Chang-ing Corporation* (New York: Basic Books, 1988), p. 87.
39. James P. Womack, Daniel T. Jones, and Daniel Roos, *The Machine That Changed the World* (New York: Rawson, 1990), p. 99.
40. Zachary Schiller, "No More Mr. Nice Guy at P&G—Not by a Long Shot," *Business Week*, February 3, 1992, p. 54.
41. Ibid.

Chapter 8: From Co-Managing the Workplace to Co-Managing the Enterprise

1. See *Iron Age*, January 13, 1949.
2. "A Motor Car Named Desire," *Ammunition* (UAW magazine), January 1949, pp. 24–30.
3. UAW Local 1853, Saturn Corporation, "Important Dates in Saturn History," *Project Saturn*, Briefing Paper, February 1989.
4. Ibid., p. 1.
5. David E. Davis, Jr., "Saturn Launch," *Automobile*, November 1990, p. 61.
6. Ibid., p. 1.
7. Don Ephlin, "United Auto Workers: Pioneers in Labor-Management Partnership," in *Teamwork—Joint Labor-Management Programs in America*, ed. Jerome M. Rosow (New York: Pergamon Press, 1986), pp. 133–45.
8. Reid Rundell (Executive Vice President, General Motors Corporation), (Speech delivered to the Harvard Club, Detroit, Michigan, September 18, 1985, mimeographed), p. 12.
9. Ibid., pp. 12–13.
10. Recognition of the UAW as bargaining representative at the Saturn Corporation was challenged by the National Right to Work Committee. The matter was litigated before the U.S. National Labor Relations Board. After full consideration of the arguments on both sides, the NLRB in 1986 dismissed the charges and upheld the right of the corporation to give recognition to the UAW.
11. Interview with Skip LeFauve in Barry Winfield, "We Have Liftoff! Saturn Puts Three Cars into Orbit," *Automobile*, November 1990, p. 64.
12. UAW Saturn Corporation "Memorandum of Agreement," sec. 10, "Structure and Decision-Making Process," July 24, 1985, p. 4.
13. Ibid., "Procedure to Modify the Agreement," p. 21. In November 1991 an amended labor contract was overwhelmingly ratified by the members of UAW Local 1853. The new agreement continues all the basic provisions of the joint action processes applicable under the previous contract but focuses on economic issues such as salary increases, pension, and

other benefit provisions, including separation allowance, retiree health care, dependent life insurance, vacations, holidays, and the savings plan.

14. Ibid. Details of the "Consensus Guidelines" are described in sec. 11, pp. 7–8.

15. Ibid., sec. 11, pp. 1–8.

16. Ibid., sec. 21, "Job Security," p. 12.

17. Statement by UAW Vice President Don Ephlin, contained in a UAW press release, July 26, 1985, p. 3.

18. UAW Saturn Corporation, "Memorandum of Agreement," sec. 19, "Classifications," July 23, 1985, p. 11.

19. Ibid., sec. 22, "Reward System," "Base Compensation," p. 13; sec. 23, "Compensation Level at Steady State," p. 14.

20. The authors visited the Saturn facility in Spring Hill, Tennessee, in January 1991 and had the opportunity to tour the plant, observing the operations in process and interviewing employees at their jobs. Meetings were also arranged with members of work units, work unit modules, and business units, and also with the local union officials and the top-level management officials.

21. See Winfield, "We Have Liftoff!" p. 62.

22. Saturn news release, October 11, 1990. According to 1991 base manufacturers' suggested retail prices (MSRP), the basic SL vehicle is priced $2,003 below Toyota Corolla and $1,495 below Honda Civic DX. The top-of-the-line SL2 sedan is priced $1,653 below Toyota Camry, while the Sport Coupe is $1,014 below the Mitsubishi Eclipse GS DOHC.

23. James V. Higgins, "Saturn Will Add Second Shift This Month," *Detroit News*, April 19, 1991.

24. Hank Guzda, "Saturn: The Sky's the Limit," U.S. Department of Labor, Bureau of Labor-Management Relations and Cooperative Programs, *Labor Relations Today* 5 (March–April 1990): 2–3.

25. The information concerning the history and the contract associated with this case was provided by Bill Kane, New Jersey area director, UAW, region 9. Bill Kane is the international representative who also services the UAW local union, Local 726, Union, New Jersey, and led the contract negotiations on behalf of the union. In our discussions with Kane, the UAW representative expressed the possibility that a successful experience at ESNA might eventually serve as a model in creating a council of all UAW-represented Harvard Industry units nationwide, operating under terms and conditions equivalent to those prevailing at the ESNA facility.

26. Material for this case study was gathered in January 1992 during eight days of interviews with members of the executive board of the University

of Hawaii Professional Assembly (UHPA), members of the University of Hawaii Board of Regents, and various officials within the University of Hawaii administration. J. N. Musto, the executive director of the UHPA; John Radcliffe, the associate executive director; and Sinikka Hayasaka, the president of UHPA provided us with valuable details about the relationship between UHPA and the university.

27. Reported in Bureau of National Affairs, *Daily Labor Report*, April 9, 1991, p. A–5.

28. Christopher Farrell and John Hoerr, "ESOPs: Are They Good for You? They Can Deter Takeovers, Save Taxes, and Boost Productivity, But . . . " *Business Week*, May 15, 1989, pp. 116–23.

29. On Professor Blasi's studies, see Bureau of National Affairs, *Daily Labor Report*, April 9, 1991, p. A-5.

30. Ibid.

31. "ESOP and EI Give Avis Competitive Edge," *Work in America Report* 14 (September 1989): 4–6.

32. Ibid.

33. The authors' copy of the "Employee Ownership" study is typewritten. The quotation is taken from page ii of the report, a preface comment by the Economic Development Administration.

34. Ibid., p. 20.

35. Ibid., pp. 36, 38.

36. As reported in the Bureau of National Affairs, *Daily Labor Report*, March 29, 1991, p. A-11.

37. In 1989 the profit-sharing plan was renegotiated and approved by membership vote in order to make available funds for urgently needed capital investment in new technology (hot mill revamp and conversion of an "obsolete" casting technology to a continuous caster process). The profit-sharing maximum was set at 35 percent of profits. In addition, it was agreed, also with employee approval, that a public offering of stock would be made to raise funds for capital investment purposes. The offering succeeded. Therefore, beginning in 1989, Weirton became a 70 percent employee-owned firm, with 30 percent owned by outside stockholders.

38. In 1991, for the first time since the employee takeover and as a result of the national economic recession coupled with production delays due largely to the installation of new technologically advanced equipment, the firm reported a profit loss for the year. With the technological improvements now substantially completed, the forecast for 1992 is for a return to profitability.

39. Originally the full complement of the board of directors was set at fourteen, comprising eight independent members, three selected by the union, with the chairman and two management executives to be selected by the chairman. The chairman elected to forgo his two appointments. Subsequently, the current chairman of the board filled the two vacancies and thus completed the full complement of fourteen.

40. In more recent years, immediately following each board meeting, a joint meeting of management staff and union officials has convened at the auditorium in the corporation's administrative office building for a briefing on the board's deliberations, with a question-and-answer period. Meetings of union officials at the union hall are still convened to discuss specific special problems that may arise.

41. "Blue Collars in the Boardroom: Putting Business First," *Business Week*, December 14, 1987, p. 126.

42. "UAW Seat on Chrysler Board: What It Means for Workers" (interview with UAW President Douglas Fraser), *Solidarity*, November 19, 1979, p. 7.

43. Douglas A. Fraser, "Labor on Corporate Boards," *Challenge* 24 (July–August 1981): 30.

44. This history of profit sharing is covered in an unpublished paper by Bert L. Metzger, president of the Profit Sharing Research Foundation, presented before a European Economic Community Forum, Dublin, Ireland, May 22, 1960, p. 6.

45. In a survey of 1,598 employers conducted in 1987 by the American Productivity Center, 32 percent reported having profit sharing. Many of these plans, however, did not extend to production workers. See Carla O'Dell and Jerry McAdams, *People, Performance, and Pay* (Houston: American Productivity Center, 1987), p. 8. In a compendium of contract settlements between 1981 and 1988, Daniel J. B. Mitchell reports that out of 1,799 agreements, 133, or 7.4 percent, included profit sharing for unionized employees. See Daniel J. B. Mitchell, "Will Collective Bargaining Outcomes in the 1990s Look Like Those of the 1980s?" *Labor Law Review* 40 (August 1989): 490–96.

46. The revised profit-sharing plans negotiated in 1990 at General Motors, Ford, and Chrysler provide for a sliding scale of profit distribution as follows, with payouts up to a maximum of 17 percent of profits:

On the first 1.8% of sales (0–1.8%), 6% of profits
On the next .5% of sales (1.8–2.3%), 8% of profits
On the next 2.3% of sales (2.3–4.6%), 10% of profits

On the next 2.3% of sales (4.6–6.9%), 14% of profits
On profits over 6.9% of sales, 17% of profits

It is interesting to note that when the UAW first submitted a profit-sharing proposal in the 1958 negotiations, management dubbed it a "radical scheme" and flatly rejected it. Even after profit sharing was agreed on in the 1961 American Motors contract, it was still rejected by the other automakers. It was not until 1982, in the course of reopening and renegotiating the national contracts, that the auto companies agreed to a profit-sharing provision.

47. Warner Gear in Muncie, Indiana, provides a good example. An EI program was introduced by agreement with the union in 1981. A steering committee comprising ten union and ten management representatives convenes monthly to provide overall direction to the process. In 1983 the parties negotiated the creation of two additional joint programs: a Joint Panel on Productivity and Quality and a Joint Union-Management Forum. The joint panel consists of eight people and implements issues relating to efficiency, productivity, and quality. The joint panel meets monthly and is cochaired by a union and management representative. Twice a year the forum meets with all the employees to discuss the status of the company's finances, its goals, new products, and so on—items that are the subject of deliberation by the top management and the Board of Directors.

48. For two excellent reviews of the impact of profit sharing and gain sharing on productivity and profits, see Daniel J. B. Mitchell, David Lewin, and Edward E. Lawler III, "Alternative Pay Systems, Firm Performance, and Productivity," in *Paying for Productivity*, ed. Alan Blinder (Washington, D.C.: Brookings Institution, 1990), pp. 15–94; and Martin L. Weitzman and Douglas L. Kruse, "Profit Sharing and Productivity," in *Paying for Productivity*, pp. 95–141.

49. Weitzman and Kruse, "Profit Sharing and Productivity," pp. 138–39. Based on these studies and others, Princeton University's Alan Blinder notes:

Boosting productivity by 3 to 11 percent would not constitute a third Industrial Revolution. But if such gains were not entirely consumed by labor—a big if, to be sure—they would transform a company's bottom line beyond recognition. And they come cheaply. No expensive investment in plant and equipment is necessary; no painstaking improvements in work-force quality are required. All that is needed is a change in the way the company compensates its employees—a veritable flick of the pen. This comes deliciously close to getting something for nothing. (Alan Blinder, *Growing Together: An Alternative Economic Strategy for the 1990s* [Whittle Direct Books, 1991], p. 53.)

Chapter 9: The Enterprise Compact

1. Neil Chamberlain, *The Union Challenge to Management Control* (New York: Harper and Brothers, 1948), p. 6.

2. *New York Times,* December 6, 1945, as quoted in ibid., p. 144.

3. In fact, at its thirteenth constitutional convention in November 1951, the Congress of Industrial Organizations (CIO) adopted a resolution demanding equal union sharing of such traditional management functions as determination of prices, production levels, rate and nature of capital investment, size and location of industrial plants, and the development and conservation of natural resources. At the time, few unions tried to implement the resolution through collective bargaining—but the success of the resolution on the floor of the CIO convention more than forty years ago indicates that the issue of management prerogatives was hardly dormant. See Gordon F. Bloom and Herbert R. Northrup, *Economics of Labor Relations,* 4th ed. (Homewood, Il.: Irwin, 1961), p. 187.

4. Chamberlain, *Union Challenge,* p. 145.

5. As quoted in ibid., p. 169.

6. From article 4 of the agreement between Snyder General Corporation, Climate Control Division, Red Bud Plant, located at 401 Randolph Street, Red Bud, Illinois, and Sheet Metal Workers International Association, Local no. 459, affiliated with the American Federation of Labor–Congress of Industrial Organizations, August 29, 1983.

7. Chamberlain, *Union Challenge,* chap. 11.

8. On these three functions, see ibid., p. 22.

9. Of course, in many firms—especially smaller ones—the CEO and the president are the same person. In this case, there are still two "functions," but they are carried out by the same individual.

10. See "1987 Local Agreements, Understandings, and Local Demand Settlements between Trenton Plant, Fisher Guide Division, General Motors Corporation and Local no. 731 United Auto Workers, Trenton, New Jersey," p. 8 (mimeographed).

11. In 1948, Neil Chamberlain wrote:

    Financial and price policies of businesses are being brought more and more under the analytical survey of union officials and their research assistants. The productive efficiency of the managers is being accorded close scrutiny. Insofar as there is union dissatisfaction with management's discharge of its functions, it may be expected that labor officials and representatives will seek to secure a voice in the determination of business standards and policies, that they may be brought in line with its objectives, whatever the latter may be. (*Union Challenge,* p. 5)

12. See "Report of the President to the Twelfth Convention of the UAW," United Auto Workers, Detroit, July 10, 1949, p. 160.

13. Letter dated August 18, 1957, noted in the "President's Report to the Seventeenth Constitutional Convention of the UAW," United Auto Workers, Detroit, October 9–16, 1959, p. 12.

14. Even in this unlikely scenario of a universal enterprise compact where wages rose less than productivity growth, prices would still decline by less than the difference between the two. This is because nonlabor costs comprise about 25 percent of the value of total output, and because some purchased inputs are foreign imports whose prices might not decline at all. Only if the remaining costs—primarily depreciation, indirect business taxes, and net interest—were to decline by the same amount as the difference between productivity and wage growth—and if the firm purchased only inputs that were declining in price—would the firm's total real costs decline by 3 percent. Only in this rarest of cases could the firm reduce its prices by the full 3 percent without reducing profits or wages.

15. One American example that commands a price premium is Maytag, the line of home appliances advertised and sold on the basis of their impeccable service records.

16. Clair Brown and Michael Reich, "When Does Union-Management Cooperation Work? A Look at NUMMI and GM–Van Nuys," *California Management Review* 31 (Summer 1989): 28.

17. W. Edwards Deming, *Out of the Crisis* (Cambridge, Mass.: Center for Advanced Engineering Study, 1982), p. 28.

18. Ronald Henkoff, "Cost Cutting: How to Do It Right," *Fortune*, April 9, 1990, p. 40.

19. Robert Levering, *A Great Place to Work: What Makes Some Employers So Good (and Most So Bad)* (New York: Avon Books, 1988).

20. For details on the 1990 UAW-GM contract, see *UAW-GM Report* (Detroit: UAW Solidarity House, September 1990).

21. David I. Levine and Laura D'Andrea Tyson, "Participation, Productivity, and the Firm's Environment," in *Paying for Productivity*, ed. Alan S. Blinder, pp. 183–243.

22. See Chamberlain, *Union Challenge*, p. 92.

23. An excellent description and history of the Textile/Clothing Technology Corp. is found in Richard Kazis, "Rags to Riches? One Industry's Strategy for Improving Productivity," *Technology Review* 92 (August/September 1989): 42–53.

24. By the end of 1984 the $(TC)^2$ had a fairly stable budget of $7 million a year, thirteen dues-paying members, and forty other contributing firms from the fibers, textile, sportswear, and tailored-clothing industries. See ibid., p. 50.

25. These provisions are found in documents 1, 2, and 3 attached to the "1987 Local Agreements."

26. See Work in America Institute, Inc., "Jointness in GM/UAW Relationships at Plant Level," Special Report, Scarsdale, N.Y., December 15, 1988, p. 10.

27. Ibid., p. 9.

28. As one example, the UAW's General Motors Department under former Vice-President Donald Ephlin retooled a number of its staff to participate in strategic decision making at various levels. In addition to carrying out their traditional bargaining responsibilities and arbitration, four members of Ephlin's staff were assigned full-time to the Saturn project to help manage the start-up of that new venture. Eight worked full-time on the joint UAW-GM Quality Network, helping to implement quality projects all across the corporation, and a large number were assigned to the joint UAW-GM Human Resource Center in Auburn Hills, Michigan, carrying out a massive, jointly administered training and education effort. All of these staff had to learn wide-ranging new skills. It appears that most of them mastered their assignments and have won praise from the union and management alike. See Donald F. Ephlin, in remarks presented at the John F. Kennedy School of Government, Harvard University, Cambridge, Massachusetts, March 22, 1989.

29. As one example, the state of Connecticut uses final offer arbitration to settle disputes between schoolteachers and school boards. If a settlement is not reached by bargaining within a specified period of time, the dispute automatically goes to mediation. If, within a short specified time, mediation fails, the case automatically goes to a three-member arbitration panel that must make a ruling within a similarly short period. There has not been a single strike in a Connecticut school district since the binding arbitration system went into effect in 1971. See Legislative Program Review and Investigations Committee, Connecticut State Legislature, "Binding Arbitration for Teachers: Briefing Package, October 12, 1989.

30. The Western Airlines case is described in Joel Cutcher-Gershenfeld, Robert B. McKersie, and Kirsten R. Wever, The Changing Role of Union Leaders, BLMR 127 (Washington, D.C.: U.S. Department of Labor, Bureau of Labor-Management Relations and Cooperative Programs, 1988); and Kirsten R. Wever, Western Airlines and Its Four Major Unions: The Air Line Pilots Association, the Air Transport Employees, the Association of Flight Attendants, and the International Brotherhood of Teamsters, BLMR 129 (Washington, D.C.: U.S. Department of Labor, Bureau of Labor-Management Relations and Cooperative Programs, 1988).

31. Wever, "Four Major Unions," pp. 18–19. Even if the unions had been given equal representation on the board, speculation suggests the situa-

tion was already beyond salvation by the time joint participation was initiated.

32. See Aaron Bernstein, "Letting Teachers Call the Shots," *Business Week*, January 28, 1991, p. 54.

33. By law, the school councils are comprised of three teachers, two parents, and the school principal. See ibid., p. 54.

34. Thomas Kochan, "Do Labor and Management Have What It Takes to Be Partners in Strategic Planning?" *Labor Relations Today* 3 (July/August/ September 1988): 3.

35. See Roger Fisher and William Ury, *Getting to Yes: Negotiating Agreement Without Giving In* (Boston: Houghton-Mifflin, 1981).

Chapter 10: Creating a Benign Climate for the
New Labor-Management Accord

1. Wallace C. Peterson, "The Silent Depression," *Challenge* 34 (July/August 1991).

2. Paul Weiler, "Who Will Represent Labor Now?" *American Prospect*, no. 2 (Summer 1990): 80.

3. Ibid., p. 79.

4. AFL-CIO Committee on the Evolution of Work, *The Changing Situation of Workers and Their Union* (Washington, D.C.: AFL-CIO, February 1985), pp. 2, 12–13, 18.

5. See W. P. Murphy, "Establishment and Disestablishment of Union Representation" (Paper presented to a symposium on "The Labor Board at Mid-Century," sponsored by the Southern Methodist University Law School, Washington, D.C., 1985).

6. See Gordon L. Clark, "A Question of Integrity: The National Labor Relations Board, Collective Bargaining and the Relocation of Work," *Political Geography Quarterly* 7 (July 1988): 213.

7. *First National Maintenance Corp. v. NLRB*, 101 S.Ct. 2573 (1981).

8. Gordon L. Clark, "Restructuring the U.S. Economy: The NLRB, the Saturn Project, and Economic Justice," *Economic Geography* 62 (1986): 297.

9. See 369 NLRB no. 162, 115 LRRM 1281 (1984). For a more detailed discussion of this case, see Clark, "A Question of Integrity," p. 219.

10. See 268 NLRB 601 (1984). See also K. Johnson, "Judicial Adjudication and the Spatial Structure of Production: Two Decisions by the National Labor Relations Board," *Environment and Planning* 18 (1986).

11. John Dunlop, "The Economic Future of the United States and the Legal Framework of Its Industrial Relations" (Keynote paper presented to a

symposium on "The Labor Board at Mid-Century," as reported in the *Daily Labor Report*, no. 194 [October 7, 1985]: 1).

12. See *NLRB v. Yeshiva University*, 444 U.S. 672 (1980).

13. Charles Heckscher, *The New Unionism: Employee Involvement in the Changing Corporation* (New York: Basic Books, 1988), p. 78.

14. See U.S. Department of Labor, Bureau of Labor-Management Relations and Cooperative Programs, *Cooperating for the Future: A New Dimension in Labor-Management Relations*, BLMR 112 (Washington D.C.: Government Printing Office, 1988), p. 2.

15. Ibid., pp. 2–8.

16. "Working Today for a Better Tomorrow" (Erie, Pa.: Northwestern Pennsylvania Area Labor-Management Council, pamphlet), p. 6.

17. Described in the "Annual Report of the New York State Industrial Cooperation Council," Albany, N.Y., 1988, inside cover page.

18. Title page of the typewritten document that sets forth the structure and purpose of the Indiana Labor-Management Council, "a not-for-profit, nonpartisan organization" conceived in 1982 by Governor Robert D. Orr.

19. See Labor-Management Development Center, *Worksite Labor-Management Cooperation Orientation and Training Manual*, 2d ed. (Marquette, Mich.: Northern Michigan University, 1989).

20. See Bennett Harrison and Barry Bluestone, *The Great U-Turn: Corporate Restructuring and the Polarizing of America* (New York: Basic Books, 1988).

21. See Aaron Bernstein, "You Can't Bargain with a Striker Whose Job Is No More," *Business Week*, August 5, 1991, p. 27.

22. As quoted in Bernstein, "You Can't Bargain," p. 27.

23. Weiler, "Who Will Represent Labor Now?" p. 83.

24. Ibid.

25. John Hoerr, "What Should Unions Do?" *Harvard Business Review* 69 (May–June 1991): 45.

Index